Analysis and Comparison of Relational Database Systems

GW00703173

Patrick Valduriez
MICROELECTRONICS AND COMPUTER TECHNOLOGY CORPORATION (MCC)

Georges Gardarin
INSTITUT NATIONAL DE RECHERCHE EN INFORMATIQUE ET EN
AUTOMATIQUE (INRIA)

 ADDISON-WESLEY PUBLISHING COMPANY, INC.
Reading, Massachusetts • Menlo Park, California • New York
Don Mills, Ontario • Wokingham, England • Amsterdam
Bonn • Sydney • Singapore • Tokyo • Madrid • San Juan

SABRINA is a trademark of INRIA.
SUPRA is a trademark of Cincom Systems, Inc.
DTACOM/DB is a registered trademark of Applied Data Research, Inc.
FOCUS is a registered trademark of Information Builders, Inc.
ORACLE is a registered trademark of Oracle Corporation.
UNIFY is a registered trademark of Unify Corporation.
dBASE III PLUS is a trademark of Ashton-Tate.
KNOWLEDGEMAN/2 is a registered trademark of mdbs Inc.
R:BASE 5000 is a registered trademark of Microrim Inc.
NOMAD is a registered trademark of U3S International Ltd.
SYBASE is a registered trademark of Sybase, Inc.

Many of the designations used by manufacturers and sellers to distinguish their products are claimed as trademarks. Where those designations appear in this book, and Addison-Wesley was aware of a trademark claim, the designations have been printed in initial caps or all caps.

The programs and applications presented in this book have been included for their instructional value. They have been tested with care, but are not guaranteed for any particular purpose. The publisher does not offer any warranties or representations, nor does it accept any liabilities with respect to the programs or applications.

Library of Congress Cataloging-in-Publication Data

Valduriez, Patrick.
  Analysis and comparison of relational database
systems.

  Includes bibliographies and index.
  1. Data base management.   2. Relational data bases.
I. Gardarin, G. (Georges)   II. Title.
QA76.9.D3V32   1989   005.75'6   88-6263
ISBN 0-201-19940-8

ABCDEFGHIJ–HA–898

PREFACE

Since its inception in 1970, the relational data model has become increasingly popular with database researchers, designers, practitioners, and end users, largely because of the simplicity and the power of the relational concepts. Unlike hierarchical and network models, the relational model provided a theoretical foundation for database management, which has motivated the database research community. The main outcomes of this research were the development of high-level data-manipulation languages and a solid basis for automating the conceptual database design process.

After ten years of research, the first relational database management systems (RDBMSs) appeared on the market. Although they had definite advantages in terms of usability and end-user productivity, they were generally restricted to decision support applications and plagued by poor performance. Since the first RDBMSs, relational database technology has shown remarkable progress in terms of usefulness and performance. Most RDBMSs today support an integrated set of fourth-generation programming language tools to enhance end-user productivity. Some provide high performance for on-line processing applications. Furthermore, an increasing number of RDBMSs provide extensive support for distributed database management. The development of fourth-generation tools and distributed database management capabilities has been facilitated by the power of the relational model.

This book examines the current systems that best implement relational database concepts. Ten RDBMSs mainly designed for mainframes and minicomputers, four RDBMSs uniquely targeted for microcomputers, and the main relational database machines are described and analyzed. The analysis criteria include both the functional capabilities and implementation choices of RDBMSs. Comparison results are summarized in tables. The list of systems presented here is not exhaustive but is a sample of the best products. The information presented here is based on the most recent version of each system that was available when we went to press.

This book is directed to a large public, including students in computer science (at the undergraduate and graduate level), computer scientists, and database users who wish to know more about RDBMSs. A basic knowledge of the principles of relational database systems is a prerequisite to understanding this book. Our recent book, *Relational Databases and Knowledge Bases,* introduces the technical vocabulary used extensively in the text. Furthermore, some familiarity with modern operating systems is assumed. The book can also be used by teachers to extend a traditional introduction to database technology. This book should enable readers to appreciate the practical superiority of the relational model for intensive database management. It also compares and criticizes the main relational database products and thus should help practitioners to choose the most suitable RDBMS. The comparison criteria can be applied to relational systems not presented here to understand and analyze their capabilities. We hope that readers will find all the systems examined here as interesting and significant as we did while preparing this book.

Many colleagues and designers of the systems we looked at helped us. They are B. Boettcher, H. Boral, E. Boughter, R. Epstein, M. Franklin, P. Hawthorn, G. Kiernan, R. Krishnamurthy, G. Lohman, R. Michel, C. Mohan, P. Neches, F. Pasquer, E. Simon, M. Smith, D. Tossan, M. Ubell, J-F. Vergnangeal, Y. Viemont, and N. Zidi. We are also grateful to the following reviewers for their comments and suggestions: Daniel Rosenkrantz, State University of New York at Albany and Dennis Shasha, Courant Institute of Mathematics. We also wish to acknowledge our debt to the RDBMS vendors (see list in Appendix) whose cooperation made the book possible. However, we must emphasize that the presentation of these systems is our own interpretation of the technical information made available to us. Finally, we would like to thank our colleagues of the Advanced Computer Architecture program at MCC, Austin, and the SABRE project at INRIA, Paris, for their support.

CONTENTS

1

INTRODUCTION

1.1 Evolution of Database Systems

Since the first *database management systems* (DBMSs) appeared in the early 1960s, they have evolved in terms of quality (functionality, performance, ease of use, and so on) and quantity (number of different products). The qualitative evolution has been driven by two complementary trends: significant progress in the areas of database theory and database technology and increasingly sophisticated requirements of database users. The quantitative evolution of DBMSs stems from the increasing number and variety of database applications and the increasing diversity of computing resources. The importance of the database arena in computer science is also exhibited by many books [Date 83, Date 86, Delobel 85, Gardarin 84, Gardarin 88, Ullman 82] and conferences.

A DBMS is characterized mainly by the data model it supports. The first DBMSs, based on the hierarchical or network model, remain the most used today. They can be viewed as an extension of file systems in which interfile links are provided through pointers. The data manipulation languages of those systems are navigational, that is, the programmer must specify the access paths to the data by navigating in hierarchies or networks.

In the early 1980s, the first systems based on the relational model appeared on the market, bringing definite advantages over their predecessors. Today a large number of relational products is available on mainframe computers, minicomputers, microcomputers, and dedicated computers (database machines), and their market is rapidly expanding. The success of the relational model among researchers, designers, and users is due primarily to the simplicity and the power of its concepts.

1.2 What Is a Relational Database Management System?

The advantages of the relational model, invented by E. F. Codd [Codd 70], have been thoroughly demonstrated by database researchers. One main advantage is the ability to provide full independence between logical data descriptions, in conceptual terms, and physical data descriptions, in terms of files. As a consequence of this physical independency, high-level data manipulation languages may be supported. Such languages free the programmer from physical details, thereby allowing query optimization to be done by the system rather than by the user. The promotion of the relational model has also been helped by database language standardization, which yields the standard Structured Query Language (SQL) [ANSI 86]. SQL provides a uniform interface to all types of users (database administrators, programmers, end users) for data definition, control, and manipulation.

The relational data model can be characterized by three features [Codd 82]:

1. The data structures are simple. These are two-dimensional tables, called *relations* (or tables), whose elements are data items. A relation can be viewed as a file; a row of a relation, called *tuple* (or row), can be viewed as a record; and a column of a relation, called *attribute* (or column), can be viewed as a data item. The relationship linking two relations is specified by a common attribute in both relations. For example, the relationship between an EMPLOYEE relation and a DEPARTMENT relation can be specified by an attribute dept _ name stored in both relations.

2. A set of eight operators (union, intersection, difference, Cartesian product, select, project, join, and difference), called *relational algebra,* facilitates data definition, data retrieval, and data update. Each relational operator takes one or two relations as input and produces one relation.

3. A set of *integrity constraints* defines consistent states of the database.

A relational DBMS (RDBMS) is a software program that supports the relational model. A definition of a relational database system has been proposed by a Relational Task Group whose results, endorsed by E. F. Codd, are given in [Schmidt 83]. Such a definition is useful to characterize systems that are claimed to be relational. A system is said to be minimally relational if it satisfies three conditions:

1. All information in the database is represented as values in tables.
2. No intertable pointers are visible to the user.
3. The system must support at least the following relational algebra operators: select, project, and natural join. These operators must not be restricted by internal constraints. An example of internal constraint that exists in some systems is that there must exist an index on join attribute to perform a join. These contraints limit the power of the database language.

A system is said to be fully relational if it satisfies the two additional conditions:

4. It supports all relational algebra operators without any restriction due to implementation.
5. Two basic integrity constraints must be supported. The first is that each relation has one or more attributes that constitute a unique key. For example, social security number is a unique key of a PERSON relation. The second constraint, often called *referential integrity constraint,* specifies that an attribute value in one relation already exists in another relation. For instance, dept _ name in relation EMPLOYEE must exist in relation DEPARTMENT.

Codd [Codd 85] has included these conditions in a more extensive set of twelve rules to characterize a fully relational DBMS. We will not use his set of rules in analyzing RDBMSs, however, because our purpose is not to decide whether a DBMS is fully relational. Rather, it is to analyze and compare the DBMSs that exhibit many relational features. All of the systems presented in this book vary between minimally and fully relational.

Most RDBMSs support the standard SQL. In addition, they generally provide an integrated set of fourth-generation tools, such as data dictionary, screen painter, application generator, and schema design aid, which improve application development and increase database programmer productivity. Some RDBMSs also provide powerful distributed database management capabilities. The realization of these capabilities has been facilitated or even made possible by the physical data independence and superior power provided by the relational model.

1.3 Misunderstandings about the Relational Model

As with any other new idea, there has been some misunderstanding about the relational model and the introduction of RDBMSs on the market. Generally, these misunderstandings fall into five categories:

1. *To be understood, the relational model requires a theoretical background.* It is true that the first presentations of the relational model

were theoretical (using set theory) and directed to a specialized public. However, the relational model can be understood without any theoretical background since its concepts are simple. Certain relational system vendors have even prohibited the initial vocabulary associated with the relational model and reused traditional terms such as *file* and *table*.

2. *The design of a normalized conceptual schema is a strong constraint.* The normalization theory as developed in the relational framework is not simple but yields many advantages in the database design process. However, normalization is not a constraint to designing a conceptual schema. Most RDBMSs can manipulate nonnormalized relations. In addition, a number of tools are available to help the database design process in a relational framework.

3. *The relational model is too poor.* This statement holds that the data structures of the model are too simple to model the real world faithfully. It has been already shown that the concepts of models with richer semantics, such as the entity/relationship model, can be easily mapped into relational concepts. The simplicity of the relational model makes this transformation easy. Furthermore, the relational model can be enriched with integrity constraints that enable the application semantics to be captured.

4. *RDBMSs have a limited set of data types.* It is true that most RDBMSs provide few data types such as integer, float, and character string. The main reason is that they have been designed for traditional data processing (business) applications that do not need rich data types. The basic notion of domain of the relational model is not constrained to particular types, however. As shown in [Gardarin 88], relational systems may well be extended with a rich typing capability in order to support new database applications such as office automation or knowledgebase systems.

5. *The performance of RDBMSs is poor.* This was one of the primary arguments against the relational model as opposed to the hierarchical or network model. It is true that the first RDBMSs did not perform well. However, since the relational model is useful at a conceptual level, a good relational system must implement efficient query optimization techniques and fast access paths to the data. Some current RDBMSs use powerful implementation techniques inspired by those of hierarchical or network systems. As we will see in this book, relational systems, and particularly relational database machines, now provide high performance.

In summary, the drawbacks of the first relational systems are now disappearing as the relational model and its associated technology gain experience. The maturity of the technology is clearly exhibited by the increasing success of relational products. And many researchers are proposing extensions to the relational model in order to support nontraditional database applications [Gardarin 84]. The most notable extensions include the support of deductive capabilities and of object orientation as demonstrated in [Gardarin 88].

1.4 Organization

The book illustrates thoroughly the application of the concepts presented in [Gardarin 88]. Chapters 2 to 7 present RDBMSs designed mainly for mainframes and minicomputers. Chapter 2 provides an overview and comparative introduction to ten RDBMSs, which are detailed in the following chapters. A standard plan to describe an RDBMS is proposed and applied subsequently in Chapter 3 to 7. Chapters 3 and 4 examine the two pioneer relational database prototypes that have become successful products. Chapter 3 is devoted to the SYSTEM R prototype, developed by IBM, and to the IBM SQL/DS and DB2 relational products derived from SYSTEM R. Chapter 4 is devoted to the INGRES system, prototyped at the University of California, Berkeley, and marketed by RTI. Chapter 5 presents the SABRINA System, designed at INRIA, France, and marketed by a consortium of three French companies. Chapter 6 describes SUPRA, a relational database system developed in an industrial environment. SUPRA has been designed by Cincom, the creator of the popular database system TOTAL. Chapter 7 provides shorter presentations of six interesting and successful systems: DATACOM/DB, FOCUS, NOMAD, ORACLE, SYBASE, and UNIFY.

Chapter 8 deals with database systems with relational features available only on microcomputers. Four popular DBMSs — DBASE III PLUS, KNOWLEDGE-MAN/2, R.BASE 5000, and EXCEL—are presented according to a similar plan. Chapter 9 is devoted to relational database machines. Four commercial products — CAFS/ISP by ICL, DBC/1012 by Teradata, DORSAL 32 by Copernique, and IDM 500 by Britton-Lee — are successively presented. Also, a number of database machines proposed by researchers are described and taxonomized.

1.5 Definitions

We will often use the following notations in describing the syntax of DBMS languages:

[a]   indicates that the element *a* is optional;
[b] . . .   indicates that the element *b* can be repeated *n* times, $n \geq 0$;
{a|b}   means that either *a* or *b* is chosen;
<p>   indicates that *p* is a parameter that must be bound to a particular value.

References

[ANSI 86] American National Standard for Information Systems, *Database Language SQL,* ANSI X3.135 – 1986, October 1986.

[Codd 70] E. F. Codd, "A Relational Model for Large Shared DataBanks," Comm. of ACM, Vol. 13, No. 6, June 1970.

[Codd 82] E. F. Codd, "Relational Databases: A Practical Foundation for Productivity," Comm. of ACM, Vol. 25, No. 2, February 1982.

[Codd 85] E. F. Codd, "An Evaluation Scheme for Database Management Systems That are Claimed to be Relational," Int. Conf. on Data Engineering, Los Angeles, February 1985.

[Date 83] C. J. Date, *An Introduction to Database Systems,* Vol. 2, Addison-Wesley Publishing Company, 1983.

[Date 86] C. J. Date, *An Introduction to Database Systems,* Vol. 2, 4th ed., Addison-Wesley Publishing Company, 1986.

[Delobel 85] C. Delobel, M. Adiba, *Relational Database Systems,* North Holland, 1985.

[Gardarin 84] G. Gardarin, E. Gelenbe, *New Applications of Databases,* Academic Press, 1984.

[Gardarin 88] G. Gardarin, P. Valduriez, *Relational Databases and Knowledge Bases,* Addison-Wesley Publishing Company, 1988.

[Schmidt 83] J. W. Schmidt, M. L. Brodie, *Relational Database Systems: Analysis and Comparison,* Springer-Verlag, 1983.

[Ullman 82] J. D. Ullman, *Principles of Database Systems,* 2d ed., Computer Science Press, 1982.

2

INTRODUCTION
TO TEN RDBMSs

2.1 Introduction

A large range of relational database systems (RDBMSs) is on the market. They
generally support several relational concepts but differ in several important ways
according to their marketing objectives and their implementation choices.

   This chapter describes the ten RDBMSs for mainframe computers and minicomputers examined in detail in the five following chapters. The systems are:
DB2, INGRES, SABRINA, SUPRA, DATACOM/DB, FOCUS, NOMAD, OR-
ACLE, SYBASE, and UNIFY. These are not the only RDBMSs available on the
market; we chose to examine these because they have a large number of relational
features, they are well documented, and they have been successful from a marketing point of view. The set of the described systems is therefore representative of
the RDBMS realm. Each system is described in detail in the following chapters.
The three first systems (DB2, INGRES, and SABRINA) are the result of a major
research project and are well documented; therefore a whole chapter (Chapters
3–5) is devoted to the study of each of them. SUPRA, a typical example of an
industrial system, is also described in a separate chapter (Chapter 6). The six
other systems are described in less detail in the same chapter (Chapter 7).

   The presentations made in this book are based on the most recent version
of each system, which will probably be improved in the future. Our objective,
however, is not to decide which of the marketed RDBMSs is the best; it is to
characterize these systems by examining their function and their design and im-

plementation choices in a systematic way. Very little information has been made available about the performance of these systems. The criteria chosen for the comparison may help the reader to analyze quickly and systematically other systems.

The comparisons made among the systems in this chapter are based on their language, their functional capabilities, and their implementation aspects. The relevant criteria indispensable for these comparisons are defined in Section 2.2. To illustrate the languages of these systems, a toy database and a set of queries, which allows one to illustrate a large range of functional capabilities, are described in Section 2.3. The ten RDBMSs are broadly introduced in Section 2.4. The characteristics of these systems are summed up in the comparative tables in Section 2.5.

2.2 Description of an RDBMS

The most distinguishing feature of RDBMSs is probably their targeted applications, which dictates most of the design and implementation choices. Most RDBMSs are designed for traditional data processing (business) applications, which can be roughly divided into two classes. The first class consists of *decision support applications,* such as project planning, which are oriented toward complex queries. The database is typically small or medium and accessed by a few (perhaps ten) concurrent users. These applications essentially require ease of use and fast response time. The second class consists of *on-line processing applications,* such as an airline reservation system, which are transaction oriented and update intensive. The database is typically very large and accessed by a large number of concurrent users. These applications need high multiuser throughput and extensive data control and availability. Although most RDBMSs may be used for both classes of applications, some of them are best for on-line processing. In introducing each RDBMS, the special support of on-line processing applications will be indicated.

The description of an RDBMS is composed of the following elements: data definition, data manipulation, semantic data control, transaction management, algorithms, architecture, additional tools, and distributed database management. We introduce each of these elements and provide the basic terminology that will be used throughout this book. For more details, we refer readers to other books dealing with principles and algorithms of relational database systems [Gardarin 88, Date 86, Ullman 82].

2.2.1 Data Definition

This section describes the data definition language (DDL) and the way the data definitions are managed by the system. We consider only the data facilities for the conceptual and physical (also called internal) schema levels. External schema-level (views) definition is included in the section on semantic data control.

The definition languages for the conceptual and physical schemas may be distinct or included in a uniform language. Conceptual data definition is guided by the data model supported by the DBMS. Although most of the RDBMSs analyzed in this chapter support a purely relational model, some support a hybrid model in which relations may be organized as hierarchies. The hybrid model of an RDBMS, however, is able to reduce to a purely relational model. The conceptual data can thus be defined by the following entities: database, relation hierarchy, relation, tuple, domain, and attribute. Tuple definition is generally subsumed by relation definition, which requires the list of attributes that constitute a tuple. Important capabilities of the conceptual DDL are the addition and deletion of database, relation hierarchy (when applicable), relation, and attribute. The addition or deletion of attributes in a relation is complex, for it requires database reorganization.

Physical data definition prescribes the way the conceptual objects should be efficiently implemented on disk. In general, this includes the specification of relation (or relation hierarchy) clustering according to a storage structure (such as hashing or B-tree), secondary indexes, and sometimes links between frequently joined relations. Relation clustering must be defined to maximize the performance of the select/project operation. A secondary index optimizes the select operation by providing fast indirect access to a relation. Similar to the use in CODA-SYL systems, a link provides efficient support for the join operation. Important capabilities of the physical DDL are the definition and redefinition of relation clustering and the addition and deletion of indexes and links. The redefinition of relation clustering is involved, for it requires database reorganization.

The compilation of the DDL statements produces conceptual and physical data descriptions, which are typically stored in a central data structure called *data dictionary*. The data dictionary is an important tool, which includes all kinds of information about data, applications, and the system. Examples of such information are semantic data control information, compiled queries, and performance information. The data dictionary is dynamic when DDL statements generate automatic database reorganizaton and changes to the data dictionary become immediately visible to concurrent users. The data dictionary can be managed as a relational database, called *metabase,* in which case it can be queried by authorized users with the same data manipulation language. The data dictionary must be efficiently managed since it is systematically accessed for compiling user queries.

The data dictionary may provide direct support for database design by allowing the storage and manipulation of various design representations. In this case, the data dictionary is generally interfaced to a database design aid tool, which interacts with the designer through a possibly graphic interface and eventually generates the conceptual and physical schemas. The design aid capability provided by some RDBMSs is of major value in automating the task of the database administrator.

2.2.2 Data Manipulation

The data manipulation language, often called *query language,* enables a user or programmer to retrieve data from the database and to update the database. We make a clear distinction between query language and user interface. The *query language* is the single user entry point to the database system. On top of the query language may be provided various *user interfaces,* each targeted for a class of applications. The user interfaces offered by the best RDBMSs are typically highly visual and combine the use of forms, menus, icons, and windows. Their description is also included in this section.

The value of the relational model is to give a solid foundation for high-level query languages. The query languages of the first DBMSs, such as hierarchical and CODASYL systems, are essentially procedural. With such languages, the user (actually a programmer) navigates in a hierarchy or a network through a "one-record-at-a-time" interface and specifies the way (procedure) the data should be accessed. Based on set theory, the relational model has permitted the development of nonprocedural set-oriented query languages, with which the user specifies the needed result without having to describe the way to produce it.

Relational query languages have a sound theoretical basis: relational algebra or relational calculus. Relational algebra [Codd 72], based on set theory, provides set operations (Cartesian product, union, difference, select, project, join, and others) to manipulate relations. Complex queries can be expressed as sequences of relational algebra operations. Furthermore, efficient algorithms exist for implementing each operator. Relational calculus-based languages [Codd 72], based on first-order logic, enable the expression of queries as logical formulas. Thus, they are more declarative than relational algebra-based languages. The major advantage of a declarative language is to minimize the amount of information necessary to specify a query. This diminishes the risk of user error, increases user productivity, and provides more opportunities for system optimization. Relational calculus is divided between *tuple relational calculus* and *domain relational calculus.* Tuple relational calculus associates tuples to each variable of a logic formula. The SQL language (see Chapter 3) is based on tuple relational calculus. Domain relational calculus associates domains to each variable of a logic formula. The QBE language (see Chapter 3) is based on domain relational calculus. An important property of relational calculus is that it can be mapped easily into relational algebra. Therefore most RDBMSs that support a relational calculus-based query language implement relational algebra operators for efficiency.

Query languages are specially designed for intensive data manipulation. In addition, they provide basic support for result presentation, such as sorting and grouping; however, their data type support and computational power are generally quite limited. The domains supported by current RDBMSs include a few primitive types such as integer, real, string, date, and time. The computation capabilities are restricted to arithmetic and aggregate functions. Furthermore, complex applications require the ability to nest several query language commands and some form of control over this nesting.

One general solution to these problems is to embed the query language into a general-purpose programming language. The programming language is a third-generation language such as C, COBOL, or Pascal (first- and second-generation languages designate machine and assembly languages, respectively). An *embedded query language* combines the database manipulation capabilities of the query language with the general computing power of the programming language. One significant problem with this approach is that the application programmer must deal with two languages, one procedural and one nonprocedural, which do not match nicely. Furthermore a different embedded query language preprocessor is necessary for each host language.

Another solution is to provide a unique language that integrates the query language capabilities with essential programming language constructs. The resulting language is termed *fourth-generation language* (4GL) and, compared to a 3GL such as COBOL, is essentially nonprocedural. There is no precise definition of 4GL. However, a typical 4GL includes query language commands, control capabilities (IF, GOTO, etc.), iteration (WHILEDO, FOR), variable manipulation, and error handling. The query language commands can be based on either relational algebra or relational calculus. Furthermore, a 4GL usually integrates in a uniform way powerful tools, such as report generator or application generator, which increase programmer productivity. Although less general than the embedded query language approach, 4GLs are a step toward database programming languages in which the database manipulation and programming capabilities are fully integrated.

2.2.3 Semantic Data Control

This section describes the way data manipulation may be controlled so that authorized users perform correct operations on the database. Semantic data control typically includes view management, security control, and semantic integrity control. These functions contribute to the maintenance of database integrity. In the relational framework, semantic data control can be achieved in a uniform fashion. Views, security constraints, and semantic integrity constraints can be defined as rules that the system automatically enforces. The violation of some rule by a user transaction, a set of database operations (see Section 2.2.4), implies generally the rejection of the effects of that transaction.

The definition of the rules for controlling data manipulation is part of the administration of the database, a function generally performed by a database administrator (DBA). The DBA is also in charge of applying the organization's policies. Semantic data control is generally specified using the DDL. Similar to data definition, the rules for semantic data control are maintained in the data dictionary.

Views enable user groups to have their particular perception of the database. In a relational system, a view is a *virtual relation,* defined as the result of a query on base relations but not materialized like a base relation stored in the database. A view is a dynamic window in the sense that it reflects all updates to the database. An external schema can be defined as a set of views and/or base relations. Besides their use in external schemas, views are also useful for ensuring data security in a simple way. By selecting a subset of the database, views hide some data. If users may access the database only through views, then they cannot see and manipulate the hidden data, which are therefore secure.

Data security, an important function of a database system, protects data against unauthorized access. Data security encompasses data protection and authorization control. *Data protection* is required to prevent the physical content of data from being understood by unauthorized users. This function is typically provided by file systems. The ultimate solution to protecting data on disk is data encryption. Encrypted (encoded) data can be decrypted (decoded) only by authorized users who know the code. *Authorization control* must guarantee that authorized users perform only operations they are allowed to on the database. Many different users may have access to a large collection of data under the control of a single system. The DBMS must thus be able to restrict the access of a subset of the database to a subset of the users. Authorization control has long been provided by operating systems as services of the file system. In this context, a centralized control is offered. The creator of an object is the central controller who may allow particular users to perform particular operations (read, write, execute) on that object. Also, objects are identified by their external names. Authorization control in database systems differs from those of traditional file systems in several aspects. Authorizations must be refined so that different users have different rights on the same database objects. This requirement implies the ability to specify subsets of objects more precisely than by name and to distinguish among groups of users. In addition, decentralized control of authorizations is of particular importance in a distributed context. In relational systems, authorizations can be uniformly controlled by DBAs using high-level constructs. For example, the controlled objects can be specified by predicates in the same way as a query qualification.

Semantic data control contributes to the maintenance of *database consistency*. A database state is said to be consistent if the database satisfies a set of constraints, called *semantic integrity constraints*. Maintaining a consistent database requires various mechanisms, such as concurrency control, reliability, protection, and semantic integrity control. Semantic integrity control ensures database consistency by rejecting update transactions that lead to inconsistent database states or by activating specific actions on the database state that compensate for the effect of the update transactions. The updated database must satisfy the set of integrity constraints. With no support from the DBMS, the traditional solution to semantic integrity control is to embed the controls in application programs. Declarative methods have emerged with the relational model to alleviate the problems of program/data dependency, code redundancy, and poor performance of the traditional solution. The idea is to express integrity constraints using assertions of predicate calculus. Thus a set of semantic integrity assertions defines database consistency. This approach allows one to declare easily and modify complex integrity assertions. However, supporting automatic semantic integrity control requires efficient algorithms since the cost of checking assertions can be prohibitive. Therefore most RDBMSs are restrictive in their support for semantic integrity control, although a few recent ones have excellent semantic integrity control capabilities.

2.2.4 Transaction Management

This section describes the solutions to transaction management in a multiuser (concurrent) environment when system and media failures occur. Database consistency can be altered by update operations. To guarantee database consistency, update operations are typically grouped into consistency units, called *transactions,* controlled by the database system. A transaction is an execution unit that, applied to a consistent database, generates a consistent but possibly different database. A transaction is *atomic:* either it is executed to completion (commits), or it is not executed at all (aborts). Concurrency control and recovery are the two aspects of transaction management. Concurrency control and recovery in RDBMSs need not be different than in nonrelational systems. A comprehensive treatment of transaction management can be found in [Bernstein 87].

Concurrency control ensures that the interleaved execution of multiple transactions produces the same result as if they were executed sequentially. Thus concurrency control makes multiuser data sharing transparent to each user. An important goal of concurrency control is to achieve a high degree of concurrency in order to maximize the system throughput. The most popular solution to concurrency control, based on *locking,* is derived from the operating system method for allocating resources to tasks. The various portions of data may be viewed as resources that may be allocated (locked) or deallocated (unlocked) to transactions. An important parameter affecting performance is the *data granule,* which can be locked or unlocked. Concurrency control granularity is both logical (transaction level) and physical (system level). A logical granule may be database, relation, domain, or tuple; a physical granule may be segment, file, or page. A logical granule corresponds to one or more physical granules. A small granule obviously maximizes the degree of concurrency but, compared to larger granules, incurs higher control overhead (in particular, the lock table is larger). A small granule (such as tuple) is best for short transactions that touch a few tuples; a large granule is best for long transactions (such as batch transactions). The well-known problem of a locking algorithm is that deadlocks may occur. The main solution, based on deadlock detection, may generate transaction aborts.

Transaction reliability guarantees that transactions are executed in a reliable way. It is achieved through fault-tolerance techniques that permit recovery from many kinds of failure. The most important types of failure that transaction reliability is concerned with are transaction, system, and media failures. The objective of reliability is to recover a consistent database state after failure while minimizing user interaction. Ideally recovery should be transparent to the user. Overall, reliability is a complex function that is not independent of other important functions such as concurrency control, buffer management, and file management. The single principle on which all reliability algorithms are based is data duplication: corrupted or lost data should always be recoverable from redundant copies. Managing this duplication is expensive, for it can increase the number of disk accesses to process updates. The most popular data structures used for duplication are logs and periodic backup copies. A log records information regarding the state of update transactions and the updated pages. The main types of information recorded in the log are before and after images. The logs are useful to start or restart the system. The procedure executed to start the system after normal termination or failure is called *recovery procedure*. The recovery procedures are based on the log and eventually on tape archives. The types of recovery procedures are: recovery after normal termination, transaction failure (abort), system failure, and media failure. Recovery after media failure is the most complex procedure since it requires the combined use of logs and backup copies.

There are two basic techniques for implementing disk page updates in conjunction with a reliability algorithm: update-in-place and shadowing. *Update-in-place* tries to keep the updated objects at their original location. *Shadowing* never keeps the updated objects at their original location. The updates of a transaction are not done in place but rather in new pages, whose old versions are called *shadow pages*. Each technique is useful for different conditions.

2.2.5 Query Processing and Storage Model

The query processing strategy and the data storage model are the key components for efficient processing of database queries. RDBMSs tend to offer high-level languages (such as SQL) that are nonprocedural and use set-at-a-time operators. When querying a relational database, the user specifies the desired result without providing the access paths to the data. Hence the system is responsible for determining how to access the data by applying a query processing algorithm that produces an access plan for a given query. Query processing is a difficult and important task that has received considerable attention in the past ten years [Jarke 84, Kim 85]. The reason is that its efficiency conditions the performance of the RDBMS in performing high-level queries and thus its usability. The performance issue is critical for relational systems because queries are uniformly used to perform various tasks, such as retrieval and update queries, schema management, and semantic data control. The first RDBMSs were strongly criticized because of their poor performance. Since then the query processing methods designed have proved to be efficient in both prototypes and the later commercial products.

The objective of query processing is to execute queries in such a way that cost is minimized. The selection of the best access plan, called *query optimization,* is known to be computationally intractable for general queries. Therefore heuristics are necessary for optimizing the cost function. This cost function typically refers to machine resources such as disk accesses and central processing unit (CPU) time. The most popular approach to query optimization is the exhaustive search of the entire solution space in which the cost of each possible access plan is estimated. Such optimization is based on the statistics regarding the database (relation cardinalities, attribute selectivities, and so on), available access paths to the data (such as clustered and secondary indexes), and algorithms for implementing relational algebra operations.

Physical database design is an important issue related to query optimization. In fact, nonrelational database systems such as IMS and System 2000 provide very sophisticated ways of organizing the physical database structure. Physical database design permits one to tailor the underlying database structure to a given data access pattern, deduced from the knowledge of database applications. Thus the power of the storage model, which prescribes the storage structures and algorithms provided by the DBMS, and the accuracy of physical database design are crucial to the efficiency of query processing.

2.2.6 Additional Tools

The additional tools that often come fully integrated with an RDBMS are designed to improve data presentation and application development and to interface with other systems. They add to database usability and the application developer's productivity.

The limited data presentation facility of a query language like SQL can be enriched by a report generator and a graphic interface. A *report generator* permits users to define rapidly complex reports with report characteristics (header, page headers and footers, group and subgroups with headings and totals) and data selected from the database. The report definitions are stored in the data dictionary. Reports can be produced by giving the report name and a query qualification to select the desired data. A *graphic interface* permits one to display the results of retrieval queries as graphic forms, such as histograms, diagrams, or curves, possibly with colors. Similar to reports, graphs are defined and stored in the data dictionary.

The development of complex data processing applications can be significantly speeded up by such tools such as the screen manager and the application generator. A *screen manager* permits the definition of custom screens for data editing, possibly using the report generator or graphic interface for data presentation. Screen definitions are stored in the data dictionary. An *application genera-*

tor performs a more complex task that combines and synchronizes the previous tools for defining rapidly complex applications. RDBMSs generally provide interfaces with other systems for integrating nonrelational data in the database. Typical interfaces are with text editors, spread-sheet programs, mail systems, or file systems.

2.2.7 Architectures

This section describes the functional and process architectures of the RDBMS. The *functional architecture* is given in terms of software modules, each performing a well-defined function, and interfaces between modules. The functional architectures of RDBMSs may be roughly divided between two types of architectures, as shown in Fig. 2.1.

The first type of architecture is based on a separate interface model with

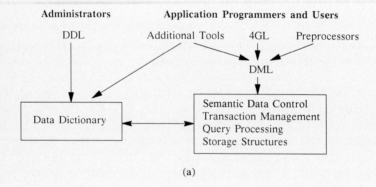

(a)

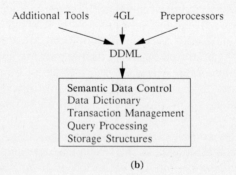

(b)

FIGURE 2.1 Functional RDBMS architectures. (**a**) Separate interface model and (**b**) uniform interface model.

two separate RDBMS languages: the DDL and the data manipulation language (DML). The various user interfaces and additional tools are built on top of the DML. With this type of architecture, the data dictionary is generally not managed as a metabase but in an internal form that requires specific manipulation capabilities. Therefore there might be some duplication of function (and code) to manipulate data dictionary information and relation information. This type of architecture generally stems from a bottom-up design approach where the data dictionary and relational features have been added on an existing file system or database system architecture.

The second type of architecture is based on a uniform interface model with a unique data definition and manipulation language (DDML). With this type of architecture, the data dictionary is managed as a relational database. Therefore data dictionary manipulation can be entirely done with the relational database management capabilities. This type of architecture stems from a top-down design approach where the RDBMS has been designed from scratch.

The *process architecture* describes the implementation of the multiuser RDBMS in the operating system. There are three basic approaches to allocate operating system processes to RDBMS transactions [Stonebraker 81], as shown in Fig. 2.2. In all approaches, there is one process per logged-on user, called *user process,* which manages user interaction (such as terminal monitor).

The simplest approach is the *process model* approach in which there is exactly one RDBMS process per user. The RDBMS processes share the same reentrant RDBMS code and some common data structures such as buffer table. Since each transaction is implemented by one process, the multitasking and scheduling facilities of the operating system may be exploited. The main disadvantage of this approach is that the number of competing users is limited by the maximum number of processes. Remember that a process is a valuable resource. Another problem is the overhead of process switching. Whenever a transaction is interrupted, for example, because of a disk access, a process switch occurs, and another process becomes active. In most operating systems, process switching is expensive in terms of CPU time. Most RDBMSs follow this approach.

Another approach is the *single server model,* in which the user processes send request messages to be served by a single RDBMS process. This approach solves most of the problems of the process model. In particular, since there is a single RDBMS process, the overhead for process switching is minimized. This approach is more complex, however, because the single RDBMS process must support some form of multitasking and scheduling of transactions to provide internal parallelism.

A third approach is the *multiple server model,* in which the user processes can send request messages to multiple RDBMS processes. This approach may avoid the main problem of the single server model (duplication of operating system code). Furthermore it provides opportunities for processing transactions in parallel by having several RDBMS processes performing different work for the same transaction.

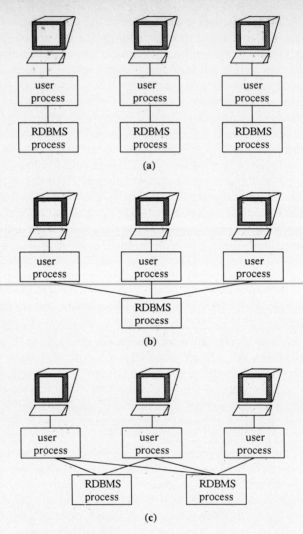

FIGURE 2.2 Different RDBMS process architectures. (**a**) Process model, (**b**) single server model, and (**c**) multiple server model.

2.2.8 Distributed Database Management

The support of remote or distributed datase is an important capability of a DBMS. Since the early 1960s, centralization of an organization's data in a large and expensive computer has been the single approach to data processing. Recent developments in the area of computer networks, minicomputers, and microcomputers have made the decentralized approach, in which the data are distributed across several machines, a cost-effective solution. A decentralized approach has three advantages. First, each group (or person) having a computer has direct control over its own information, resulting in increased data integrity and more efficient data processing. Second, compared to the centralized approach in which the data must be transferred from each group to the central computer, the communication overhead is reduced. Third, the decentralized approach is the natural solution to data processing in a geographically distributed organization.

The need to integrate and share the data located in and managed on different computers is often very strong. Such data sharing requires the interconnection of the various computers through a local or general network and specific software support to manage and process distributed data. Most RDBMSs offer solutions to distributed data sharing. These solutions, given in increasing degree of functionality, are remote database, homogeneous distributed database, and heterogeneous distributed database.

A *remote database* (Fig. 2.3) is a database located on a computer other than where the user (or application) is executing. In general, the user is aware of the remote database location, which must be specified to access the data. A data communication component is necessary for accessing the remote database. A local database may also reside on the computer the user is running. The user can then download remote database data to the local database. Recent advances in microcomputer technology have favored the workstation/server organization, in which the remote database is managed on a mainframe server by an RDBMS and private databases are managed on workstations by a microversion of the same RDBMS. The interconnection server/workstation is typically handled by a local network.

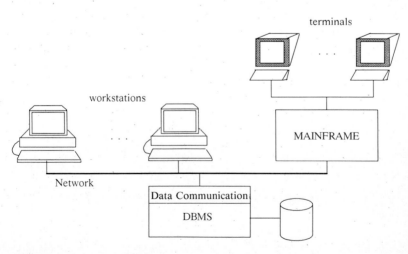

FIGURE 2.3 Remote database.

A *distributed database* [Ceri 84, Ozsu 89] is a set of cooperating databases that reside on different machines, called sites, interconnected by a computer network. The main difference from a remote database is that the user is not aware of data location and perceives the distributed database as a single database. This important feature is usually called *location transparency*. For increasing reliability and locality of references, some data can also be replicated on several computers. *Replication transparency* makes such replication invisible to the user. The management of a distributed database requires the following system components at each site: a data communication component, a local DBMS, and a distributed DBMS (DDBMS). The DDBMS has four main functions:

1. Management of a global data dictionary to support location and replication transparency.
2. Distributed data definition and control.
3. Distributed query processing, including distributed query optimization and remote database access.
4. Distributed transaction management, including distributed concurrency control, recovery, and commit protocol.

A distinguishing property of a distributed database is to be homogeneous or heterogeneous (Fig. 2.4). A *homogeneous distributed database* is one where all the local databases are managed by the same DBMS. This approach is the simpler one and provides incremental growth, by making easy the addition of a new site

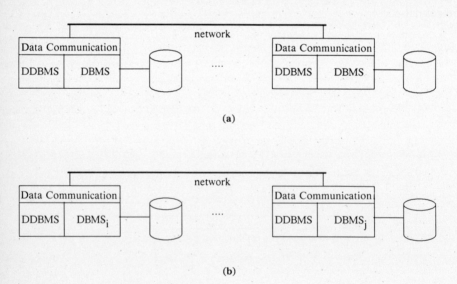

FIGURE 2.4 Distributed databases. (**a**) Homogeneous (same local DBMSs) and (**b**) Heterogeneous (different local DBMSs).

in the network, and increased performance, by exploiting the parallel processing capability of multiple sites. A *heterogeneous distributed database* is one where the local databases need not be managed by the same DBMS. For example, $DBMS_i$ can be a relational system and $DBMS_j$ a hierarchical system. This approach is more complex but enables the integration of existing independent databases without requiring the creation of a completely new distributed database. In addition, the DDBMS must provide interfaces between the different DBMSs. The typical solution used by RDBMSs is to have gateways that convert the language of each different DBMS into the language of the RDBMS.

2.3 The Toy Database

The toy database is a WINES database modeling an agricultural company supplying wines to customers, called drinkers. The basic schema is shown in Fig. 2.5. The drinkers are characterized by a number (attribute D#), a name, and a type of drinker ("heavy," "average," "light"). The wines are described by the attributes wine number (W#), vineyard, vintage, percentage of alcohol (PERCENT), and price. The wines are made by producers who are characterized by a number (P#), a name, and a region. The information regarding wines drunk in a certain quantity, at a specific date and place, is collected in the DRINK relation. The quantities of wines harvested by the wine producers are collected in the HARVEST relation. In Fig. 2.5, the attributes that participate in the key of each relation are printed in boldface type.

Different types of queries are now defined in English. They are supposed to test thoroughly the data manipulation language's expressive power. Three retrieval queries (R1, R2, R3), an insert query (I1), a modification query (M1), and a view definition query (V1) are the constituents of the set of queries that will be expressed in the language of each system. For each query, we give its result based on the instantiation of the WINES database illustrated in Fig. 2.6.:

R1: This type of retrieval query illustrates the use of the project, select, and join operators. It returns the names of producers of 1982 or 1984 Julienas. The result is:

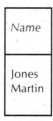

Name
Jones
Martin

R2: This type of retrieval query performs a select operation in which the search qualification involves a simple string pattern matching and null values (unknown values). It returns the names of the drinkers having

DRINKER (**D#**, NAME, TYPE)
WINE (**W#**, VINEYARD, VINTAGE, PERCENT, PRICE)
PRODUCER (**P#**, NAME, REGION)
DRINK (**D#, W#, DATE, PLACE,** QTY)
HARVEST (**P#, W#,** QTY)

FIGURE 2.5 WINES database

WINE

W#	VINEYARD	VINTAGE	PERCENT	PRICE
W1	Julienas	1982	13.2	null
W2	Beaujolais Village	1987	12.9	7
W3	Julienas	1984	12.8	10
W4	Pommard	1983	12.3	14
W5	Medoc	1978	11.5	25
W6	Chianti Classico	1985	11.9	10
W7	Chardonnay	1985	13.5	null
W8	Pommard	1984	12.1	12
W9	Montbazillac	1983	11.8	12
W10	Cabernet	1986	null	14

PRODUCER

P#	NAME	REGION
P1	Pierre	Bourgogne
P2	Jones	Beaujolais
P3	Dupuy	Bordeaux
P4	Bertolli	Chianti
P5	Martin	Beaujolais
P6	Smith	California
P7	Puig	Dordogne

HARVEST

P#	W#	QTY
P1	W4	10
P2	W1	20
P2	W2	15
P4	W6	12
P5	W1	30
P6	W7	null
P6	W10	20
P7	W9	null

DRINKER

D#	NAME	TYPE
D1	Jones	average
D2	Dupont	heavy
D3	Bertolli	heavy
D4	Paul	light
D5	Doe	null

DRINK

D#	W#	DATE	PLACE	QTY
D1	W6	04/12	Paris	5
D1	W3	09/25	Austin	2
D2	W10	04/12	Paris	7
D2	W5	09/25	Austin	7
D5	W1	09/25	Austin	3

FIGURE 2.6 Example of WINES database

drunk a wine whose vineyard's name begins with "C," and whose percentage of alcohol is between 11 and 13 or unknown. The result is

Name
Jones
Dupont

R3: This type of retrieval query performs a select operation with the use of aggregates in the project list and search qualification. It computes the average percentage of alcohol per vineyard for only those vineyards whose minimum percentage of alcohol is more than 12. The result is

Vineyard	Average Percentage
Julienas	13
Beaujolais Village	12.9
Pommard	12.2
Chardonnay	13.5

I1: This type of update query inserts a set of tuples into a base relation from a temporary relation resulting from a selection in the database. It inserts the producers of the Bourgogne region having harvested a 1983 wine, in the DRINKER relation, having for drinker's number, the producer's number, and an unknown type. The DRINKER relation becomes

D#	Name	Type
D1	Jones	average
D2	Dupont	heavy
D3	Bertolli	heavy
D4	Paul	light
D5	Doe	null
P1	Pierre	null

M1: This type of update query modifies a set of tuples by computing a new attribute value from an existing value. It increases by 10 percent the quantity of Julienas harvested in 1982. The HARVEST relation becomes

P#	W#	Qty
P1	W4	10
P2	W1	22
P2	W2	15
P4	W6	12
P5	W1	33
P6	W7	null
P6	W10	20
P7	W9	null

V1: This type of query provides the definition of a multirelation view, which is recorded in the data dictionary. The JULIENAS-HARVEST view indicates, for each producer of Julienas, the producer number, the name, and the quantity. The materialization of this view (be selecting all its information) would produce

P#	Name	Qty
P2	Jones	20
P5	Martin	30

2.4 Overview of Ten Relational Systems

2.4.1 DB2 and SQL/DS

DB2 and SQL/DS form the family of IBM's relational products. Both products offer the high-level language SQL and have the same functional capabilities; they differ only by their operating system environment and targeted applications. SQL/DS is best for decision support applications, while DB2, specifically designed for large configurations, is targeted for on-line processing applications. Besides the SQL language, these systems also support original solutions to data control, transaction management, and query optimization. The storage structures are based on B-trees. SQL/DS works on IBM minicomputers under DOS/VSE and VM/CMS, whereas DB2 is implemented on IBM mainframes under MVS and MVS/XA. Two optional products — QMF (Query Management Facility) and DXT (Data Extract) — may be used with SQL/DS or DB2.

2.4.2 INGRES

INGRES is an RDBMS originally designed for the minicomputer environment. It is marketed by Relational Technology Inc. INGRES supports the high-level QUEL and SQL languages, and it provides original solutions to data control and query decomposition. In addition, it supports powerful and user-friendly tools for application development based on the concept of visual programming. The INGRES implementation is based on B-trees, ISAM, and hashed storage structures. INGRES runs on many minicomputers, including DEC VAX under UNIX and VMS, IBM under VM/CMS, Appolo, DATA GENERAL, HP, ICL, NCR, SUN, and UNISYS. A MICRO-INGRES version is available for microcomputers based on the microprocessor MC 68000 under UNIX. Furthermore INGRES includes INGRES/STAR, the first commercial version of a heterogeneous distributed database system.

2.4.3 SABRINA

Designed by a group of researchers from INRIA and the University of Paris 6, France, and later marketed by a group of French companies (INFOSYS, EUROSOFT, SAGEM), SABRINA is an SQL-based RDBMS. The SABRINA product provides a rich set of user interfaces, including SQL, a form-oriented version of SQL, and a multilanguage interface for host programming languages, and integrated tools for application development. The distinguishing features of the SABRINA system are complete and efficient semantic integrity control, the support of nonnormalized relations at the internal schema level, a single storage structure called predicate tree with which many kinds of multiattribute hashing methods can be specified, an efficient hash-based join algorithm that exploits large main memories, and an original integrated solution to transaction management. SABRINA is operational on DPS8 under MULTICS, on SM90/SPS7 under UNIX, and more generally on all UNIX-based systems.

2.4.4 SUPRA

Designed by Cincom Systems, the creator of the well-known product TOTAL, SUPRA is a heterogeneous DBMS that exhibits many relational features and supports various internal data structures, such as preexisting TOTAL or VSAM files. SUPRA is uniquely designed for on-line processing applications. The support of various internal data structures is achieved through sophisticated conceptual-internal schema mappings. SUPRA includes a powerful algebraic 4GL and a complete set of 4GL application development tools, including a database design aid.

SUPRA is available on IBM mainframes. A version of SUPRA, called ULTRA, is also available on the DEC VAX computers.

2.4.5 DATACOM/DB

Designed by Applied Data Research, DATACOM/DB is a heterogeneous RDBMS targeted for large on-line processing applications. DATACOM/DB is derived from an advanced inverted-list DBMS. It allows applications to access various internal data structures such as VSAM and DL/I files. DATACOM/DB supports SQL and comes with several other 4GL tools for application development, including a COBOL generator and a database design facility. Furthermore, DATACOM/DB is included in a homogeneous distributed database system. DATACOM/DB implements a peculiar storage model, based on a compound index, and sophisticated query optimization. DATACOM/DB and associated products are uniquely targeted for IBM operating environments.

2.4.6 FOCUS

Produced by Information Builders Inc., FOCUS is a hybrid DBMS that provides a relational as well as a hierarchical model. The relations are segments that may be arranged hierarchically in a file. However, FOCUS can be used as a pure RDBMS. FOCUS offers an extensive set of 4GL interfaces and fourth-generation tools for application development. Read/write interface facilities enable users to read and update external files (VSAM) or external databases (IMS, DB2, SQL/DS, and others) uniformly within the FOCUS environment. The implementation is based on the BDAM and B-tree organizations. FOCUS is available on several operating environments, including IBM mainframes, DEC VAX, and WANG VS computers. A microversion is available on PC/XT microcomputers.

2.4.7 NOMAD

Produced by MUST Software International, NOMAD is a hybrid DBMS that can be relational as well as hierarchical. Similar to FOCUS, many relations may be arranged hierarchically within a file. NOMAD provides an extensive set of 4GL components. One of its unique capabilities lies in the possibilities of defining a virtual database as a unique relation (universal), thus avoiding the specifying of the joins. The implementation is based on the BDAM organization. NOMAD is uniquely designed and optimized for the IBM operating environments and compatible systems under MVS, MVS/XA, MVS outside TSO, and VM/CMS. A microversion is available on IBM PC and compatibles.

2.4.8 ORACLE

Designed by Oracle Corporation, ORACLE is an SQL-based RDBMS. ORACLE optimizes the execution of relational operations using efficient storage structures — in particular, multirelation clustering. ORACLE comes with a set of 4GL tools that interface the RDBMS through SQL. This includes a 4GL, a form-oriented application generator, a report writer, a database design help, a color graphics facility, and an easy-to-learn spread sheet. Furthermore ORACLE supports relational distributed database management. ORACLE is highly portable and therefore available on a large variety of operating environments, including mainframes, minicomputers, and microcomputers.

2.4.9 SYBASE

Produced by Sybase Inc., SYBASE is the newest SQL-based RDBMS. It is specifically optimized for on-line data processing applications. Therefore it provides complete semantic data control, including triggers, and high multiuser performance. SYBASE consists of two subsystems, the DataToolSet and the DataServer. The DataToolSet provides a powerful SQL-based 4GL for data definition, data manipulation, and data control and includes a complete set of form-oriented tools for application development and maintenance. The DataServer provides the database management functions and includes a homogeneous distributed database management capability. SYBASE is primarily designed for DEC VAX computers under VMS and UNIX, and SUN computers.

2.4.10 UNIFY

Designed by Unify Corporation, UNIFY is an RDBMS that is uniquely targeted for on-line transaction processing applications in the UNIX environments. UNIFY is available on all UNIX-based operating environments. UNIFY's access model includes four access methods, each optimized for a specific access type: hashing for random access, multiple attribute B-trees for range queries and wildcard search, links for joins, and buffered sequential access for efficient scan. UNIFY comes with a number of form-oriented tools for data management, which access uniformly the DBMS through a unique low-level interface. UNIFY also can be part of an integrated development environment, ACCEL, that combines the capabilities of application generators, windowing interfaces, 4GLs, and relational database management.

2.5 Comparative Tables

This section summarizes the functional capabilities and implementation choices of the ten RDBMSs. Details regarding the elements constituting the description of these RDBMSs are given in comparative tables. In each table, the ten RDBMSs are listed by row in order of presentation. Since the IBM systems SQL/DS and DB2 provide the same function, we will list only DB2 except in the last table, in which both SQL/DS and DB2 are presented. For each table, we give some explanation of each column from left to right.

Table 2.1 summarizes the data definition capabilities of each system. The data model indicated is the one that is supported to define the schema viewed by the users. A hybrid model is one that is hierarchical but can reduce to a purely relational model. A few systems support three schema levels. The absence of external schema stems from the lack of view support. The absence of internal schema means that conceptual and internal levels are almost identical since a relation is implemented as a single file and one or more indexes. The support of internal schema allows access to various external files or the implementation of several relations in a single file for avoiding join operations. The basic conceptual definition unit is either a single relation (relation, or logical view) or several relations (hierarchical file, or base). In the second case, changing a relation schema implies redefining the entire file or base. The redefinition of a relation schema is supported when the addition (extend) or removal (restrict) of attributes implies the automatic relation's reorganization. If not supported, changing a relation schema must be done by the DBA using a loading-unloading facility. All systems support an active data dictionary to maintain data definitions. The data dictionary is fully integrated with the DBMS when organized as a metabase (relational database). In this case, it can be accessed with the same data manipulation language. Otherwise the data dictionary is managed in an ad hoc way, that is, differently from the base data. We say that a database design aid is supported when conceptual and/or internal schemas may be automatically generated from a high-level descripion of the attributes and their dependencies.

Table 2.2 summarizes the facilities offered by the systems to manipulate the database. The data manipulation language is SQL for most systems or algebraic (relational algebra operators with programming constructs). Most systems provide direct support for null values. A form-oriented version of the data manipulation language allows the user to express queries by forms displayed on the screen. Other types of user interface are a menu-based version of the language or a limited natural language (English) interface. In general, the data manipulation language is embedded in host programming languages through the precompiler approach or a CALL interface.

Table 2.3 summarizes the view, authorization, and semantic integrity support of each system. Relational views are supported if they instantaneously reflect the database updates. This definition thus excludes the static views (snapshots) that are copies of a database subset. On the other hand, it must be possible to

TABLE 2.1 Data definition

	Data model	Schema levels[a]	Conceptual definition unit	Relation change[b]	Data dictionary	Database design aid
DB2	Relational	E,C	Relation	E	Metabase	No
INGRES	Relational	E,C	Relation	E	Metabase	No
SABRINA	Relational	E,C,I	Relation	E,R	Metabase	Expert system
SUPRA	Relational views	E,C,I	Logical view	E,R	Ad hoc	Yes
DATACOM/DB	Relational	E,C,I	Relation	E,R	Ad hoc	No
FOCUS	Hybrid	C,I	File	E,R	Ad hoc	No
NOMAD	Hybrid	C,I	File	E,R	Ad hoc	No
ORACLE	Relational	E,C,I	Relation	E	Metabase	Yes
SYBASE	Relational	E,C	Relation	E	Metabase	No
UNIFY	Relational	E,C	Base	No	Metabase	No

[a]Schema levels: E: external, C: conceptual, I: internal.
[b]Relational change: E: expand (add attributes), R: restrict (remove attributes).

29

TABLE 2.2 Data manipulation

	Language	Null values	Query by forms	Other user interfaces	Host PL interface
DB2	SQL	Yes	Limited QBE	No	Precompiler
INGRES	QUEL, SQL	Yes	Yes	No	Precompiler
SABRINA	SQL	Yes	No	Menus	Precompiler
SUPRA	Algebraic	No	No	Menus, English	CALL interface
DATACOM/DB	Allgebraic, SQL	No	No	Menus	CALL interface COBOL interface
FOCUS	Algebraic	Yes	No	Menus, English	CALL interface COBOL interface
NOMAD	Algebraic	Yes	No	Menus	CALL interface
ORACLE	SQL	Yes	Yes	Menus	Precompiler CALL interface
SYBASE	SQL	Yes	Yes	Menus	Unique PL interface
UNIFY	Limited SQL	No	Limited QBF	No	Precompiler

TABLE 2.3 Semantic data control

	Relational views	Updatable views	Authorization control	Password protection	Encryption	Integrity control[a]
DB2	Yes	Select-project	Decentralized	No	No	K
INGRES	Yes	Select-project	Centralized	No	No	D,K
SABRINA	Yes	No	Decentralized	No	No	A,D,F,K,R,T
SUPRA	Yes	DBA-supplied update rules	Decentralized	No	No	K,R
DATACOM/DB	Yes	Select-project	Centralized	No	Yes	D,K
FOCUS	No	No	Centralized	No	Yes	D,K
NOMAD	No	No	Centralized	Yes	Yes	D,K,R
ORACLE	Yes	Select-project	Decentralized	Yes	No	D,K
SYBASE	Yes	Select-project	Centralized	No	No	D,K,R triggers
UNIFY	No	No	Centralized	Yes	No	D,K,R

[a]Integrity constraints: A: aggregate, D: domain, F: functional dependency, K: unique key, R: referential, T: temporal.

define from several relations a relational view. Update through views may be automatically supported when they result from select-project operations or when update rules have been specified by the DBA.

The authorization control is said to be decentralized when a constituent (a database, a relation, or a view) administrator possesses a command that grants somebody the right to be the constituent administrator. Otherwise the control is centralized, in which case the system generally supports the explicit notion of database controlled by a unique administrator. Data security may be increased by password protection and/or encryption. Semantic integrity control is also included in the table.

Table 2.4 summarizes the transaction management support of each system. A transaction may include several queries or may be a program that can be arbitrarily complex. The concurrency granule is the unit on which the exclusions of conflictual accesses between transactions are applied. Variable granularity (relation, tuple, set of qualified tuples) facilitates the application's control adequacy. All systems but one support concurrency control by two-phase locking with deadlock detection. Multistep transactions allow users to commit updates when needed, before the end of transaction. Multistep transactions are particularly useful for long and complex transactions. Most systems implement updates in place, and two systems use the shadow page mechanism. All the systems provide a mechanism for recovering after media failure, as well as after system and transaction failure.

Table 2.5 summarizes the storage structures and access paths, the query processing technique of each system. The two first columns (storage structures and access paths) are explicit. The optimization timing is *static* (if optimization is done before executing the query) or *dynamic* (if optimization takes place at run time). The static approach, generally based on the exhaustive search algorithm with heuristics, is able to save access plans in compiled form for future executions. The dynamic approach is employed when complex query optimization, which requires join ordering, is not supported. In this case, optimization reduces to the choice of the best access path per operation. The hybrid approach is initially static but incorporates run-time decisions. Most systems only implement the nested-loop join algorithm possibly combined with index access. The sort-merge join algorithm or hash-based join algorithm may complement the nested-loop join algorithm for joins with low selectivity or no index. The last column indicates interesting features of the storage model or query processing.

Table 2.6 summarizes the additional tools for data manipulation and presentation, application development, and other tools. The table is explicit and needs no further explanation.

Table 2.7 summarizes the functional and process architectures of each system. The functional architecture is based on either the separate interface model or the uniform interface model. In the latter case, there is a single entry point for both users and administrators. Most systems implement the process model. One

TABLE 2.4 Transaction management

	Transaction type	Concurrency granule	Concurrency control	Multistep transaction	Implementation of updates	Media recovery
DB2	Multiquery	Variable	Locking	Yes	In place	Yes
INGRES	Multiquery	Relation or page	Locking	Yes	In place	Yes
SABRINA	Multiquery	Page	Locking	No	Shadowing	Yes
SUPRA	Program	Tuple	Locking	No	In place	Yes
DATACOM/DB	Multiquery, Program	Tuple	Locking	No	In place	Yes
FOCUS	Program	Tuple	Versioning	No	Shadowing	Yes
NOMAD	Program	Relation or tuple	Locking	No	In place	Yes
ORACLE	Multiquery	Relation or tuple	Locking	Yes	In place	Yes
SYBASE	Multiquery	Relation or tuple	Locking	Yes	In place	Yes
UNIFY	Program, Query	Variable	Locking	Yes	In place	Yes

TABLE 2.5 Query processing and storage model

	Storage structures[a]	Access paths[b]	Optimization timing	Complex query optimization	Join algorithms[c]	Other
DB2	B	I,S	Static	Yes	NL,SM	
INGRES	H,B	H,I,S	Static	Yes	HJ,NL,SM	Data compression
SABRINA	Predicate tree	I,M,S	Static or dynamic	Yes	HJ,SM	Filtering
SUPRA	B,H,HR	H,I,L,S	Dynamic	No	NL	
DATACOM/DB	B	I,S	Hybrid	Yes	NL	Data compression
FOCUS	B,HR	I,L,S	Dynamic	No	NL	
NOMAD	B,HR	I,L,S	Dynamic	No	NL	
ORACLE	B,M	I,S	Static	Yes	NL	Data compression
SYBASE	B	I,S	Static	Yes	NL	
UNIFY	B,H	H,I,L,S	Dynamic	No	NL	Dynamic links

[a]B: B-trees, H: hashing, M: multirelation, HR: hierarchy.
[b]H: hashing, I: index, L: link, M: multiattribute clustering, S: scan.
[c]HJ: hash-based join, NL: nested loop, SM: sort-merge.

TABLE 2.6 Additional tools

	Result presentation[a]	Screen management[b]	4GL	Application generator	Decision support
DB2	RG	No	No	No	No
INGRES	RG, G	SM	Yes	Yes	No
SABRINA	RG	SM	No	No	No
SUPRA	RG	SM	Yes	Yes	Yes
DATACOM/DB	RG	SM	Yes	Yes	Yes
FOCUS	RG, G	SM	Yes	Yes	Statistics Spread sheet
NOMAD	RG, G	SM	Yes	Yes	Statistics Financial
ORACLE	RG, G	SM	No	Yes	No
SYBASE	RG	SM,WM	Yes	Yes	No
UNIFY	RG	SM,WM	No	No	No

[a]G: graphics, RG: report generator.
[b]SM: screen manager, WM: window manager.

(SYBASE) implements the single server model with its own multithread management, and another one (DATACOM/DB) implements the multiple server model. System portability is an interesting feature but must be traded off for performance. For example, a system uniquely designed for IBM machines can better exploit both the operating system and the machine architecture, as indicated in the last column. The uniform access to external data from the same environment is an important advantage that allows the integration of existing data.

Table 2.8 summarizes the distributed database management capabilities of the six listed systems (the others do not support distributed database management). Notice that FOCUS and NOMAD have a very limited distributed capability.

Table 2.9 summarizes the operating environments in which each system is available.

TABLE 2.7 Architectures

	Functional architecture	Single entry point	Process architecture[a]	Portability	Access to external data	Others
DB2	Uniform	SQL	PM	IBM	No	Exploits N-way processors
INGRES	Uniform	QUEL	PM	Medium	No	
SABRINA	Uniform	SQL	PM	UNIX	No	Own IO subsystem
SUPRA	Separate		PM	IBM	Yes	Exploits N-way processors
DATACOM/DB	Separate		MSM	IBM	Yes	Exploits N-way processors
FOCUS	Separate		PM	Low	Yes	
NOMAD	Separate		PM	IBM	Yes	Exploits virtual memory
ORACLE	Uniform	SQL	PM	High	No	
SYBASE	Uniform	SQL	SSM	Medium	No	
UNIFY	Uniform	Database routines	PM	UNIX	No	Own IO subsystem

[a]PM: process model, SSM: single server model, MSM: multiple server model.

TABLE 2.8 Distributed database management

	Distributed database	Location transparency	DBMS transparency	Replication transparency	Distributed query optimization	Distributed transaction management
INGRES	Heterogeneous	Yes	Yes	Yes	Yes	Yes
DATACOM/DB	Homogeneous	Yes	No	Yes	Yes	Yes
FOCUS	Remote (PC-server)	No	No	No	No	No
NOMAD	Remote (PC-server)	No	No	No	No	No
ORACLE	Homogeneous	Yes	Yes	No	Yes	Yes
SYBASE	Homogeneous	Yes	No	No	No	Yes

TABLE 2.9 Operating environments

	Mainframes	Minicomputers	Microcomputers	Operating systems
DB2	IBM			MVS
SQL/DS		IBM		VM/CMS DOS/VSE
INGRES		IBM, DEC, HP, SUN, etc.	UNIX based	VM/CMS, VMS, UNIX, etc.
SABRINA	Bull (DPS8)	Bull (SPS7)	UNIX based	MULTICS, UNIX
SUPRA	IBM	IBM		MVS, VM/CMS, DOS/VSE, etc.
DATACOM/DB	IBM	IBM		MVS, DOS/VSE, VSE/SP, etc.
FOCUS	IBM	DEC, VAX, Wang, AT&T, NCR, etc.	Under PC-DOS and MS-DOS	MVS, VSM, VS, AT&T, UNIX
NOMAD	IBM	IBM	Under PC-DOS and MS-DOS	MVS, VM/CMS, MVS/XA
ORACLE	IBM	IBM, DEC, AT&T, Sequent, etc.	Under UNIX, PC-DOS, MS-DOS, Micro VMS	MVS, VM/CMS, GCOS, DYNIX, etc.
SYBASE		DEC,SUN		VMS, UNIX
UNIFY		UNIX based	UNIX based	All UNIX systems

2.6 Conclusion

Detailed comparison criteria of RDBMSs and their application to ten marketed systems have been described. The characteristics of these systems, which are detailed in the following chapters, have been summed up in comparative tables, which give a general view. All of these systems offer a relational conceptual model; however, two of them allow relations to be organized as hierarchies. These systems differ on several points, mainly by their function, architecture, and implementation choices.

The function and architecture of a system stem essentially from the targeted applications: decision support and/or on-line processing applications. Although all systems can support both types of applications, we believe that DATACOM/DB, SUPRA, SYBASE, and UNIFY are best for on-line processing, while the others are best for decision support. Another important difference lies in the functional architecture model. The most recent RDBMSs (DB2, INGRES, SABRINA, ORACLE, SYBASE, and UNIFY) implement the uniform interface model, which allows efficient and uniform processing of all data. The other systems, based on the separate interface model, are probably not as efficient in processing certain data (such as a data dictionary) but allow access to heterogeneous sources of data (for example, DL/I or VSAM files).

Only two systems (SABRINA and SYBASE) provide extensive semantic integrity control. Most of the systems handle the domain constraints and key uniqueness. Only a few support referential constraints. The main reason for these limitations is that the implementation of complete and efficient integrity control is difficult. When the integrity control provided is restricted, complex processing may be specified by procedures stored in the schema. This last approach exhibits certain drawbacks (redundant code and optimization by the programmer, for example) that may burden the DBMS applications.

Seven systems support SQL for data manipulation, and four systems provide an algebraic 4GL. Furthermore five systems have user form-oriented interfaces (QBE or QBF type). The systems supporting a declarative language (SQL) usually implement a query optimization algorithm. The fundamental difference between declarative and algebraic is that the choice of the best operation ordering is entirely made in the first case by the system and partially made in the second case by the user (with the problems of program dependency upon data). In other words, with an algebraic language, the optimization, which consists of the ordering of relational operators, is done by the programmer.

The transaction management facilities of these systems, which are all multiuser oriented, can be compared. These systems differ especially by the implemented access methods: hashed files, B-trees, and others. Most of the systems offer a quite full set of 4GL tools for data presentation and application development. The integration of these tools with the DBMS is largely facilitated or rendered possible by the relational model. Some provide remote base access or dis-

	No index		With secondary index		With clustered index	
	100	1000	100	1000	100	1000
INGRES–U	53.2	64.4	59.2	78.9	7.7	27.8
INGRES–C	38.4	53.9	11.4	54.3	3.9	18.9
ORACLE–O	53.2	72.5	7.3	53.5	4.5	31.6

Note: Selection was on 10,000 tuples; time expressed in seconds; result written in a relation.

FIGURE 2.7 Performance of ORACLE vs INGRES for select [Bitton 83, Oracle 84]

	No index		With secondary index		With clustered index	
	After a selection		After a selection		After a selection	
	100	1000	100	1000	100	1000
INGRES–U	9.6	10.2	1.66	2.11	2.34	4.49
INGRES–C	2.6	1.8	1.71	0.9	1.8	1.97
ORACLE	?	?	1.2	1.3	1.5	2.3

Note: join of 10,000 x 10,000 tuples; time expressed in minutes; the result written in a relation.

FIGURE 2.8 Performance of ORACLE vs INGRES for join [Bitton 83, Oracle 84]

tributed database management capabilities. For six systems, a microcomputer version is already available.

Readers may find that it is regrettable that comparisons based on more quantitative criteria such as performance measures of different relational queries have been omitted. This can be explained by the extreme difficulty to compare objectively the performance of systems designed (and optimized) to run in different contexts. Nevertheless, research has been undertaken in [Bitton 83] on the systematic comparison of RDBMS performance. A set of representative queries on a database adapted to exhaustive measures has been tested on different systems, including INGRES and ORACLE. Figs. 2.7 and 2.8 illustrate partially the results obtained in [Bitton 83] for the prototype INGRES-U (University), the product INGRES-C (Commercial), and ORACLE systems. The results for ORACLE come from ORACLE Corporation, which has applied the same benchmark [Oracle 84]. We should emphasize that these numbers are quite old and that the benchmarked systems made significant progress in terms of performance. For instance, ORACLE version 5 processes a 10000 × 10000 tuples join in 135 seconds without index and 57 seconds with index. Unfortunately more recent benchmarks have not been published. A performance evaluation methodology in a multiuser context has been introduced in [Boral 84].

References

[Bernstein 87] P. A. Bernstein, V. Hadzilacos, N. Goodman, *Concurrency Control and Recovery in Database Systems,* Addison-Wesley Publishing Company, 1987.

[Bitton 83] D. Bitton, D. J. DeWitt, C. Turbyfill, "Benchmarking Database Systems: A Systematic Approach," Int. Conf. on VLDB, Florence, Italy, 1983.

[Boral 84] H. Boral, D. J. DeWitt, "A Methodology for Database System Performance Evaluation," ACM SIGMOD Int. Conf., Boston, June, 1984.

[Ceri 84] S. Ceri, G. Pelagati, *Distributed Databases: Principles and Systems,* McGraw-Hill, 1984.

[Codd 72] E. F. Codd, "Relational Completeness of Data Base Sublanguages," in *Database Systems* (R. Rustin, ed.), Prentice-Hall, 1972.

[Date 86] C. J. Date, *An Introduction to Database Systems,* Vol. 1, 4th ed., Addison-Wesley Publishing Company, 1986.

[Gardarin 88] G. Gardarin, P. Valduriez, *Relational Databases and Knowledge Bases,* Addison-Wesley Publishing Company, 1988.

[Jarke 84] M. Jarke and J. Koch, "Query Optimization in Database Systems," ACM Computing Surveys, Vol. 16, No. 2, 1984.

[Kim 85] W. Kim, D. S. Reiner, D. S. Batory, *Query Processing in Database Systems,* Springer-Verlag, 1985.

[Oracle 84] Oracle Corp., *ORACLE Corporation Response to the DeWitt Benchmark,* Menlo Park, Calif., March 22, 1984.

[Ozsu 89] T. Ozsu, P. Valduriez, *Principles of Distributed Database Systems,* Prentice-Hall, 1989.

[Stonebraker 81] M. Stonebraker, "Operating System Support for Database Management," CACM, Vol. 24, No. 7, July 1981.

[Ullman 82] J. D. Ullman, *Principles of Database Systems,* 2d ed., Computer Science Press, 1982.

3

SYSTEM R, SQL/DS, AND DB2

3.1 Introduction

IBM was among the first organizations to recognize the potential benefits of the relational model and to conduct extensive research and development in relational database technology. The first major research effort, initiated in 1975 at the San Jose Research Laboratory, California, led to a complete RDBMS prototype, called System R, which was operational in 1979. The most significant contributions of System R were the design and specification of SQL, a unified language for relational database management, and efficient techniques for SQL query compilation and transaction management. System R had a major impact on the RDBMS market, evidenced by the fact that most RDBMSs support or are committed to support the standard SQL language. From 1979 to 1984, an experimental adaptation of System R to a distributed environment, called R*, was pursued at the same laboratory. Parallel to System R, another RDBMS project, called QBE, was investigated at the Yortktown Heights Research Laboratory. The emphasis in QBE was on an easy-to-use form-oriented database language. QBE was subsequently adapted to an integrated office automation system, called OBE. QBE and OBE also had a significant impact on the RDBMS market, particularly in the area of user-friendly interfaces fully integrated with the database system.

The techniques explored in System R, and to some extent in QBE, have been incorporated into the IBM products SQL/DS and DB2. DB2 is the most recent of IBM's relational products, each of which offers the SQL language and works on the main IBM operating systems. These products are similar since all derive from System R. The transfer of the technology used in System R was applied first in SQL/DS for the DOS/VSE environment in 1981, then in SQL/DS release 2 for VM/CMS in 1982, and finally in DB2 for MVS in 1983. DB2 and SQL/DS provide similar interfaces for application programming and query. Nevertheless different physical components were developed to satisfy the different requirements of large systems (MVS) versus smaller systems (VSE).

A full understanding of the DB2 and SQL/DS products can be reached only by the detailed presentation of the research prototype System R, which is given in Section 3.2. In Section 3.3, we introduce QBE. The development of System R into the SQL/DS product and its adaptation to DOS/VSE and VM/CMS environments are explained in Section 3.4. The DB2 product, as well as its associated products, QMF and DXT, are described in Section 3.5; QMF and DXT are distinct products that may be used with DB2 as well as with SQL/DS. Finally, we give a short presentation of R* in Section 3.6.

3.2 System R

System R was an experiental DBMS, built to demonstrate the advantages of a system based on the relational model and its feasibility in real environments [Astrahan 76, Blasgen 81]. The objective was to offer full functional capacities to a wide population of concurrent users, thus giving a performance level that can be compared to that of the more classical systems such as IMS. The system was written in PL/I.

3.2.1 Data Definition

The SQL language, originally called SEQUEL [Chamberlin 74], invented by System R designers, constitutes a unified approach to data manipulation, definition, and control. The notion of database does not exist in System R; the relations are directly manipulated by the users. The CREATE TABLE command allows one to establish a new base relation (physically implemented) with the names of attributes and their type. The creation of the relation DRINKER may be defined as follows:

```
CREATE TABLE DRINKER

    (D#          INT NOT NULL,
    NAME         CHAR (20),
    TYPE         CHAR (5));
```

Inversely, a relation that has become useless may be suppressed by the DROP TABLE command. The definition of a relation may be completed by the specification, at any time, of clustered or secondary indexes on some attributes by the CREATE INDEX command. The following command creates an index on a unique key, D#:

CREATE UNIQUE INDEX DRINKIND ON D#;

An index may be defined by a combination of attributes, which individually may be in ascending (ASC) or descending (DESC) order:

CREATE INDEX DRINKIND2 ON DRINKER (TYPE ASC, NAME DESC) ;

The key word CLUSTERING preceding INDEX specifies that the relation's data are clustered according to the sorted attributes of the index. Two other commands facilitate the data description. KEEP TABLE makes permanent a temporary relation resulting from a query; however, the KEEP TABLE command has not been implemented. EXPAND TABLE is used to add a new attribute to an existing relation. The existing tuples are then read as null values in the new attribute until they are explicitly updated. The set of information related to the description and data control (metadata) is stored in the data dictionary organized as a set of relations (metabase) and therefore may be managed like all other data. A user may thus query the subset of the data dictionary of interest and modify it indirectly by using the preceding commands.

3.2.2 Data Manipulation

The SQL Language

Set-oriented data manipulation may be made with the SQL language. This language has all the functions of the tuple relational calculus, plus functions for sorting, grouping, arithmetic, and aggregates such as SUM and AVERAGE. The initial definition of SEQUEL was based on nested blocks, where each block defined a selection and the nesting that of the join of two blocks. SQL not only permits nested query blocks but also the nonprocedural specification of queries. Null values are processed by using the key word NULL in a selection criteria. The facilities of SQL are demonstrated in the following queries on the WINES database.

R1: SELECT DISTINCT NAME
     FROM PRODUCER P, WINE W, HARVEST H
     WHERE P.P# = H.P# AND H.W.# = W.W#
         AND W. VINEYARD = "Julienas"
         AND W. VINTAGE = 1982 OR W.VINTAGE = 1984

R2: SELECT D.*
FROM DRINKER D, WINE W, DRINK R
WHERE D.D# = R.D# AND P.W.# = W.W#
    AND W.VINEYARD LIKE ''C%''
    AND (W.PERCENT BETWEEN 11 AND 13
        OR W.PERCENT IS NULL)

R3: SELECT VINEYARD, AVE (PERCENT)
FROM WINE
GROUP BY VINEYARD
HAVING MIN (PERCENT) > 12;

I1: INSERT INTO DRINKER (D#, NAME)
SELECT P.P#, NAME
FROM PRODUCER P, HARVEST H, WINE W
WHERE REGION = ''Bourgogne''
    AND P.P# = H.P# AND H.W# = W.W#
    AND VINTAGE = 1983;

M1: UPDATE HARVEST
SET QTY = QTY * 1.1
WHERE W# IN
    (SELECT W.W.#
    FROM WINE W, HARVEST H
    WHERE H.W.# = W.W#
        AND VINEYARD = ''Julienas''
        AND VINTAGE = 1982);

SQL Embedded in a Programming Language

The integration of SQL commands into a programming language (PL/I, COBOL, FORTRAN, ASSEMBLY) is based on a precompiler. Its function is to analyze a source module written in a programming language and to identify the SQL commands so as to replace them with CALLS to the DBMS. The module thus precompiled may then be processed by the SQL compiler. Each SQL command isolated by the precompiler is compiled into an execution plan, stored in a catalog. During the execution of the application program, the presence of a CALL gives control to the DBMS, which can then put into action the corresponding execution plan and the tuple transfers to or from the program (depending on whether it is an insertion or a retrieval). The conversion from the SQL *set-oriented processing* mode into the *procedural* mode of a programming language is attained by using *cursors*. A cursor is the name assigned by the programmer to a set of tuples (for example, the result of a query) as well as a *current pointer* of a tuple belonging to the set, as shown in Fig. 3.1. OPENing of a cursor engenders the execution of the query and places the current pointer on the first resulting

```
Program PL/I-SQL ;
   •
   •
   •

EXEC SQL BEGIN DECLARE SECTION;
  DCL VAR1 CHAR (20) ;
  DCL VAR2 INT ;
EXEC SQL DECLARE SECTION;
   •
   •
   •

EXEC SQL DECLARE C CURSOR FOR
   SELECT VINEYARD, VINTAGE
   FROM WINE
   WHERE PERCENT = 11
   •
   •
   •

EXEC SQL OPEN C ;
DO WHILE "NON END C"
   begin
   EXEC SQL FETCH C INTO : VAR1, : VAR2;
   < process the tuple of C >
   end ;
```

FIGURE 3.1 Example of SQL statements embedded in a PL/I program.

tuple. Each tuple is explicitly materialized in the program by the FETCH command against the appropriate cursor. This has the effect of delivering the current tuple and moves the pointer onto the following tuple. Thus the tuple received by the program may be processed inside a loop that completes when there are no remaining tuples in the set. The concept of cursor facilitates the integration of SQL in a programming language.

3.2.3 Semantic Data Control

Semantic data control is performed by using four tools: views, authorizations, integrity constraints, and triggers.

Views

A *view* is a relation derived from one or more base relations; it is considered the result of an SQL query. It is specified by the DEFINE VIEW command. A view is a *virtual relation* (not physically implemented) that instantaneously reflects the updating of the base relation(s) from which it is derived. It can therefore be considered a dynamic database window. The definition of the view JULIENAS-HARVEST is expressed by:

> **VI** : CREATE VIEW JULIENAS-HARVEST AS
> SELECT H.P#, P.NAME, H.QTY
> FROM WINE W, PRODUCER P, HARVEST H
> WHERE H.W# = W.W# AND H.W# = P.P#
> AND W.VINEYARD = ''Julienas''

A view is interrogated in the same way as are base relations. Some users may be authorized only to manipulate a view without having access to the constituent relations. A view of system R may be updated only when it derives, by restriction-projection, from only one relation, thus leaving out the views defined by a join, aggregate, or something else. For example, it is impossible to propagate the updating of a view of the average percentage in alcohol of the Julienas wines to the WINE relation. A query on a view is executed by the transformation of that query into one that can be applied to the base relations. The query qualification is merged with the qualification defining the view so that it can then be processed by the query optimizer. This method is similar to the INGRES query modification method (see Chapter 4).

Authorization

The authorization method of system R [Griffiths 76, Fagin 78] is based on privileges that are given by the SQL GRANT command and denied by the REVOKE command. The creator of a new object (relation, view), who must be at least authorized to create objects, is granted all privileges to operate on them (retrieval, update, suppression, and so on). This person therefore becomes the administrator of the object and may selectively grant privileges to other users or suppress them if necessary. In particular, the GRANT of management rights may be transferred by the GRANT privilege. The granularity of authorization is in general the relation but can be the attribute for updates. The following command illustrates the definitions of privileges on the DRINKERS relation:

> GRANT ALL PRIVILEGES ON DRINKER TO PAUL;
> GRANT SELECT, UPDATE (NAME, TYPE) ON DRINKER TO JOHN;

The authorization method therefore offers the possibility of a more flexible control that may be centralized by a unique administrator, completely decentralized, or hybrid. A closer control of privileges on subsets of objects may be attained by the *view mechanism*. A view enables one to hide from users who do not have access to base relations, tuples, or attributes of a relation (for example, restrain access to the average of quantities of DRINK by PLACE). To expand the view method's adaptability, the key word USER is interpreted as an identifier (user-id) of the current user. Thus the following command defines a view of all the producers from the same region as the current user:

```
CREATE VIEW W-PRODUCER AS
SELECT * FROM PRODUCER P1, PRODUCER P2
WHERE P1.REGION = P2.REGION AND P1.NAME = USER;
```

Semantic Integrity

Data *semantic integrity* is controlled by maintaining *integrity constraints*. The integrity method of System R is described in [Eswaran 75]. The tool is rather complete, although its implementation is restricted to unique key control. The definition of an integrity constraint is established by an assertion, expressed by SQL predicates, on a relation or view. The ASSERT command gives an assertion that is verified on the existing data and stored in the catalog if it is declared true. Data updates that violate an integrity constraint are rejected. Any constraint that may be expressed by predicates in WHERE clauses may be defined:

Domain: (for example, PERCENT < 14).

Referential: a wine drunk in DRINK must exist in WINE.

With aggregate: the average of the alcohol percentage is less than 14.

Temporal: the quantity of a wine harvested is superior to that of the old quantity. The key words NEW and OLD are indispensable to state temporal constraints. For example, the last constraint is expressed by:

```
ASSERT ON UPDATE TO HARVEST: NEW QTY > OLD QTY
```

Furthermore it is possible to specify that an attribute is the key of a relation. The integrity constraints are checked at the end of the transaction (set of SQL requests in the order defined by the user) by a *detection* method. The updates of the transaction are made to the copy of the base relation, and the assertions are verified according to the new values. If the constraints are violated, the state of the base relation prior to the transaction is restored by application of the recovery mechanism. Nevertheless it is possible to declare a constraint IMMEDIATE, which is then checked during each set manipulation (SQL request). Furthermore *integrity points,* in which the assertions are checked, may be established by the user. This restricts the possible transaction restart until the last integrity point. Although they are very attractive, none of these capabilities was implemented.

Triggers

The last aspect of data control, the trigger, is an interesting aspect even though it was never implemented in System R or any subsequent products. A trigger enables one to execute a series of SQL statements as the result of executing some other SQL statement. For example, suppose that the relation DRINKER contains a supplementary attribute DRINK-NB describing the number (quantity) of drinks. This value may be automatically incremented by the following trigger:

```
DEFINE TRIGGER D-WINE
ON INSERTION OF DRINK
UPDATE DRINKER
SET DRINK-NB = DRINK-NB + 1
WHERE W# = NEW DRINK.W#
```

3.2.4 Transaction Management

Basic Concepts

An SQL *transaction* is an ordered set of SQL commands embraced by a COMMIT WORK statement and the previous such statement. A transaction is processed as an *atomic unit,* meaning that either all or none of its updates are integrated into the database. Therefore a transaction may not be partially executed unless the system uses *save points.* A save point, inside a transaction, is specified by the SAVE command, which commits the updates in the base. Save points are transparent to the user; that is, the SAVE command is not visible to the user. It is automatically specified by the system when necessary. A specific mode enables one to define implicitly the SAVE command after each set-oriented manipulation. During a transaction, the user may, with the RESTORE command, undo the updates and come back to the situation as of the last save point or, if no SAVE has been given, to the initial situation at the beginning of the transaction.

The transaction is a unit that guarantees the consistency of the database. The consistency of the database may be altered by two types of problems: concurrent updates and failures. Each of these crucial types of problem has been given original and efficient solutions in System R.

Concurrency Control

To allow a large number of users to work simultaneously, System R manages concurrency control based on the locking of logical objects (relation, tuples, and so forth) or of physical objects (page) [Gray 76]. At the logical level, the system ensures the synchronization of concurrent transactions and overcomes the classical problems of the loss of updates or the introduction of inconsistencies. At the physical level, the locking mechanism is put into effect to resolve internal conflicts. Even in the absence of logical conflicts between two transactions — for example, when each transaction has access to a different tuple belonging to the same relation — a physical conflict may arise if the two tuples are on the same page. Seen by the mechanism of concurrency control, an SQL request is defined as a set of simple operations manipulating one tuple at a time. The physical locking is done by locks on one or several pages acquired during the execution of a simple operation. The logical locking is made by setting locks on the objects such as segments (physical space that contains several relations), relations, tuples, or key value intervals [Eswaran 76], which are maintained until the end of the transaction. The functions necessary to logical or physical locking are managed by the system, thus making the concurrency control totally transparent to the user. Nevertheless it is possible to use the explicit locking operators in exclusive or shared mode on large granules.

The overhead added by concurrency control can be important with a large number of transactions having access to data. To obtain good performance, System R offers three levels of increasing consistency, the level required being chosen at the beginning of the transaction. For these three levels, the system guarantees that data modified by a transaction will not be altered by another before the end of the transaction. This rule is indispensable for the restart of the transaction, independent of the modifications carried out by the others. With the highest level of consistency (level 3), the user perceives System R as though it is a mono-user system. The evaluation of the System R prototype by real users has shown that the level 3 is generally used [Chamberlin 81a]. However, subsequent use of SQL/DS has demonstrated that users also want level 2 consistency.

In order to ensure good performance in a large range of applications, System R provides a variable locking granule. Transactions having access to a small volume of data need only lock tuples, whereas batch programs having access to a large volume of data prefer to lock entire relations. Variable granularity is achieved by obeying a hierarchical locking protocol so that different locks may be associated with each granule, such as a segment, a relation, and a tuple. A lock on a relation therefore implies that locks are implicitly acquired on the tuples of the relation. When a transaction accumulates a large range of locks on small granules (for example, on tuples), the system may exchange them for a lock on a larger granule (for example, on a relation).

The classical problem engendered by a locking mechanism is a deadlock situation between several concurrent transactions. System R uses a deadlock detection technique and selects one or several transactions to be restarted in the event of a deadlock. Periodically the waiting graph between transactions is constructed. The detection of a cycle in this graph, which signifies the presence of a deadlock situation, implies the selection of a victim. In general, the transaction chosen for recovery is the youngest one, which has usually the smallest number of locks. This transaction is then undone by the recovery mechanism until the most recent save point preceding the locking request. Again this is all transparent to the user.

Reliability

The recovery mechanism restores the database to a consistent state after failure [Gray 79]. A database is consistent when it does not contain partially completed transaction updates. Furthermore the set of integrity constraints must be fulfilled. Three types of failure may arise: secondary media (disk) failure, system failure, or transaction failure. Although different, all the recovery algorithms for these types of failure are based on the use of a valid copy of data when the data are lost. The implicit and realistic hypothesis of the recovery system is that the primary data and their copy cannot be lost simultaneously. The first two types of failures require restarting the system and using system checkpoints. Checkpoints may be established when transactions are still active.

When there is a media failure, the most infrequent but difficult case, the information stored on disk is assumed to be lost. The recovery mechanism put into action after such a failure, often called a *cold start,* calls on archives on tape and on a log of data images before and after modification to provide the copy of valid data. Periodically, during long checkpoints, the data image on disk is archived on tape. Only the data that have been modified since the last recovery point are recorded, making the checkpoint incremental. The use of two logs stored on two different disks enables one to recover after the failure of a disk containing a log. In initiating the cold start, the database is reconstructed from the most recent image provided by the archives on tape and after images specified by the log are applied to the database from the last checkpoint. This procedure is followed by a system restart.

When a system failure arises, the information in main memory is assumed to be lost. The recovery mechanism after such a failure, often called *warm start,* uses the log of before- and after-images and the page copies on disk called *shadow pages* [Lorie 77]. When a page of the base is updated, it is not written in the same place but in a different location. Therefore the original page is always available on disk, although the new page may still be in core memory. The old and new location of each page is contained in a catalog. During short checkpoints, which are more frequent than those used for cold starts, the system records on disk the new pages that could still be stored and marks in the log the checkpoints. After each save point or, in their absence, at the end of each transaction, the images before and after modification made by a transaction are recorded in the log. After a system failure, some of the new pages on disk may be in an inconsistent state. This may happen when the modified pages were still in main storage when the failure occurred. A consistent database state may be obtained by restoring the old pages that were written at the last checkpoint. The after-image log is then applied to the transactions that have been validated. When there is a transaction failure, all the modifications made by the transaction must be undone until the last checkpoint of the transaction. This procedure may be dictated by the user (by the ROLLBACK WORK statement) or by the system (for example, by the detection of deadlocks). Transaction recovery consists of applying before images by consulting the log until the checkpoint, thus undoing the modifications made by the transaction. As opposed to the other two mechanisms, this one does not entail a restart of the system.

3.2.5 Query Processing and Storage Model

Storage Structures
Data are stored in a set of logical spaces, called *segments,* used for the control of physical clustering. Segments contain users' data, access paths data, data dictionary information, and intermediate query results. All tuples of a relation are contained in a unique segment, whereas a segment may contain several relations. This decision was essentially linked to the initial idea of clustering the tuples of different relations that satisfy certain criteria so that the join operations may be accelerated. Nevertheless the extra cost of maintaining interrelation links seemed too high for update operations, and the idea was dropped. Different types of segments are predefined for precise purposes. For example, one type of segment is adapted to the storage of temporary relations and does not provide for concurrent access and recovery. The allocation of space on the disk for segments is done by groups of pages called *extents* so that the base can easily be expanded. The logically adjacent pages of a segment may be physically close so that sequential or selective access inside the segment may be accelerated. For each segment, a table is maintained that translates a logical address into its disk address. Such a table is divided into fixed-size blocks. A page request is satisfied by allocating a page in a main memory buffer shared by concurrent users and reading the page from disk to that buffer. In fact, two separate buffers are managed — one for the page table blocks and one for pages themselves. The pages and blocks are fixed in memory until their explicit liberation by the system. When a page is liberated, it becomes a candidate for replacement, and, if needed, the buffer manager replaces the liberated page that was the least recently requested.

Access Paths
The two access paths supported by System R are the *segment scan* (sequential scanning) and the *index scan.* System R access paths facilitate the search for any number of tuples based on the order of certain keys. Other methods, such as hashing, could have improved the performance of transactions having access to a limited number of tuples but are not good for range queries.

The main access paths provided by System R are indexes sorted according to one or several attributes. A relation may have zero or more indexes on one or more attributes, each in ascending or descending order. The indexes enable one to have direct access to one or several tuples according to key value, as well as ordered sequential access to a subset of a relation from one key value to another.

Each index is maintained in a multilevel structure composed of one or several pages contained in the same segment as the relation. The pages of an index are organized in a B+ — tree form, an efficient variation of B-tree [Bayer 72], a structure well adapted for dynamic data (of which the volume and distribution varies rapidly) that has engendered the VSAM access method [IBM 75]. To each tuple, a unique logical address called Tuple Identifier (TID) is associated; it is composed of the page number and an indirect address (offset) in the page.

Each index page is a node of the tree containing a sequence of index entries. An entry of nonterminal node is a couple (attribute value, pointer to a low subtree). In addition to the node's entries, there is a pointer to the left-most subtree. An entry of a terminal node contains a key value and a list of TIDs identifying the tuples having that attribute value. The leaf pages are chained in a list to support sequential access from leaf to leaf. In order to obtain multikey indexes, an original encoding mechanism [Blasgen 77a] is used to generate a unique key from several keys by conserving the key values order, thus making multikey searching efficient.

Only one index defined on a relation can be clustered; that is, the tuples of a relation are clustered physically according to the key values of the index. Therefore the tuples of close or equal key value may be found on the same page. This property is important for reducing the number of disk accesses and favors queries bearing on clustering attributes. On the other hand, access to tuples according to the order of nonclustering index keys implies the use of a large number of random accesses to data pages (at worst an access per tuple), since the probability that two tuples with close key values are on the same page is small. The difference between the two types of index is illustrated by Figs. 3.2 and 3.3.

The Optimizer

The *optimizer* is a system module that translates an SQL query into an optimal execution plan for accessing stored relations. The optimizer's first task is semantic analysis of the query and composition of views, if necessary. If the definition of a view contains search predicates, these are merged (by AND) with the query,

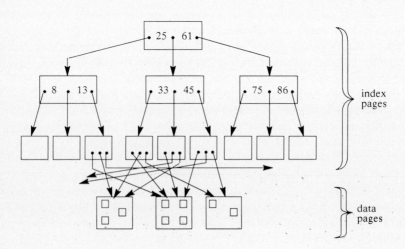

FIGURE 3.2 Example of nonclustered index.

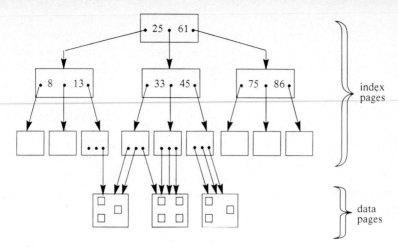

FIGURE 3.3 Example of clustered index.

which, thus modified, refers to real relations only. The query is formulated into conjunctive normal form — that is, OR-predicates connected by AND.

The most complex task of the optimizer is to generate the execution plan of the query. This is where the heart of optimization is. The System R approach to optimization is based on exhaustive search of the solution space, where the best execution plan is selected among (almost) all possible plans. It is the most popular approach because it is cost-effective. This approach performs static optimization based on statistical information. The originality of the algorithm proposed in [Selinger 79] is threefold: (1) it takes into account IO cost, CPU cost, and existing access paths; (2) it does not apply systematically the heuristics that push all selections down the tree because it can have a dramatic effect on performance; and (3) it considers the ordering of the result tuples produced by an execution plan. In this section, we briefly describe the algorithm in [Selinger 79].

A calculus query is first decomposed into a relational algebra tree. Transformation rules are then used to generate alternative processing trees, each corresponding to an execution plan. The optimizer attempts to choose the best execution plan for the query by predicting the cost of each candidate processing tree. Because the number of candidate trees can be large, some of them are ignored. A first heuristics is to eliminate all trees involving Cartesian products (the most expensive operation). Furthermore when two joins are equivalent by commutativity, only the cheaper one is kept. Finally selection operations must be done either before a join operation (pushed down the tree) or during the processing of the join, in which case the selection predicate is tested when the join predicate is satisfied [Blasgen 77b]. The cost of each candidate execution plan is evaluated by the formula:

$$Cost = IOs + W * instructions.$$

This general cost function measures the disk access time (IOs) and the CPU time (instructions). W is a coefficient, adjustable according to the system, between IO time and CPU time. Thus the choice of the plan of minimal cost for the processing of a query minimizes the use of resources.

The calculation of cost takes into account index selectivity and access path properties. Statistics regarding relations, attributes, and indexes are used to assign a selectivity factor to each of the disjunctions of predicates of the query. The product of the selectivity factors by the cardinalities of the relations gives the cardinality of the query's result.

The exhaustive search approach can be viewed as searching the best strategy among all possible ones. The possible strategies for executing a query are generated by permutation of the join ordering [Smith 75]. With n relations, there are $n!$ possible permutations. The algorithm can be conceptually seen as:

> **for each** $n!$ permutations **do**
> > **begin**
> > build the best strategy to join $R_1, \ldots R_n$
> > compute cost
> > **end**
> select strategy of minimum cost

The System R algorithm does not actually generate all $n!$ permutations. The permutations are produced dynamically by constructing a tree of alternative strategies. For each pair of strategies for joining two relations equivalent by commutativity, the strategy of highest cost is dropped.

We now detail the System R algorithm. The optimizer first takes into consideration the selection operation and determines the cheapest access path to a relation by evaluating each possible access path. The cost of each access path, as well as the order it produces, are predicted. This order is useful for queries whose results need to be sorted or grouped in that order or if duplicate elimination is required for the final projection. Two access paths of minimal cost are then considered: the cheapest access path that gives the sorted tuples in a useful order and the cheapest access path that does not generate any order.

Estimating the cost of an access path is based on the cardinality of the operation result. This cardinality can be calculated from statistics on base data and formulas to compute selectivity factors. The statistics maintained by System R include:

1. The number of distinct values present for each attribute A, denote by ndist (A).
2. The minimum and maximum values of each numerical attribute.
3. The cardinality of each relation R, denoted by card (R).

Other statistics concern the size of the relations and indexes. The cardinality of the result of a selection operation on relation R is

$$S * \text{card } (R)$$

where S is the selectivity factor (proportion of selected tuples) of the selection predicate. S is estimated by the following formulas:

$S (A = \text{value}) = 1/ \text{ndist} (A)$.
$S (A > \text{value}) = \max(A) - \text{value} / (\max(A) - \min(A))$.
$S (A < \text{value}) = \text{value} - \min(A) / (\max(A) - \min(A))$.
$S (A \text{ in } \{\text{values}\}) = S (A = \text{value}) * \text{card} (\{\text{values}\})$.
$S (P \text{ and } Q) = S (P) * S (Q)$.
$S (P \text{ or } Q) = S (P) + S (Q) - (S (P) * S (Q))$.

These formulas assume that attribute values are uniformly distributed within their domain and that attributes are independent.

If the query is monorelation and the order of the result is unimportant, the cheapest access path is chosen. If the order of the resulting tuples is required or if the query contains joins, the cost of the cheapest access path that gives a useful order is compared with the cost of the cheapest access path added to the cost of sorting the resulting tuples. The cheapest alternative is selected in the execution plan.

The optimization then takes into consideration the joins so as to choose between two algorithms to process them, one of which is optimal in a given context. These two algorithms are the *nested-loop* and the *sort-merge* join algorithms.

The nested-loop join algorithm is the simpler one. For each tuple of one relation, called the *external relation,* each tuple of the other one, called the *internal relation,* is accessed based on the join attribute value of the external tuple, and a joined tuple is formed if the two tuples match. If there is no index on the join attribute of the internal relation, the complexity of this algorithm is prohibitive since sequential scan must be used.

The sort-merge join algorithm [Blasgen 77b] consists of sorting both relations on the join attribute and completing the join operation by a merge-type operation. Because of its logarithmic complexity, the sort-merge join algorithm is efficient relative to other algorithms (such as nested loop with an index on the internal relation) when the sizes of the operand relations are large.

The evaluation of the cardinality of a join result is simple and is calculated in the same way as the product of the operand cardinalities divided by the constant 10. That amounts to assuming that the result of a join is large but still smaller than the result of the Cartesian product. This estimation can be largely inaccurate.

The dynamic construction of alternative join orderings begins by considering the join of each relation based on its best monorelation access path with every other relation. For each pair of equivalent binary joins (R, S) and (S, R), the one of minimum cost is kept. Then joins of three relations are considered. For each pair of joins (R, S, T) and (R, T, S), the one of minimum cost is kept. The algorithm proceeds until joins of n relations have been treated.

We illustrate this algorithm with the following example query on the WINES database:

"Names of wines produced in the Bourgogne region"

The query expressed in SQL is:

(R4)   SELECT   W.VINEYARD
        FROM   WINE W, PRODUCER P, HARVEST H
        WHERE   W.W# = H.W# AND
                 H.P# = P.P# AND
                 P.REGION = "Bourgogne"

Let us assume the following indexes on the relations involved in R4:

WINE: index on W#.
PRODUCER: index on P#, index on REGION.
HARVEST: index on W#, index on P#.

Let us assume that the best monorelation access paths to these relations for R4 are:

WINE: sequential scan.
PRODUCER: index on REGION.
HARVEST: sequential scan.

There are 3! possible join orders for that query. CP denotes Cartesian product and JN denotes join:

1. JN (CP (WINE, PRODUCER), HARVEST)
2. JN (CP (PRODUCER, WINE), HARVEST)
3. JN (JN (HARVEST, WINE), PRODUCER)
4. JN (JN (HARVEST, PRODUCER), WINE)
5. JN (JN (WINE, HARVEST), PRODUCER)
6. JN (JN (PRODUCER, HARVEST), WINE)

Strategies 1 and 2 are ignored by the algorithm because they contain a Cartesian product. Among the remaining strategies, all but number 6 require a sequential scan of the first relation and indexed access to the other relations. Only strategy 6 has indexed access to all three relations. Assuming that the predicate REGION = "Bourgogne" has good selectivity, strategy 6 is chosen by the optimizer.

The exhaustive search approach is used in many systems because it is cost-effective. The compile time optimization of a query can be amortized over multiple executions. However, the complexity of the algorithm is impressive. For a query involving n relations, the worst-case time complexity of the algorithm is $0(n!)$, which is prohibitive when n is large (greater than 10). The use of dynamic programming and heuristics, as in System R, reduces the complexity to 2^n, which is more practical.

3.2.6 Architecture

The process structure of System R is based on the process model, introduced in Section 2.2.7. We will detail it in the context of SQL/DS and DB2. System R's functional architecture is represented in Fig. 3.4. It is based on a uniform interface model using SQL as a single entry point. The system functions are divided into two subsystems: the Relational Data System and the Relational Storage System.

Relational Storage System

The *Relational Storage System* (RSS) can be considered a low-level DBMS. It supports an internal interface that supplies one-tuple-at-a-time access operators to base relations. Calls on the RSS must explicitly specify which segments and

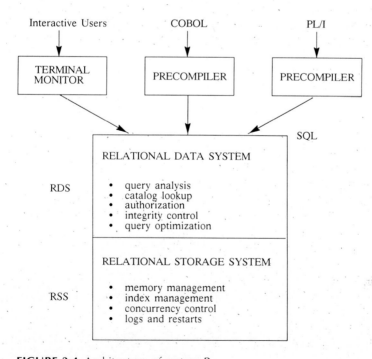

FIGURE 3.4 Architecture of system R.

indexes are to be used. The interface is navigational and supports the scanning of tuples according to the access path specified. The RSS is a full storage subsystem since it manages the secondary storage allocation, buffer pool, and transaction control (concurrency restart), and it secures the reliability of the system. Moreover, it automatically maintains the indexes. The RSS therefore offers certain functions that can be found in other relational or nonrelational systems. Nevertheless most design problems have led to original solutions detailed in the preceding sections, which improve the DBMS's functionality. For example, a new attribute may be added to a relation with the ALTER statement without having to unload and reload the relation.

Relational Data System

The *Relational Data System* (RDS) offers the external SQL interface that can be directly called from an interactive transaction or from programming languages. It carries out two distinct functions:

1. *Compiling SQL commands in access modules generated in machine language:* This function precompiles the SQL commands that are integrated into a program written in host language, in which case the access modules are stored in the database for repeated use, as shown in Fig. 3.5.
2. *Execution control of access modules,* which invokes the RSS, as in Fig. 3.6.

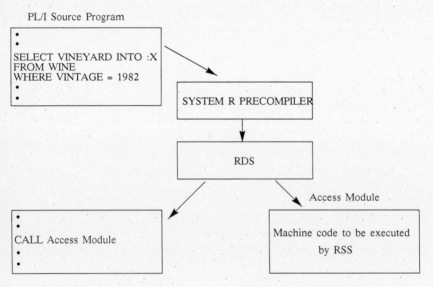

FIGURE 3.5 Precompilation of a PL/1 program with an SQL query.

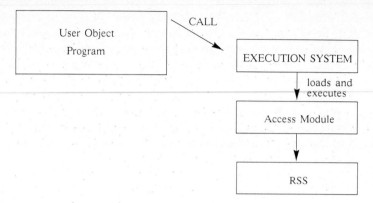

FIGURE 3.6 Execution of a compiled module.

The RDS carries out data definition, control, and manipulation, as well as optimization of queries. Furthermore because the RSS uses internal names generated by the system for database objects, it manages the catalog of external names. To have acceptable performance, System R has adopted a compilation rather than an interpretation approach to SQL for DML statements only. An SQL DML command is compiled in three stages. Syntactical analysis of the command is the first stage. The second stage is optimization of the query, which is itself divided into several tasks: resolution of the query's symbolical names, checking authorizations, composition of views (if any), and building up an optimized plan of the query expressed in Access Specification Language. During the last stage, the execution plan is translated into a set of compact and efficient routines in machine language, called an *access module*.

The Compiling Approach

Translation of an execution plan into machine language requires selection of fragments written in machine language from a library containing about a hundred fragments [Lorie 79]. This compiling approach has considerable effect on both predefined transactions and interactive queries in System R. In an environment of predefined transactions, the access module is called on during the program execution to interact with the database. Thus the compilation cost is recovered since analysis, authorization checks, and query optimization are not repeated. In an interactive environment, compilation is direct, and the query is executed only once. The advantages of compilation compared with interpretation are less clear. Some measures [Chamberlin 81b] have shown that generating the plan in machine language increases the optimization cost by approximately 25 percent. Because the resulting routine (of low level) is more efficient than an SQL interpreter (of high level), the added cost of compilation is quickly recovered when the query is complex.

Since access path selection is decided during compilation, it is possible that subsequent modifications of the database will invalidate some access modules. For example, an index used as an access path may be DROPped from the database. In that case, all the modules so affected are marked as invalidated in the catalog. When an invalid module is called, it is recompiled, this being transparent to the user.

Performance comparisons between System R and IMS have shown the benefits of the compilation approach [Chamberlin 81b]. An airplane reservation system, a particular application installed by ad hoc programs, was processed by IMS and System R. The performance criterion applied was the number of short transactions that can be processed in a second. The results can be summarized as follows:

Ad hoc solution: 100 transactions per second.
IMS: 20 to 50 transactions per second.
System R: Interactive, 2 transactions per second; predefined, 20 transactions per second.

This result shows the benefits of predefining and therefore of compiling the queries to obtain a level of performance that can be compared to that of classical systems.

3.3 Query by Example

Query By Example (QBE) [Zloof 77] is a language based on domain relational calculus. Unlike SQL, where variables range over tuples, QBE variables range over domains. QBE supports capabilities not available in SQL, such as transitive closure of a relation [Zloof 76]. Its most distinguishing feature is that it is especially designed for interactive use from a graphical terminal on which the relation skeletons can be visualized. The basic idea of the language is that the user formulates a query by specifying an example of a possible answer using the relation skeletons. This visual style is generally easy to learn for non – data processing professionals. Another objective of QBE is that the user should type as few characters as possible so that errors are minimized. QBE was fully operational by 1977.

A query example is given using key words, constants, and variables typed in column entries. Key words are useful for various operations such as printing attributes (P.), grouping (G.), sorting (for example, AO. for ascending order), or aggregates (AVE., MIN., and so on). (Key words must end with a dot.) Constants are directly entered in the columns and may be preceded by a key word or comparison operator other than equal (which is implicit). Domain variables are example values preceded by the "_" character for distinguishing from constants. The results of a query are simply displayed in the corresponding relation skeletons.

To illustrate the query expression facility in QBE, we will use the examples detailed in SQL in Section 3.2.2.

(R1)

PRODUCER	P#	NAME	REGION
	_200	P.	

WINE	W#	VINEYARD	VINTAGE	PERCENT	PRICE
	_100	Julienas	1982		
	_100	Julienas	1984		

HARVEST	P#	W#	QTY
	_200	_100	

Note: two lines in the same columns are used to indicate the OR operator.

(R2)

DRINKER	D#	NAME	TYPE
	P._100	P.	P.

DRINK	D#	W#	DATE	PLACE	QTY
	_100	_200			

WINE	W#	VINEYARD	VINTAGE	PERCENT	PRICE
	_100	like 'C'		_X	

CONDITIONS
11 < _X < 13 or _X null

Note: a complex condition may be entered in a predefined CONDITIONS box instead of the columns of the relation skeletons.

(R3)

WINE	W#	VINEYARD	VINTAGE	PERCENT	PRICE
		P. G.		P. AVE. _X	

CONDITIONS
MIN. _X > 12

(I1)

DRINKER	D#	NAME	TYPE
	_100	_Dupont	

PRODUCER	P#	NAME	REGION
	_100	_Dupont	

HARVEST	P#	W#	QTY
	_100	_200	

WINE	W#	VINEYARD	VINTAGE	PERCENT	PRICE
	_200	Bourgogne	1983		

(M1)

HARVEST	P#	W#	QTY
U.		_100	_QX
		_100	_QX * 1.1

WINE	W#	VINEYARD	VINTAGE	PERCENT	PRICE
	_100	Julienas	1982		

The view JULIENAS-HARVEST (denoted by JH) can be defined as follows:

(View)

I. VIEW JH	P#	NAME	QTY
	_100	_Dupont	_1

PRODUCER	P#	NAME	REGION
	_100	_Dupont	

HARVEST	P#	W#	QTY
	_100	_200	_1

WINE	W#	VINEYARD	VINTAGE	PERCENT	QTY
	_200	Julienas			

Note: the key word I. indicates to QBE that it is a view definition to be inserted in the data dictionary. The view JH can then be manipulated like any other view in SQL by typing its name JH, which displays the relation skeleton:

JH	P#	NAME	QTY

3.4 The SQL/DS Product

3.4.1 Environment

During 1978, the Endicott Programming Center of IBM was commissioned to develop the System R prototype into a product, SQL/Data System, for the environment of the operating system DOS/VSE. A history of the development of System R into a commercialized product is detailed in [Chamberlin 81a]. DOS/VSE is a system for batch processing that can support three other IBM products: DL1, CICS, and ICCF. DL/1 (Data Language/1) gives access to hierarchical databases. CICS (Customer Information and Control System) is a transaction and communication management system. ICCF (Interactive Command and Control Facility) provides the possibility of session-oriented time sharing. The

DOS/VSE system thus completed may support batch jobs, time-sharing applications, and transactions. SQL/DS is accessible to all applications of the DOS/VSE environment. Furthermore CICS can have access to DL/1 data as well as to SQL/DS data. Finally, a utility provides for the conversion of DL/1 data into SQL/DS relations.

3.4.2 Architecture of SQL/DS

SQL/DS was designed as a system having its own partition in the DOS/VSE environment rather than as a system sharing the CICS partition. This decision has made SQL/DS more independent from CICS and more adaptable to other operating systems. The decision was put into effect in 1983 by the creation of SQL/DS Release 2 for the VM/CMS environment. These two versions of SQL/DS differ only by their operating system environment and provide the same functions. The location of SQL/DS in its own partition gives better protection to the database against unauthorized CICS users. Nevertheless a CICS transaction issuing an SQL request generates communications and transfers between two partitions that may degrade performance. CICS has therefore been adapted to facilitate the use of SQL/DS.

The architecture of SQL/DS in a DOS/VSE environment is illustrated in Fig. 3.7. Communication between the CICS partition or the batch partition and the SQL/DS partition is made by different links that transmit the requests and results in the form of messages. These links connect the processes, which execute an SQL interface program inside the CICS partition or batch, with the "agent" processes that execute the SQL/DS requests. The different agents inside the

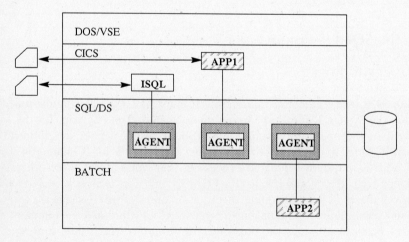

FIGURE 3.7 Integration of SQL/DS in DOS/VSE.

SQL/DS partition share reentrant code. Fig. 3.7 shows three different uses of the system. The APP1 application program is initiated from a terminal in the same way as a CICS transaction. It calls on the routine of the SQL interface program of CICS, which directs the request by a link toward an SQL/DS agent. When the request has been processed, the agent sends the result to the APP1 program by the same link. The ISQL application corresponds to an interactive CICS transaction. The APP2 program is batch processed under DOS/VSE control.

A CICS transaction may interact simultaneously with the SQL/DS and DL/1 database systems. The reliability mechanisms of CICS, SQL/DS, and DL/1 have to be coordinated in such a way that the atomicity of the CICS transaction and consistency of the data under control of the three systems can be ensured. CICS is dedicated to coordination of the two other systems. The restart procedure of CICS is extended so that it can operate on both SQL/DS and DL/1 data. This is done by a two-step commit protocol [Gray 78] that commits the protocols of all three systems. When a CICS transaction is ready to carry out its updates, it sends to the other systems the message "READY TO COMMIT." If the two other systems answer that they are ready, CICS makes its own updates and commands the others to do the same. If one of them does not answer, CICS undoes its updates and orders the others to do the same.

3.4.3 Additional Tools

In addition to the adaptations and improvements described, SQL/DS has new functions that increase its usability and give a better correspondence with the real environment. Among the improvements can be found the following:

- An extraction utility was written to simplify the transfer procedure of DL/1 data into SQL/DS relations.
- The interface to SQL was improved and made easier for the user.
- A report generator was added.
- A direct log facility was provided to improve the restart procedure of System R.
- A "HELP" command was added by using educational information stored in the SQL/DS database.

3.5 The DB2 Product

3.5.1 Environment

During 1983, the DB2 relational DBMS (IBM Database 2) was announced for the MVS operating system (MVS/370 and MVS/XA). An entire book is devoted to DB2 [Date 83]. MVS is a large system, compared, for example, with

DOS/VSE, which can cooperate with IMS (MVS version of the DOS/DL/1 DBMS), CICS, TSO (time-sharing system), and more recently with APL2 systems. DB2 is large-size database oriented. The physical data management component for DB2 differs substantially from that of SQL/DS. For example, the requirements of MVS users are a logging and recovery protocol to handle large databases and heavy workloads and the need to support N-way multiprocessors [Kahn 84]. A DB2 application may be executed under the control of one of three subsystems: IMS, CICS, or TSO. DB2 is therefore concurrently accessible to all applications of the MVS environment [Haderle 84]. A DB2 application under the control of either CICS or IMS may have access to IMS or DB2 data. With DB2, two other products, QMF and DXT, appeared. QMF (Query Management Facility) is a user-friendly interrogation program and report generator for DB2 (under TSO) and SQL/DS (under VM/CMS). DXT (Data Extract) is a data extraction program for recording IMS/VS DL/1, VSAM, and SAM data in a sequential file of adequate format for entering into a DB2 or SQL/DS database.

3.5.2 Architecture of DB2

The conception of DB2 has benefited from experience acquired during development of SQL/DS in the DOS/VSE environment. Thus DB2 occupies its own address spaces in the MVS environment. It is therefore more independent. In the same way as with SQL/DS, the subsystems MVS have been adapted so that the use of DB2 can be facilitated. Functionally, DB2 and SQL/DS are similar, although their internal format of data storage is different.

Nevertheless utilities make possible the transformation of SQL/DS data into DB2 data, and conversely. The essential difference between DB2 and SQL/DS is that DB2 is made for a wider environment. For example, the size of an SQL/DS database is restricted to 64 billions of bytes, whereas a DB2 database is restricted by the size of the secondary storage available on-line. The reason is that the on-line DB2 code, without any consideration of control structures, requires more than 3 megabytes. Moreover the transaction management mechanisms are more sophisticated than those of SQL/DS, since it may have a higher number of concurrent users. A two-step commit protocol [Gray 78] has also been developed so that different systems (CICS, IMS, and DB2) may be able to validate data updates from the same application program.

DB2's implementation takes advantage of a number of MVS features not available in other environments. These features affect mostly the private and buffer space management. DB2 exploits the MVS cross-memory organization to manage data and code in virtual address space efficiently [Cheng 84]. Virtual space of MVS is exploited specifically by two DB2 components: the Environmental Descriptor Manager and the Buffer Manager. The Environmental Descriptor Manager optimizes access to the frequently accessed database descriptors (data dictionary information) and compiled queries (used repeatedly). The Buffer Manager uses four buffer pools, three holding 4K-byte pages and one holding 32K-byte pages. The 32K-byte page buffer pool is used for reading/writing relations with record sizes greater than 4K bytes that are stored in files with a page size of 32K bytes. The DB2 buffer manager replacement algorithm (LRU) is extended to take into account the fact that pages have been updated [Teng 84]. Finally DB2 employs two different sort algorithms: vs Sort, which is efficient for sorting large relations but has a substantial initialization (optimization) overhead, and DB2 Sort, which is more efficient for sorting small relations (in buffer space).

DB2 incorporates most of the solutions implemented in the Relational Data System of the System R prototype. As for SQL/DS, semantic integrity control and triggers have not been implemented. Only the unique key control can be made by the index definition, with specification of unique key. Other types of control therefore are created by the user. It is probable that the integrity control mechanism specified by the designers of System R will be implemented in DB2 and SQL/DS.

3.5.3 New Products

Two different and optional products are now available under DB2 and SQL/DS, QMF, and DXT. QMF (Query Management Facility) provides, in addition to the SQL interface, a powerful report generator and the QBE interrogation language, which are both user friendly. The report generator is easy to use, and the specification of reports from DB2 or SQL/DS databases may be carried out by SQL or QBE. The QBE language of DB2, less complete than the one designed by Zloof, does not support aggregate functions or grouping. Therefore the query R3 could not be expressed with the product, whereas it can be in the original QBE. Reports may be edited from a relation in graphical form. DXT (Data Extract) is separate from QMF, although it is possible to use QMF to manipulate or to produce data extraction reports. DXT's aim is to extract data belonging to an IMS database (or DOS/DL/1), or SAM, or VSAM files and to make up a file that will be entered into an SQL/DS or a DB2 database. This product thus secures compatibility among different IBM products.

3.6 R*

The R* system exemplifies the way an RDBMS can be extended to work in a distributed context. R* [Williams 82] was an experimental DDBMS that incorporates many techniques of System R adapted to a distributed environment. R* provides cooperation between autonomous sites, each managing a local database with the same RDBMS (an extension of System R) and interconnected through a local or general network. This cooperation is transparent to the user who sees a single database. R* was fully operational by 1983.

3.6.1 Objectives

The main objectives of R* were location transparency, site autonomy, and minimal performance overhead. Location transparency makes the use of R* equivalent to that of a centralized DBMS. Queries involving relations stored at different sites need not specify the relation locations. Therefore the database may be physically reorganized by moving relations to different sites, without any impact on the queries that access them.

Site autonomy is an important characteristic that enables any operational site to process independently its local data, despite the failure of any other site. Therefore each site must store all data dictionary information necessary to be autonomous without relying on a centralized global data dictionary.

The performance overhead added by distributed data management functions should be minimal. In particular, local queries, which do not require remote data access, should be processed almost as efficiently as if the system were not distributed. Furthermore the cost of processing distributed queries should also be minimized.

3.6.2 Extensions to System R

All of these objectives were achieved in the implementation of R*. The main extensions to System R for supporting distribution concerned data definition and authorization control, query compilation and optimization, query execution, and transaction management.

Data definition and authorization control were extended for managing distributed objects and users. In particular, naming was modified so that the internal name of an object is system-wide unique and never changes. Internal name generation can be done at the object creation site independent of other sites. Such a naming convention provides both location transparency and site autonomy. The SQL language was supplemented with two new statements. An INTRODUCE DATABASE statement enables the addition of a new site in the system. The introduction of a new site is done on a site-pair basis whereby two sites, an existing one and the new one, mutually agree to share their data and exchange their data dictionary information. This avoids synchronizing all sites to add a new one and thus achieves site autonomy. The MIGRATE TABLE statement enables relocating a relation to another site where it is used the most.

Query compilation and optimization was extended to deal with queries involving distributed objects [Lohman 85]. R* performs distributed compilation whereby a single site, called *master site,* makes global decisions, and other sites, called *apprentice sites,* subsequently make local decisions. The master site is the one where the query is issued; the apprentice sites are the remaining sites that store data involved in the query. The optimizer of the master site makes all intersite decisions, such as the selection of the sites and the method for transferring data, and generates a global access plan, which is then sent to all apprentice sites. The apprentice sites make the remaining local decisions (such as the ordering of joins at a site) and generate the local access plans. The objective function of R*'s optimizer is a general total cost function including local processing (similar to System R function) and communications cost. The optimization algorithm is also based on the exhaustive search of the solution space. As in the centralized case, the optimizer must select the join ordering, the join algorithm (nested loop or merge join), and the access path for each relation. In addition, the optimizer must select the sites of join results and the method of transferring data between sites.

Query execution in R* may require the coordination of distributed processes when the query involves multiple sites. Similar to System R, R* uses the process model. A single R* process is initially allocated at the user site to interact with the user application program. This process is maintained until the application program terminates. Thus it may serve more than one transaction of the same user. Compared to the pure process model, which creates one process per transaction, R* reduces process creation overhead. When remote data access is required for that user, a dependent R* process is created at the remote site. Any dependent process may, in turn, generate the creation of a dependent process at another site. Intersite communication is done between R* processes, that is, under full control of R*.

Transaction management underwent significant changes to deal with distributed transactions. Concurrency control in R* is based on a locking algorithm that supports both local and global deadlock detection. The atomicity of a transaction that runs on several sites is achieved through a two-step commit protocol.

3.6.3 Architecture of R*

The architecture of an R* site is illustrated in Fig. 3.8. Similar to DB2, R* runs in the MVS environment. It uses the TSO, VSAM, and CICS subsystems of MVS. TSO controls the execution of application programs or query interfaces that invoke R* and handles terminal IOs. VSAM is used to store and access the database files. Unlike SQL/DS, R* runs in the CICS partition. Communication between R* systems is done through the Inter-System Communication facility of CICS. R* is composed of four components: RDS*, RSS*, TM*, and DC*. The RDS* extends the RDS of System R to support distributed database management. It performs SQL compilation, which includes parsing, data dictionary management, authorization control, and query optimization, and controls the run-time execution of the compiled access plans. The RSS* provides low-level support for file management and transaction management. The TM* (R* Transaction Manager) performs the various functions for controlling distributed trans-

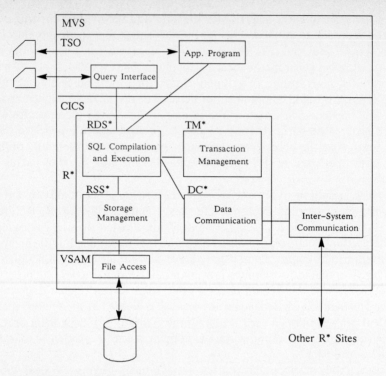

FIGURE 3.8 Architecture of R*.

actions. It performs two-step commit coordination, deadlock detection, and recovery. The DC* (R* Data Communication component) provides message communication between CICS and the other R* sites.

3.7 Conclusion

In this chapter we have examined IBM's relational products by taking as the starting point a detailed description of the solutions implemented in the research prototype System R from which they are derived. System R validated the idea of a DBMS based on the relational model and its feasibility. It offered full data definition, control and manipulation, transaction management, query optimization, reliability, and recovery functions. The most significant contributions of System R were the design of SQL, now the standard relational language, and efficient techniques for SQL compilation and transaction management. Acceptable performance is obtained by compiling the SQL language. We also briefly described two other major IBM prototypes of relational systems: QBE, a user-friendly database language, and R*, an extension of System R to a distributed environment.

The SQL/DS product for the DOS/VSE operating system was the first development of System R into a commercial product. The SQL/DS release 2 for VM/CMS and the DB2 product for the MVS environment have followed recently. Two optional products to DB2 and SQL/DS, DXT and QMF, have also been presented. They provide for easier data manipulation and for progressive migration from a more classical system such as IMS to a relational system such as SQL/DS or DB2. This set of products makes up a series of relational DBMSs for the IBM systems, which will probably develop further to make information management easier.

References

[Astrahan 76] M. M. Astrahan et al., "System R: A Relational Approach to Database Management," ACM TODS, Vol. 1, No. 2, June 1976.

[Bayer 72] R. Bayer, C. McCreight, "Organization and Maintenance of Large Ordered Indexes," Acta Informatica, Vol. 1, No. 3, 1972.

[Blasgen 77a] M. W. Blasgen, K. P. Eswaran, R. G. Casey, "An Encoding Method for Multifield Sorting and Indexing," Comm. ACM, Vol. 20, No. 11, November 1977.

[Blasgen 77b] M. W. Blasgen, K. P. Eswaran, "Storage and Access in Relational Databases," IBM Systems Journal, Vol. 16, No. 4, 1977.

[Blasgen 81] M. W. Blasgen et al., "System R: An Architectural Overview," IBM Systems Journal, Vol. 20, No. 1, February 1981.

[Chamberlin 74] D. D. Chamberlin, R. F. Boyce, "SEQUEL: A Structural English Query Language," ACM-SIGMOD Workshop on Data Description, Access and Control, May 1974.

[Chamberlin 81a] D. D. Chamberlin, A. M. Gilbert, R. A. Yost, "A History of System R and SQL/Data System," Int. Conf. on VLDB, Cannes, 1981, IEEE Ed.

[Chamberlin 81b] D. D. Chamberlin et al., "Support for Repetitive Transactions and Ad Hoc Query in System R," ACM TODS, Vol. 6, No. 1, March 1981.

[Cheng 84] J. M. Cheng, C. R. Loosley, A. Shibamiya, P. S. Worthington, "IBM Database 2 Performance: Design, Implementation and Tuning," IBM Systems Journal, Vol. 23, No. 2, 1984.

[Date 83] C. J. Date, *A Guide to DB2,* Addison-Wesley Publishing Company, 1983.

[Eswaran 75] K. P. Eswaran, D. D. Chamberlin, "Functional Specifications of a Subsystem for Database Integrity," Int. Conf. on VLDB, Framingham (USA), September 1975, ACM Ed.

[Eswaran 76] K. P. Eswaran, J. N. Gray, R. A. Lorie, I. L. Traiger, "The Notions of Consistency and Predicate Locks in a Database System," Comm. ACM, Vol. 19, No. 11, November 1976.

[Fagin 78] R. Fagin, "On an Authorization Mechanism," ACM TODS, Vol. 3, No. 3, December 1978.

[Gray 76] J. N. Gray et al., "Granularity of Locks and Degrees of Consistency in a Shared

Database," IFIP Working Conf. on Modelling of Database Management Systems, FreudenStadt (RFA), January 1976.

[Gray 78] J. N. Gray, "Notes on Database Operating Systems," in *Operating Systems: An Advanced Course,* Springer-Verlag, 1978.

[Gray 79] J. N. Gray et al., *The Recovery Manager of a Data Management System,* IBM Research Report RJ2623, San Jose, Cal., June 1979.

[Griffiths 76] P. P. Griffiths, B. W. Wade, *An Authorization Mechanism for a Relational Database System,* ACM TODS, September 1976.

[Haderle 84] D. J. Haderle, R. D. Jackson, "IBM Database 2 Overview," IBM Systems Journal, Vol. 23, No. 2, 1984.

[IBM 75] IBM Corp., *Planning for Enhanced VSAM under OS/VS,* pub. GC 26 – 3842, IBM Corp., White Plains, N.Y., 1975.

[Kahn 84] S. Kahn, "An Overview of Three Relational Database Products," IBM Systems Journal, Vol. 23, No. 2, 1984.

[Lorie 77] R. A. Lorie, "Physical Integrity in a Large Segmented Database," ACM TODS, Vol. 2, No. 1, March 1977.

[Lorie 79] R. A. Lorie, B. W. Wade, *The Compilation of a High Level Data Language,* IBM Research Report RJ 2598, San Jose, Cal., August 1979.

[Lohman 85] G. Lohman et al., "Query Processing in R*," in *Query Processing in Database Systems,* Springer-Verlag, 1985.

[Selinger 79] P. G. Selinger et al., "Access Path Selection in a Relational Database Management System," ACM SIGMOD Conf., Boston, May 1979.

[Smith 75] J. M. Smith, P. Y. Chang, "Optimizing the Performance of a Relational Algebra Database Interface," Comm. ACM, Vol. 18, No. 10, 1975.

[Teng 84] J. Z. Teng, R. A. Gumaer, "Managing IBM Database 2 Buffers to Maximize Performance," IBM Systems Joural, Vol. 23, No. 2, 1984.

[Williams 82] R. Williams et al., "R*: an Overview of the Architecture," 2d Int. Conf. on Databases, Jerusalem, June 1984.

[Zloof 76] M. M. Zloof, *Query by Example: Operations on the Transitive Closure,* IBM Research Report RC 5526, Yorktown Heights, N.Y., 1976.

[Zloof 77] M. M. Zloof, "Query by Example: A Database Language," IBM Systems Journal, Vol. 16, No. 4., 1977.

4

INGRES

4.1 Introduction

The INGRES (Interactive Graphics and Retrieval System) project was conducted at the University of California, Berkeley, from 1973 to 1980. Like IBM's System R, it represented a first major effort to build and experiment with an RDBMS prototype. A complete INGRES prototype was running in 1977 under the UNIX operating system [Ritchie 74] on PDP 11/40 and 11/70. The most significant contributions of INGRES were the design and specification of QUEL, a unified language for data description, manipulation, and control, and the development of original solid solutions to semantic data control and query optimization. QUEL has common points with SQL in that it is based on tuple relational calculus; however, it is more regular and powerful than the original SQL. Another important contribution is the design of a form-oriented user interface, fully integrated with INGRES, which speeds up the development of data processing applications. From 1977 to 1983, INGRES was extended to Distributed INGRES to run on a collection of computers interconnected through a high-speed network.

The INGRES project has achieved its primary goal of demonstrating the feasibility and usefulness of an RDBMS in a minicomputer environment. As a result, INGRES has been marketed since 1981 [RTI 83] by Relational Technology Inc. (RTI). Extensive testing of the prototype by external users in 1979 led to the identification of a number of problems that were subsequently corrected in the product, which now offers a high degree of performance and a variety of uses. It supports the standard SQL and provides a full set of form-oriented integrated tools for application development and data manipulation based on the concept of visual programming. In addition, it includes the first commercial version of a heterogeneous distributed database system, INGRES/STAR, which allows the cooperation of different DBMSs running on remote machines. INGRES is available on a number of operating environments, including DEC VAX/VMS and UNIX, IBM mainframes and compatibles with MVS, VM/CMS and UTS, and most of the UNIX operating system-based computers. A more restricted version, MICRO-INGRES, is available for a large range of microcomputers based on the MC 68000 microprocessor under UNIX and IBM PCs under MS DOS and PC DOS. Detailed information on the INGRES prototype and the INGRES product can be found in [Stonebraker 86] and [Date 87], respectively.

The INGRES prototype is described in detail in Section 4.2. In Section 4.3, we briefly look at Distributed INGRES. In Section 4.4, the INGRES product with the main adaptations added by RTI is detailed. Finally, Section 4.5 presents the INGRES/STAR DDBMS.

4.2 The INGRES Prototype

The INGRES prototype [Held 75] is an RDBMS designed as an external layer of the UNIX system. The design and implementation choices that led to the first prototype are reported in [Stonebraker 76a]. INGRES was written in C, a standard system programming language used to develop UNIX. INGRES' initial objective was to offer high-level interfaces to diversified applications (management, geographical, statistical, and others) in a minicomputer environment. Most of the prototype's solutions were improved in the product, except for the transaction management and query processing modules, which were completely redesigned.

4.2.1 Data Definition

In INGRES, data definition, control, and manipulation are made with the QUEL language [Zook 76], a high-level nonprocedural language that has many commonalities with the SQL language since it is based on tuple relational calculus.

INGRES supports the explicit notion of database, a collection of relations under the control of a database administrator. To log on INGRES, the INGRES <base name> command must be invoked. The user is therefore introduced and may work on the specified base. This notion furthers the control of the access rights to base relations by a unique administrator. Nevertheless it restricts access to data of a single base and makes difficult, or even impossible, access to several bases. An authorized user may initialize a new database by using the command CREATEDB <dbname>.

The creator of a database becomes its administrator endowed with particular privileges, such as the possibility to destroy an empty base by using the DESTROYDB <dbname> command. With the CREATE command, a new relation in the current base may be built with the names of the attributes and their type.

The creator of a relation becomes its owner. Only the administrator may create relations, which are shared between different users; a nonadministrator user that is authorized may create only private relations. The creation of the DRINKER relation is defined as follows:

```
CREATE DRINKER
(D# = i2,                    (integer encoded on two bytes)
NAME = c20,
TYPE = c5)
```

A relation may be destroyed by its owner by using the command DESTROY <relation name>. Filling the relation by the insertion of tuples may be established with the help of the data manipulation language or a utility loading a file created by a text editor. The physical clustering of a relation is defined by the MODIFY command by specifying the storage structure chosen among those described in Section 4.2.5 and the keys.

The following command clusters the DRINKER relation into a hashed file:

MODIFY DRINKER TO HAS ON D#

Secondary indexes on an existent relation may be specified by the INDEX command on one or several attributes — for example:

INDEX ON DRINKER IS DRINKIND (TYPE)

The index DRINKIND is represented as a relation associating with each type of drinker an identifier (logical address) of tuples in the DRINKER relation. The index is thus treated like a relation, although it is automatically updated when the indexed relation is modified. Only the owner of the relation may use the MODIFY and INDEX commands.

The redefinition of an existent relation — for example, adding a new attribute — must be made by loading the relation into a file followed by its loading into the relation with a different format and by using the preceding commands (DESTROY, CREATE). The SAVE UNTIL <date> command extends a temporary relation, which is the result of a query, to a certain date.

Information that concerns data description and their control is stored in a data dictionary, organized as a metabase, which contains the relations RELATION, ATTRIBUTE, INDEX, PROTECTION, and INTEGRITY. A user may then be authorized to query some of the metabase information with QUEL commands. Updating of the data dictionary can be made only by using data description or control commands.

4.2.2 Data Manipulation

Data manipulation is completely handled by QUEL, the main INGRES entry point. However, various user interfaces have also been designed and built on top of QUEL. In this section, after illustrating data manipulation with QUEL, we present the main user interfaces that have been successively developed in the INGRES project: EQUEL, an embedding of QUEL in C; RIGUEL, a database programming language; and FADS, a form-oriented application development tool. Other user interfaces, not reported here, have also been proposed, including CUPID [McDonald 75], a graphical interface to QUEL, and GEO-QUEL [Go 75], a geographical interface that provides data presentation in map format.

QUEL
The QUEL language provides set-oriented data manipulation. It has the power of tuple relational calculus enriched with sorting, grouping, arithmetical, and aggregate functions. In opposition to SQL, which may be used with nested blocks, QUEL is purely nonprocedural. Nevertheless, variable definition is compulsory even when attributes may be named without ambiguity. The processing of null values is allowed by specifying the key word ' ', meaning "null," in the right part of the selection criterion. QUEL's facilities are illustrated by the following queries defined in Chapter 2 on the WINES database.

> **R1:** RANGE OF P IS PRODUCER
> RANGE OF W IS WINE
> RANGE OF H IS HARVEST
> RETRIEVE UNIQUE P.NAME
>   WHERE P.P# = H.P# AND H.W# = W.W#
>   AND W.VINEYARD = "Julienas"
>   AND W.VINTAGE = 1982 OR W.VINTAGE = 1984

> **R2:** RANGE OF D IS DRINKER
> RANGE OF W IS WINE
> RANGE OF R IS DRINK
> RETRIEVE D.ALL
>   WHERE D.D# = R.D# AND R.W# = W.W#
>   AND W.VINEYARD = "C*"
>   AND (W.PERCENT ≥ 11 AND W.PERCENT ≤ 13
>   OR W.PERCENT = ' ')

R3: RANGE OF W IS WINE
RETRIEVE W.VINEYARD,
AVE (W.PERCENT BY W.VINEYARD WHERE MIN (W.PERCENT
> 12)

I1: RANGE OF P IS PRODUCER
RANGE OF H IS HARVEST
RANGE OF W IS WINE
APPEND TO DRINKER
(D# = P.P#, NAME = P.NAME, TYPE = ' ')
WHERE P.REGION = ''Bourgogne''
AND P.P# = H.P# AND H.W# = W.W#
AND W.VINTAGE = 1983

M1: RANGE OF H IS HARVEST
RANGE OF W IS WINE
REPLACE H (QTY = QTY * 1.1)
WHERE H.W# = W.W#
AND W.VINEYARD = ''Julienas''
AND W.VINTAGE = 1982

EQUEL

Like all other query languages, QUEL was insufficient for developing actual data processing applications. As a consequence, QUEL was initially integrated into the C programming language, creating the EQUEL language (embedded QUEL) described in [Allman 76]. An EQUEL instruction is either a C command or a QUEL command preceded by two special characters (# #). The program's variables, which are preceded by # #, may be used in QUEL queries. Fig. 4.1 gives an example of an EQUEL program. During the execution of an EQUEL program, the occurrence of an INGRES statement gives control to the DBMS either for the execution of QUEL queries or for the transfer of a tuple with the program. The conversion from the set-oriented processing mode of QUEL into the procedural mode of C is quite simple. The call of the QUEL query may be compared to the initialization of a program's loop (such as WHILE in Pascal). This call generates the query execution, which assigns the variables. The beginning and end of a loop are specified respectively by (and). The instructions between (and) correspond to the procedural processing of a tuple, which comes from or will be sent to the DBMS. The loop ends when there are no more tuples to be processed. The notion of cursor, explicit in System R, is therefore implicit in EQUEL.

A precompiler transforms an EQUEL program into a C program by copying the C commands and adding C code to communicate with INGRES. The resulting C program can then be compiled. The approach to precompilation of

```
main ( )
        •
        •
        •

# CHAR VAR 1 [20];
# INT VAR2
        •
        •
        •

# RANGE OF W IS WINE
# RETRIEVE (VAR1 = W.VINEYARD, VAR2 = V.VINTAGE)
# WHERE W.PERCENT = 11
#      {
           •
         < process one retrieved tuple >
           •
           •
           •
#      }
```

FIGURE 4.1 Example of EQUEL program.

INGRES (Fig. 4.2) is very different from that of System R, which replaces the SQL statements by CALLs to the DBMS. The precompiler generates a C program in which the QUEL statements are included as strings. For each QUEL statement in the EQUEL program, the precompiler requests INGRES to parse it. The parsed QUEL statement is then inserted into the C program as a string. Code necessary at run time to transmit the parsed QUEL statement to INGRES and to read tuples from INGRES is added to the C program. Compared to the System R approach in which the compiled SQL code is stored in a library, the object code produced by the EQUEL precompiler is larger.

RIGUEL
As an embedded query language, EQUEL suffers from the so-called impedance mismatch, which stems from the set-oriented operation mode of the query language coupled with the procedural operation mode of the programming language. RIGUEL [Rowe 79] was an attempt to provide the same functionality as EQUEL while eliminating the impedance mismatch. RIGUEL is a database programming language, a general-purpose programming language that includes database access primitives and the database data types of relation, tuple, and view. The approach is similar to Pascal/R [Schmidt 77], which supplements the Pascal programming language with a relation type. The programming constructs of RIGUEL are similar to those of Pascal and MODULA and include modules

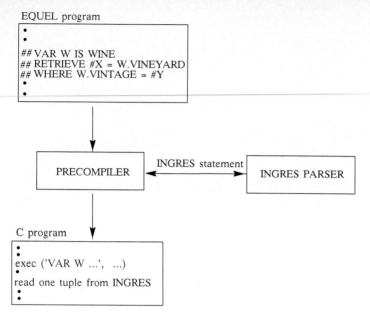

FIGURE 4.2 Precompilation of an EQUEL program.

and procedures. For example, the WINE relation may be declared in a RIGUEL module as follows.

```
name: type = array 1..20 of char;
WINE : relation
      W#: integer;
      VINEYARD: name;
      VINTAGE: name;
      PERCENT: real;
      key W#;                    (*W is the key of the WINE relation *)
```

Key constraints may be specified with the relation definition. Such a module may be imported by all RIGUEL programs that use the WINE relation.

The manipulation of the tuples in a relation or a view is done with the FOR-statement, which has particular semantics when used on a relation. The FOR-statement generates a sequence of values (tuples) specified by the FOR-condition and then applies the same instruction block to each element of the sequence. For example, the EQUEL program of Fig. 4.1 could be expressed in RIGUEL by the program in Fig. 4.3.

View manipulation is a distinguishing feature of RIGUEL. Views may be declared in a module together with procedures that specify the way a view update

```
program RIGUEL.
        •

VAR1: type = array 1..20 of char;
VAR2: type = integer;
        •

        •

        •

FOR W IN WINE WHERE W.PERCENT = 11 DO
        VAR1 := W.VINEYARD;
        VAR2 := W.VINTAGE;
        •

        < process one WINE tuple >
        •

        •

END;
```

FIGURE 4.3 Example of RIGUEL program.

is mapped into an update of base relations. Since the rules for updates through views are entirely specified, all kinds of views may be updated.

FADS

Most of the time for developing data processing applications is spent on screen definition, which is tailored to end-user needs. A form-oriented system permits application development to speed up by supporting directly the high-level constructs needed for screen definition. FADS (Form Application Development System) [Rowe 82] is an interactive form-oriented database programming language that provides direct access to an INGRES database. FADS integrates in one language a screen definition language, a database query language, and a programming language. It was one of the first proposals toward an application development tool fully integrated with an RDBMS. Sophisticated tools based on this approach are now available in commercial systems.

The basic objects manipulated by a FADS application are frames, forms, data types, and operations. Two built-in data types, relation and tuple, are directly supported. The objects that constitute an application are stored in the INGRES data dictionary. A frame is the display of one or more forms on the screen and a set of associated operations. The user can enter data in a form or see data retrieved from the database by triggering the required operations. An example of frame is given in Fig. 4.4. This frame permits the editing of tuples from the WINE relation. By typing 220 in the W# field and executing the FIND operation, information on the WINE 220 gets displayed. Operations associated with a form are defined in a QUEL-like language. Let us call WINEFORM the

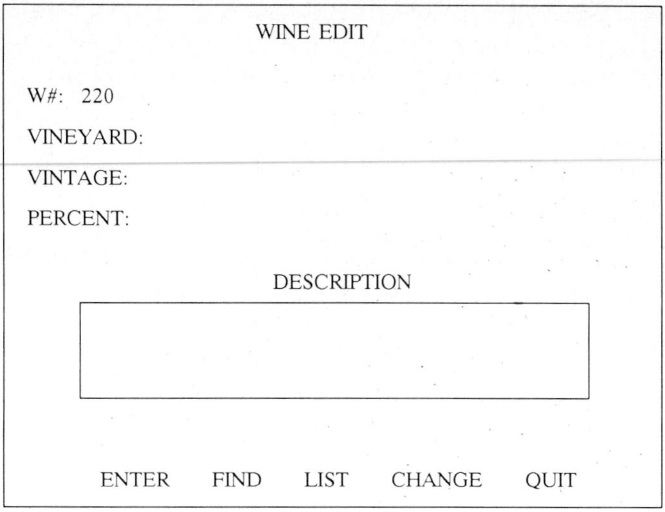

```
                              WINE EDIT

    W#:  220

    VINEYARD:

    VINTAGE:

    PERCENT:


                             DESCRIPTION



         ENTER    FIND    LIST    CHANGE    QUIT
```

FIGURE 4.4 Example of frame.

form with the fields W#, VINEYARD, VINTAGE, and PERCENT in the frame of Fig. 4.3. The operation definition for FIND can look like:

    WINEFORM = (RETRIEVE (WINE.ALL)
                 WHERE WINE.W# = WINEFORM.W#)

where WINEFORM.W# is the W# entered by the user.

A FADS application can be entirely developed or modified by manipulating a built-in frame, called *application editor,* with specific operations to edit frames and forms. In addition, the semantic consistency of an application may be checked.

4.2.3 Semantic Data Control

Data managed by INGRES are under the control of three mechanisms: views, protection, and integrity constraints. Semantic data control is uniformly handled by an elegant technique called *query modification.*

Views

A view is a virtual relation defined from relations in the database by the DEFINE VIEW command. The definition of a view may be specified as a subset of attributes of the base relations by using an analogous qualification to that of a RE-

TRIEVE statement. All types of retrieval qualification are allowed in the view definition. The person who defines the view must be the owner of the base relations. For example, the definition of the view V1 is specified by:

```
V1:  RANGE OF W IS WINE
     RANGE OF P IS PRODUCER
     RANGE OF H IS HARVEST
     DEFINE VIEW JULIENAS-HARVEST
        (H.P#, P.NAME, H.QTY)
        WHERE H.W# = W.W# AND H.P# = P.P#
        AND W.VINEYARD = "Julienas"
```

A view may be interrogated as a relation since it is derived from base relations, but it cannot always be updated as such. A view may be used to hide the base relations from some users, showing them only external schemes of the database. The update of a view is possible only if it is equivalent to the update of the base relations, whatever their instantiation is. The only updates allowed by INGRES are those of views defined by a monovariable (ranging over only one relation) that have no aggregates, such as SUM or AVE. The conversion of a query on a view into a query on base relations is made by query modification [Stonebraker 75] by merging the view and the query criteria.

Protection

INGRES's protection mechanism [Stonebraker 74, Stonebraker 76b] provides a centralized control of data access based on the notions of database and DBA. The DBA is the only person entitled to have control of the database. This person may create shared relations or views and associate with them access rights, may destroy all the temporary relations whose validity date has expired, or destroy any relation of the base. The decision of not offering a decentralized control as in System R was made to simplify the control and because it was thought not to be useful. The DBA has all powers and may concede the rights to perform operations on the relations of that database (RETRIEVE, INSERT, DELETE, UPDATE). Nevertheless the DBA may not grant the administration right. The selective specification of protection constraints is made by the PROTECT command. The following commands illustrate the definition of rights on the DRINKER relation:

```
RANGE OF D IS DRINKER
PROTECT DRINKER FOR ALL TO PAUL
PROTECT DRINKER FOR RETRIEVE, REPLACE
   (D.NAME, D.TYPE) TO JOHN
```

The PROTECT command includes the definition of subsets of objects that are to be controlled by the WHERE clause. This avoids the use of the view mechanism for access control. The key word "*" is understood as an identifier (user-id) of the current user (who is logged in). Therefore with the following command, the current user can read the information regarding all the producers of the same region as him or her:

```
RANGE OF P1 IS PRODUCER
RANGE OF P2 IS PRODUCER
PROTECT PRODUCER FOR RETRIEVE
WHERE P1.REGION = P2.REGION
    AND P1.NAME = *
```

The control of protection consists of the modification of an initial query of a user into a query that does not violate data access authorizations.

Semantic Integrity

Semantic integrity of data is maintained by the verification of integrity constraints expressed on the relations. The definition of an integrity constraint is expressed by an assertion as a QUEL qualification, which must be true of the data of a base relation (and not a view). The INTEGRITY CONSTRAINT command states an integrity constraint; it is designed to verify the relation's data, to check whether they are true, in which case they are stored in the data dictionary. The integrity constraint is then checked at each update operation of the relation. Although algorithms for processing all types of constaints that may be expressed by predicates are given in [Stonebraker 75], the implementation was restricted to monovariable constraints without aggregates. The only supported constraints are the domain constraints and the temporal constraints, of which processing is very efficient.

At each query, the integrity constraints are controlled by a prevention method rather than a detection method, wich could cost more when a transaction is undone. The qualification of a relation's update query is enriched by the predicates of the integrity constraints associated to the relation (by AND). This query modification mechanism is a unified approach to process view, authorizations, and integrity constraints.

Query Modification

A query on a view is modified into a query on base relations by integrating the protection and integrity predicates. To illustrate the query modification algorithm, we shall consider the following relation:

EMPLOYEE (NAME, DEPARTMENT, SALARY, AGE, DIRECTOR)

and the definition of a view of the young employees:

```
RANGE OF E IS EMPLOYEE
DEFINE YEMP (E.NAME, E.SALARY, E.AGE)
    WHERE E.AGE < 30
```

The following integrity constraint sets the minimum salary at $20,000

```
RANGE OF E IS EMPLOYEE
INTEGRITY CONSTRAINT IS E.SALARY > 20000
```

The following definition specifies that the only person allowed to update a salary is the director of the employee:

```
RANGE OF E IS EMPLOYEE
    PROTECT EMPLOYEE FOR ALL (E.SALARY, E.NAME)
        WHERE E.DIRECTOR = *
```

We shall now consider the example of Mr. Smith's query, which decreases Johnson's salary:

```
RANGE OF Y IS YEMPL
REPLACE Y(SALARY = 0.9 * Y.SALARY)
    WHERE Y.NAME = "JOHNSON"
```

This query updates the relation **EMPLOYEE** through the YEMP view. The view-processing algorithm consists of changing the variable and adding the predicate that defines the view:

```
RANGE OF E IS EMPLOYEE
REPLACE E (SALARY = 0.9 * E.SALARY)
    WHERE E.NAME = "JOHNSON"
        AND E.AGE < 30
```

The algorithm then adds the protection and integrity predicates to obtain the final query:

```
RANGE OF E IS EMPLOYEE
REPLACE E (SALARY = 0.9 * E.SALARY)
    WHERE E.NAME = "JOHNSON"
    AND E.AGE < 30
    AND 0.9 * E.SALARY > 20000
    AND E.DIRECTOR = "SMITH"
```

Johnson's salary will be modified only if all the predicates on the qualification are true. Thus modified, the query is processed by the query decomposition module (see Section 4.2.5). This method is very efficient because it need not access the base data; only schema information is consulted. Therefore the query that has been enriched by AND is more selective.

4.2.4 Transaction Management

Objectives

The INGRES's transaction management system was designed to be simple and efficient. These objectives were initially dictated by the small main memory size (64K bytes on PDP 11/40 in 1975) since efficient transaction management consumes much main memory. Therefore the transaction is defined as a unique QUEL query, which becomes the atomic unit for concurrency control and recovery. For example, the transfer operation of a credit from one bank account to another is done by two transactions (one for credit and the other for debit). Between these two transactions, the database is inconsistent, and the user has to take this inconsistency into account. This choice makes easier, or rather possible, the management of concurrent transactions with little overhead. A user may abort a transaction by pressing the ''break'' key of the terminal, leaving the database in its initial state. To cope with the threat of concurrent accesses and failures, INGRES ensures concurrency control of transactions and recovery after system failure. Recovery after media failure is not directly supported.

Concurrency Control

The concurrency control mechanism consists of the lock of a rough granule (full relation). The choice of such a granule reflects the minicomputer environment, which has little storage space for the lock table. With such a granule, the cost of concurrency control is very low, but it favors transactions processing a large number of tuples rather than short transactions. Nevertheless concurrency control at tuple or page level burdens considerably the system's performance. It was confirmed by simulation [Ries 77, Ries 79] that in the majority of applications, a large granule was an excellent solution but one that excluded debit/credit transaction types. This research showed that the best solutions are those in which the granule is a function of the transaction, as it is, for example, with predicate locking [Eswaran 76].

The classical deadlock problem, which arises when single locking techniques are used, is resolved quite easily by INGRES. The transaction being a QUEL query, the strategy is to avoid deadlocks by locking in advance all the necessary resources. This would have been impossible with QUEL multiquery transactions.

Reliability

INGRES supports recovery after transaction, system, and media failures; however, media recovery after media failure relies on the UNIX backup capability and is quite inefficient.

The three recovery mechanisms use the differed update techniques, which always guarantee a valid data copy in case primary data are lost. Transaction and system recovery is based on a data copy on disk, whereas media recovery requires tape archives, checkpoints, and logs.

The atomicity of the transactions is ensured by the differed update technique. This technique is very simple. All update (APPEND, DELETE, REPLACE) is processed by recording in a temporary file on disk all the tuples that might be updated (tuples that are to be added, suppressed, or modified). At the end of a transaction, the temporary file may be integrated into the database, and the affected indexes may be updated by using an atomic action. Update processing is simplified by the isolation of the temporary data from the database. Furthermore the differed updates file constitutes a log of the updates to be performed.

A transaction failure restart, which occurs only when the user decides to cancel it, consists of destroying the temporary file associated with the transaction. The differed update mechanism simplifies restart procedures but remains an expensive technique in terms of memory space (storage of a temporary file) and processing time.

System failure assumes that the content of main memory is lost. System recovery is initialized by the RESTORE command. If the integration of the updates into the database had not started before the failure, the temporary file is destroyed, which amounts to cancelling the effects of the nonvalidated transactions. If the integration of updates of some transactions had already started, then the differed update file is fully processed so as to commit the started updates. Therefore all or none of the updates of a transaction are integrated into the database. The differed update file may eventually be maintained on tape and, in this case, provides a log for recovery from media failure.

Media recovery, after loss of information on disk, uses the tape archives and the logs. System checkpoints may be periodically set up to save the content of the database on tape by using the UNIX backup scheme. These checkpoints are installed when there are no active transactions. As INGRES logs all the interactions, the recovery procedure consists of restoring the database state at the last checkpoint and in applying the interaction log (or tape containing the file of the differed updates, if it exists). This procedure is quite slow.

4.2.5 Query Processing and Storage Model

Storage System

The access methods are built as an external layer of the UNIX file system. The alternative, to develop an ad hoc storage subsystem, a decision made by System R's designers, was not taken up because it was thought to be much more complex and to make the system less portable.

The data of each relation are stored in a separate UNIX file, made up as a set of logically adjacent pages. The clustering of several relations in the same file was impossible for two reasons: page size is small (initially 512 bytes), and the pages, which are logically adjacent in a UNIX file, were not physically close on disk. Consequently clustering of data that verifies a certain criterion, such as key order, in pages that are logically close is changed by the UNIX file system, which clusters the pages based on the insertion order. The essential problem that arises when this system is used is the degradation of performance [Stonebraker 80]. UNIX converted a logical address into a physical address by using a hierarchical catalog. If it is a large relation, three or four accesses to the catalog may be necessary. The access methods built on top of UNIX add some I/O operations. New versions of UNIX ensure that pages that are logically close are also physically close.

Storage Structures

Data placement in a UNIX file may be established according to five different storage structures, each favorable to a certain access pattern. Four of these structures are based on key, the access to a tuple in a file being a function of the value of certain attributes (the key) of the tuple. They are the hashed [Knuth 73], ISAM [IBM 66], compacted hashed, and compacted ISAM organizations.

The first structure is the *heap* organization (not sorted), which stores the tuples in the file independent of their value. This structure is the cheapest one and is ideal for applications that require a full file scanning. Tuples are clustered in the file according to the given insertion order. The occupancy ratio of the file (the proportion of the useful size to the effective occupancy size) is then maximized. This organization is used for small relations, for some intermediate query results, and for the files used for loading and unloading data between the DBMS and other systems. The heap structure is the most favorable when the selectivity of the majority of the selections is poor, and a very large subset of the file must be selected.

The *keyed structures* are designed to favor the access to specific subsets of the file when the key values are provided. The access key may be a combination of different attributes. It decides in which page the tuples are to be located. A tuple must be totally contained in a page. It is designated by a unique tuple identifier (TID). A TID is composed of a logical page number, the UNIX file, and an offset of an indirection table, stored in a page. A table entry contains the tuple's address in the page. Therefore the reorganization (sorting) of the tuples of a page does not affect the TIDs taken into consideration.

A number of primary pages is allocated to a file. The increase of the relation's size implies the allocation of overflow pages chained by pointers to the associated primary pages. The order of tuples btween the different pages is not preserved. Consequently tuple access by key can be made only by having access to all the tuples of the same chain. This is the major inconvenience of a static data structure, which adapts itself to the variations of data volume by overflows [Stonebraker 80], thus requiring periodic reorganizations. The alternatives are the dynamic structures such as extendible hashing [Fagin 79] or B-trees [Bayer 72].

With INGRES, two types of conversions of key into address (TID) can be made: by hashing or according to the key order. In hashing, the tuples in the primary pages of the file are evenly distributed by using a function applied to the key. This method is the fastest for direct access to a tuple that verifies the key value. A file that ensures the key order is organized with ISAM. The file is sorted according to certain keys, with an index that associates with each highest key value a primary page address. The index may be hierarchical with several levels. An example of an ISAM file is given in Fig. 4.5. The ISAM organization is useful for range access (defined by key value limits) or for sequential access sorted on key value.

These two keyed structures represent the tuples in fixed length. They may be combined with compression techniques when the extra coding-decoding cost is redeemed by a better storage occupancy. This type of technique is frequently used in statistical databases [Shoshani 82] for both improved access performance and good disk space occupancy. The implemented compression technique consists of suppressing blanks and indicating the part of the tuple identical to that of the preceding tuple (by storing the length). An example of compression is given in Fig. 4.6.

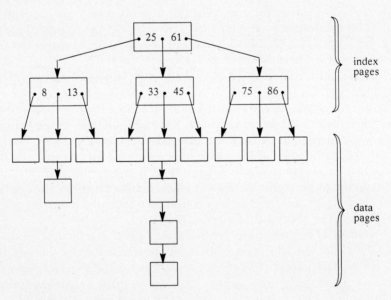

FIGURE 4.5 Example of ISAM-like file.

GEORGES, PAUL			0 GEORGES, PAUL	
GEORGES, PETER	} 38C		9 PETER	} 24C
GEORGES, JOHN			8 JOHN	

FIGURE 4.6 Example of compression.

Access Paths

The access method associated with a storage structure of a file constitutes its privileged access path since it is based on the physical clustering of tuples. Secondary indexes may be defined on a relation that associates with each secondary key value a TID corresponding to each key value. A secondary index is stored in a file organized according to one of the four keyed structures. The fact that TIDs remain invariant except during static reorganizations has the advantage of never having to generate the update of secondary indexes of the existing tuples. Furthermore the TID found in the secondary index enables access to the tuples. However, if the file is large, several disk accesses may be necessary to find a tuple based on its TID since the UNIX file system catalog (which is hierarchical) must be accessed. INGRES therefore offers a large range of access paths that enables the DBA to optimize different types of queries.

Query Processing

The evaluation of a complex query is made by a query processing algorithm based on decomposition [Wong 76]. This algorithm performs two main functions. First, a multivariable query is decomposed into a sequence of one-variable queries. Second, each monovariable query is processed by a one-variable query processor (OVQP), which invokes the access method interface. This algorithm consists of defining in a dynamic way the execution plan of the query by using simple heuristics in the choice of the first operations and in taking into account the size of the intermediate results to order the subsequent operations. This algorithm does not therefore manage statistical information for the evaluation of the execution plans. In this section, we first detail the decomposition algorithm, for it was an important alternative to the System R exhaustive search approach. Then we describe the way one-variable queries are processed.

The Decomposer

The objective of this is the efficient execution of complex queries (on several relations). The main query, which is used as a basis for others, is the RETRIEVE query. The decomposer processes the updates by generating retrieval queries of tuples that are to be modified and records the modification in the differed update file. The aim of query decomposition is to minimize the size of the intermediate results in the sequencing of the operations and to make the most selective operations as soon as possible. The basic assumption is that the cost of an operation is proportional to the size of the operands. The algorithm replaces an N-variable query Q by a series of queries $Q_1, Q_2, \ldots, Q_N$, where each query Q_i uses the result of the query Q_{i-1}. It is mainly based on two query transformation techniques, *detachment* and *substitution*. All queries generated by the decomposer are monovariables and hence processed by the OVQP.

Detachment is a transformation that divides a query into two subqueries, each having a single common relation. With the detachment, a query Q may be decomposed into two successive queries Q' and Q'', each having only one relation in common, which is the result of Q'. The detachment enables the simpler operations to appear. These operations are selections and projections, the only operations that can be detached. They are easily recognized because they are monorelation.

Not all the queries can be decomposed by detachment. A query in which no detachment is possible is said to be *irreducible*. The semijoins are irreducible. A fortiori, the joins are irreducible. Furthermore the cyclic queries are irreducible [Bernstein 81]. The irreducible queries are converted into monorelation queries by tuple substitution.

Tuple substitution transforms an N-relation query Q into a set of queries of $(N-1)$ relations by replacing one relation by its actual tuples. The recursive application of tuple substitutions until the chain of all queries are monorelation can be seen as a general nested-loop solution. For example, the application of tuple substitution to query $Q(R_1, R_2, \ldots, R_N)$, where R_i a relation, can lead to the following nested-loop evaluation (described in Pascal-like formalism):

for each tuple t_1 **in** R_1
    for each tuple t_2 **in** R_2
        •
        •
        •
        for each tuple t_n **in** R_N
          if $P(t_1, t_2, \ldots, t_N)$ **then**
            apply $F(t_1, t_2, \ldots, t_N)$

where P is a predicate and F is the function defining the effect of Q (for example, projection, update, and so on).

Each step of tuple substitution corresponds to one "for each" statement. In order to generate the smaller number of subqueries, the relation chosen to be substituted is the one with the lowest cardinality. Since the query is dynamically executed, the exact cardinalities of the operand relations (already computed) are provided.

The decomposition algorithm applied to a given query Q can be summarized as follows:

1. Detach all separable subexpressions in Q into subqueries.
2. Execute all monorelation subqueries (selections and projections) generated by step 1.
3. Apply tuple substitution recursively to the remaining n-relation subqueries by increasing order of substituted relation cardinalities.

We illustrate this algorithm with the query R4 defined in Chapter 3 on the WINES database. The query expressed in QUEL is:

```
(R4)      RANGE OF W IS WINE
          RANGE OF P IS PRODUCER
          RANGE OF H IS HARVEST
          RETRIEVE W.VINEYARD
               WHERE W.W# = H.W# AND
                     H.P# = P.P# AND
                     P.REGION = "Bourgogne"
```

One selection can first be detached, thereby replacing R4 by R41 followed by R4', where P1 is an intermediate relation.

```
(R41)     RANGE OF P IS PRODUCER
          RETRIEVE P.P# INTO P1
               WHERE P.REGION = "Bourgogne"
```

```
(R4')     RANGE OF W IS WINE
          RANGE OF P IS P1
          RANGE OF H IS HARVEST
          RETRIEVE W.VINEYARD
               WHERE W.W# = H.W# AND H.P# = P.P#
```

After successive detachments, query R4' may be replaced by the following two subqueries:

```
(R42)     RANGE OF P IS P1
          RANGE OF H IS HARVEST
          RETRIEVE H.W# INTO H1
               WHERE P.P# = P.P#
```

```
(R43)     RANGE OF W IS WINE
          RANGE OF H IS H1
          RETRIEVE W.VINEYARD
               WHERE W.W# = H.W#
```

Query R4 has been replaced by the sequence R41 → R42 → R43. Query R41 is monovariable and is executed as is. Queries R42 and R43 that are not monovariable must be further reduced by tuple substitution.

The execution of monorelation queries generated by the decomposition algorithm exploits the existing access paths to the relations. The result of a monovariable query may be stored with a particular file organization for optimizing the processing of the subsequent operation. For instance, the result of a selection operation followed by a join (generated by tuple substitution) will be stored in a file hashed on the join attribute so that a hash-based join algorithm may be used.

The reduction approach exhibits several advantages: it is relatively simple; it does not require maintaining statistics about the database; and the dynamic ordering of joins based on exact cardinalities of relations minimizes the probability of generating a bad execution of a query. There are serious problems with this approach, however. The systematic execution of selections before joins may lead to low performance, for example, if selections have poor selectivity. The main disadvantage is that decomposition and optimization, two expensive tasks that require access to schema information, are done at run time. In particular, they must be repeated for every execution of the same query.

Processing of Monovariable Queries

The OVQP receives the monovariable queries generated by the decomposer; its objective is fast access to tuples of relations satisfying a given criterion. Information on data access paths of a relation is found in the data dictionary. This module chooses the best access path according to the query qualification and calls upon the access method interface. The access possibilities are determined by verifying the access paths' compatibility using the selection criteria. For a hashed file, the equality predicate is necessary; furthermore if the key is a combination of several attributes, all have to be specified. With an ISAM file, the specification of value intervals may be made, and only the specification of the most discriminant attributes of a composed key is needed.

The possibilities are sequenced in a priority order: hashed primary relation, hashed index, ISAM primary relation, ISAM index, and sequential scanning. This priority order is defined by taking into account the number of logical accesses to the pages of the relation so as to find a tuple. The overflow pages are not taken into account.

A tuple in a hashed file is located in one access by using a random function applied to the key. The access by hashed index enables one to find an index tuple in one access and the tuple in the file in a supplementary access. Access to an ISAM file requires as many accesses as there are numbers of levels of the index part of the file (generally two or three) plus an access to the file. Access by ISAM index requires one more access than the preceding access path. Sequential scanning carries out an access for each page of the file. These costs do not take into account the number of supplementary accesses (between one and four) to the catalog of the UNIX file system.

4.2.6 Architecture

Functional Architecture

The functional architecture of INGRES is represented by Fig. 4.7. It is based on a uniform interface model using QUEL as single entry point. The system is decomposed into three subsystems, which are in charge of query control, query execution, and various utility functions.

The query control subsystem receives QUEL queries, either directly from an interactive transaction or from a C program in execution. It carries out the syntactic and semantic analysis of the query and applies the query modification technique for uniform processing of protection, integrity control, and views. This

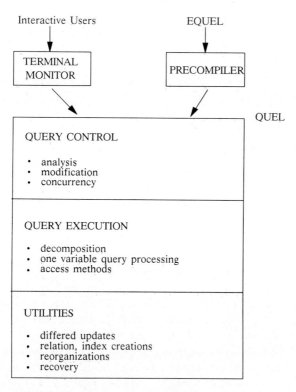

FIGURE 4.7 Architecture of INGRES.

module manages concurrency control by conveying the query to the following module once all its required resources are locked.

The execution subsystem interprets QUEL queries. An update is converted into a retrieval command so as to isolate the tuples that are to be altered. After modification, the tuples are written down in the differed update temporary file. A multivariable RETRIEVE query is decomposed into a sequence of monovariable queries, each of which is processed by the OVQP. The latter then has access to data by using the access methods.

The last subsystem supports a set of utilities (to create or destroy relations, indexes, and so on). It also integrates the updates into the base at the end of transaction and ensures the recovery tasks.

INGRES may be considered an interpreter of the QUEL language. One difference between System R and INGRES is that in the latter, all queries pass through the three subsystems without being coded into a low-level compiled format. This approach tends to favor interactive queries, which are executed one time, rather than the predefined queries. This technique makes possible dynamic generation of the query's execution plan. Nevertheless a query is analyzed, decomposed, and controlled systematically. That these costly tasks have to be repeated at each query execution is the major drawback of the interpretation approach [Stonebraker 80].

INGRES's Implementation under UNIX

INGRES is built around the UNIX system, a popular operating system because of its simplicity and the power of its concepts. Two of its important properties have had an influence on INGRES's design: file management and process management.

UNIX provides a hierarchical file system in which each file is either a data file or a referential catalog for the descending files of the system. The file system is managed as a virtual address space. When a file page is requested, it is directly given by UNIX if it is in main memory without having to generate any IO operation. If the page is not in main memory, a free space is found so as to transfer into it the requested disk page. The strategy used to select space in main memory is the classical "least recently used" buffer replacement algorithm. Nevertheless it has been shown in [Stonebraker 81] that this method is not well adapted to database operations, particularly sequential scanning. The INGRES system was designed as a UNIX user application. This decision enables INGRES to be portable on a standard UNIX. Furthermore UNIX storage management is used.

The UNIX process management is useful in making INGRES's functional architecture operational in a multiuser context. A UNIX process was a limited address space (64K 8 bit-bytes on PDP 11/40 in 1976) and is a unit controlled by the process manager. The communication system is based on interprocess links called *pipes*. A pipe may be declared a unidirectional link; it is materialized by a file containing messages, written by a producer process, and read by a consumer process. Because UNIX has no shared storage capabilities, data structures ex-

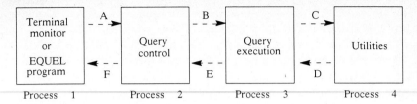

FIGURE 4.8 Process structure in INGRES.

changed between processes are communicated by pipes. Information that is to be exchanged may thus be coded by the producers and decoded by the consumers. INGRES's multiusers' management is simple and is dictated by the pipe communication mode. Each INGRES user is associated with a separate process, which shares INGRES's reentrant code and has its own data segments.

INGRES's functional architecture is implemented according to the address space offered by the computer. INGRES essentially implements the process model. With a 64K byte space, each of INGRES' subsystems is a UNIX process, the interprocesses communication being done by pipes. INGRES may be called by UNIX or by a QUEL program in execution. Fig. 4.8 illustrates the INGRES process structure for one transaction. Procedure calls are made by the pipes A, B, and C, and results and error messages are given by the pipes D, E, and F. For calls made by UNIX, a terminal monitor is added in front of INGRES to manage interaction with users. It essentially maintains a workspace for the user, enabling him or her to formulate, print, modify, and trigger INGRES's commands execution. When invocation from a program occurs, the C program in execution under UNIX calls on the DBMS.

The process structure represented by Fig. 4.8 is due to storage space considerations. Processes 2 and 3 are essentially at their maximum size (64K byte), and process 4 is divided into several overlays. This functional division is better than having a single process controlled and paginated by the system. With a 300K byte space (on PDP 11/70), the three subsystems are in only one process. The final implementation of the INGRES prototype on PDP 11/70 is divided into two processes per transaction: a user process and a DBMS process.

4.3 Distributed INGRES

Distributed INGRES [Stonebraker 77] is an extension of INGRES to run in a distributed environment. Compared to R* (see Section 3.6), Distributed INGRES has not reached a fully operational state although it "more or less" works [Stonebraker 86]. Its implementation has been painful because of the lack of distributed debugging tools. A short section on Distributed INGRES has been included

because of its peculiar objectives and original solutions to distributed query optimization. Distributed INGRES enables the management of data distributed
among a collection of computers, each running the same DBMS (an extension of
INGRES). The computers can be interconnected through either a general (slow)
network or a local (fast) network. A prototype has been developed on a few VAX
computers interconnected through the Ethernet network.

4.3.1 Objectives

The main objectives of Distributed INGRES are location transparency and increased performance. Location transparency hides the data distribution. Using
Distributed INGRES is basically equivalent to using INGRES. Location transparency is supported by having for each distributed database a global data dictionary replicated at each site storing relations of that database.

In 1977, increased performance was an unusual objective for a distributed
DBMS. It can be achieved in the context of a high-speed network by exploiting
parallel processing. The goal was to provide throughput that was linear in the
number of computers across which the data were distributed. The main idea was
that a powerful computer could be built out of several smaller and less powerful
ones. This idea also led to some parallel database machine designs [Stonebraker
79]. Performance improvement is obtained by carefully distributing the data
across many computers so that parallelism is maximized when processing a distributed query. This objective was partly achieved. However, an important result
could be demonstrated [Stonebraker 86]. If the data are appropriately distributed
across all computers for a given query, throughput improves linearly as computers are added. The open issue remains to distribute the data so that most of
the queries get processed in parallel. We will address this issue in the context of
database machines in Chapter 9.

4.3.2 Extensions to INGRES

The main extensions for INGRES to run on multiple computers concerned data
definition, query optimization, query execution, and transaction management.

The QUEL data definition facility was supplemented with a number of new
statements to define distributed databases or distributed relations. A new distributed database can be created with the statement:

DCREATEDB < dbname > AT < site list >

where site list is a list of logical site names. Thus a distributed database is explicitly defined over a number of sites, each storing a copy of the data dictionary
for that database. The site list initially associated with a database may be ex-

tended any time to incorporate new sites with an EXPAND <dbname> statement. Similar to INGRES, distributed relations may be created within a specified database with the statement:

DCREATE <relation specification> AT <site list>

where the site list is a subset of the site list associated with the database. Furthermore a relation may be subsequently extended to new sites.

Query optimization was extended to handle distributed relations and exploit parallel processing. The query optimization algorithm of Distributed INGRES [Epstein 78] is derived from the algorithm used in centralized INGRES. Therefore it consists of dynamically optimizing the processing strategy for a given query. The objective function of the algorithm is to minimize communication cost and response time. Because these two objectives are conflicting (increasing communication cost may well decrease response time), the function can give a greater weight to one or the other. The algorithm takes into account the network topology: general or local (broadcast) network. In broadcast networks, the same data unit can be transmitted from one site to all the other sites in a single transfer, and the algorithm explicitly takes advantage of this capability; for example, broadcasting is used to replicate fragments of relations and then maximize the degree of parallelism. This algorithm is based on a fragment and replicate technique.

Query execution in Distributed INGRES is based on a master/slave process structure. There is a single "master INGRES" process that interacts with the user's application program at the user site, and there is a "slave INGRES" process at each site that stores data useful to the user's application. The master process sends commands directly to its slave processes. When a slave process needs to send a relation to another site, a receptor process is dynamically created at that site to receive the relation.

Transaction management has been extended in two important directions to handle distributed transactions. First, concurrency control, based on a two-phase locking algorithm, has been enhanced with a global deadlock detection algorithm. Global detection is applied by a single process, called *scoop*. Second, a two-step commit protocol has been added to achieve the atomicity of distributed transactions.

4.4 The INGRES Product

Around 1980, the company RTI was originated by industrials and key members of the INGRES research group so as to market a product based on the INGRES prototype. The product was initially implemented on VAX machines under VMS and UNIX. Since then, INGRES has been ported on many environments, including IBM mainframes and compatibles, workstations such as SUN and Apollo, and IBM PCs. RTI's essential contribution was to develop INGRES so as to make it useful and to adjoin to it powerful management tools. INGRES is portable to different operating systems. Portability is achieved through the use of a compatibility library that includes all operating system calls used by INGRES. This library contains about sixty routines dependent on the operation system. Therefore INGRES can be ported to a new environment by writing the compatibility library. Taking into account the self-criticism expressed in [Stonebraker 80], a first effort was made to improve the functions and performance of the DBMS. The main components thus affected are transaction management and query optimization. Furthermore perception of the urgent need for user-friendly tools resulted in the development of information processing by forms subsystems. These different tools include a processing by form interface, a report generator, and a graphical package. Finally INGRES offers an outstanding distributed database management capability for heterogenous environments.

4.4.1 Architecture

INGRES's architecture for VMS environment is illustrated in Fig. 4.9 (the architecture under UNIX is similar). VMS provides a file system somewhat adapted to data management. Logically adjacent pages of a file are nearly always adjacent on disk. (Berkeley's UNIX Version 4.2 offers services comparable to the VMS file system.) The INGRES product uses the operating system's file system. Nevertheless it controls main memory management, thus making possible the implementation of page replacement algorithms adapted to database operations and the sharing of buffers containing data pages between different transactions. A random page replacement algorithm is used and is generally the best and the simplest [Stonebraker 81].

The process structure is that of the final prototype that has two processes per transaction: a terminal monitor that controls interaction with users and a server process that performs DBMS functions. Fig. 4.9 illustrates the two potential usages of INGRES; T1 and T2 are two terminal monitor processes associated to two transactions. Each user process sends messages and receives results via the terminal monitor process, which communicates with an INGRES process to execute queries. PA1 is a process that executes a COBOL application program controlled by the VMS execution system.

4.4.2 Improved Functions

Data Manipulation

The basic QUEL language was improved to make it easier for use. Because range variables can be specified as relation names, variables are not necessary for single relation queries. Functions were also added so as to facilitate the definition and

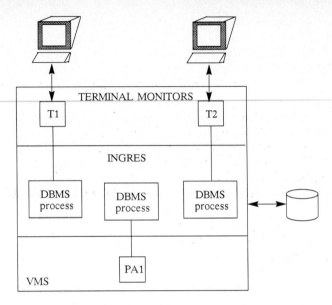

FIGURE 4.9 Architecture of INGRES in VMS.

control of QUEL statements (commands with differed execution, macrodefinition, and so on). RTI has also developed a QUEL version compatible with the standard SQL. The EQUEL language is integrated into several programming languages: Basic, C, COBOL, FORTRAN, and Pascal. A precompiler has to be used for each host language.

Semantic Data Control

The specification of data control commands is enriched by practical facilities. The types of data supported are integer, real, text (up to 2000 characters), date, and money. The definition of complex conditions is made possible by authorization control. For example, "The updating of the drinker's number and of the quantity drunk in the relation is allowed to Georges from 12 to 4 P.M. on Mondays if the quantity does not exceed the average quantity drunk of the same wine" may be expressed as:

    DEFINE PERMIT REPLACE ON E(D#,QTY) TO GEORGES
    FROM 12:00 TO 16:00 ON MON TO MON
    WHERE E.QTY ≤ AVE (E.QTY BY E.W#)

Transaction Management

INGRES guarantees complete and efficient transaction management. A transaction is defined as a set of QUEL or SQL queries preceded by the BEGIN command and ended by the END command. A user may at any moment suppress a transaction in execution with the ABORT command. INGRES's transaction management subsystem constantly maintains an update transaction journal and manages system checkpoints, which are periodically specified by the INGRES administrator. For each update, a temporary differed update file is maintained and integrated in the database at the last stage. A two-step commit validation protocol [Eswaran 76] guarantees that all or none of the updates are taken into account. Automatic recovery procedures enable one to restore database consistency after media or system failure.

To favor a large number of concurrent transactions, INGRES uses a variable locking granule. By default, the granule is the page but can be automatically exchanged for a larger granule (relation) when INGRES detects it as more efficient. Furthermore the user may specify locking at the relation level. Deadlock situations are detected and corrected by killing one of the locking transactions.

Query Optimization

The query processing algorithm designed for the prototype was considerably improved. The generation of a query execution plan is now static and based on the exhaustive search approach (see Section 3.2.5). A predefined query execution plan is stored in library under a compiled form, thus avoiding repeated query analysis, modification, and optimization tasks. The interpretative approach is therefore replaced by a compilation approach, similar to that of System R. Actually INGRES does not always perform a complete exhaustive search among all alternative execution plans. The optimization terminates when the time spent searching for the best execution plan exceeds a time-out. The time-out is an estimate of the average time needed to process the query. This trades off compilation time for run time.

The prediction of the cost of an access plan uses statistical information managed by INGRES on relations and indexes. Besides, for each attribute useful in qualifications, two informations are maintained: the number of unique values and a histogram with a variable number of value intervals. This last information avoids the classical assumption of uniform distribution of values in a domain and permits accurate estimation of intermediate relation cardinalities. These statistics are initialized during object creations and periodically updated by using the OPTIMIZEDB command. These statistics are important in the selection of monovariable access paths and in the join ordering in a query.

Another considerable improvement is the adjunction of an efficient sort-merge join algorithm [Blasgen 77] to the tuple substitution technique (nested-loop join algorithm). This algorithm is best for large operand relations and poor join selectivity.

The last aspect is that the size of pages has reached 2K bytes. The last version of INGRES, among other contributions, provides for a dynamic storage structure of B-tree type [Held 78], which is an alternative to the ISAM static structures. Thus INGRES provides four types of storage structures: HEAP (sequential), B-trees, hashed, and ISAM.

4.4.3 New Functions

One major problem in data processing is the development of complex applications. To reduce development time, INGRES provides a complete set of integrated tools for terminal control, report generation, graphic interface, interactive data manipulation, and application development. Each tool incorporates an interface with INGRES that is qualified as "visual programming" by its designers. Visual programming is based on the manipulation of forms directly on the screen. This concept is inherited from FADS. These tools use a data dictionary managed by INGRES so as to store necessary information for form definition. These tools work on INGRES databases.

Visual programming is based on the usage of forms displayed on the terminal for interaction with the DBMS. Forms make up a particular type of data presentation, adapted to the display of results as well as to information entry. Forms call on visual and intuitive concepts that are easily assimilated. A form is the display of different components on a terminal: heading, attributes describing the data's different fields, and window. A data window is a space in the form reserved for display or addition of data. A form may be combined with a range of data manipulation operations. The use of forms requires a few techniques that all tools have in common:

- Navigate on the form by using a cursor.
- Enter/edit data on the form.
- Switch from edition mode to operational control.
- Select/execute operations.

INGRES provides five subsystems that use the concept of the form:

1. *Query by forms (QBF)* is a data manipulation language by form. It has the power of tuple relational calculus. It provides for retrieval, insertion, modification, and suppression of existing data of a unique relation. The latest version offers multirelation data manipulation, which was not available in FADS.
2. *Visual forms editor (VIFRED)* is a form editor that makes possible form manipulation (creation, suppression, modification, edition). The form description is stored in a data dictionary managed by INGRES. Forms may be defined for use by QBF or by an application program.
3. *Report by form (RBF)* enables one to define data reports from forms created with VIFRED. RBF makes possible the manipulation of report characteristics (heading, column, titles, data format, line sorting, and so on). RBF may also select commands from INGRES's powerful report generator, which has a complete report specification language.
4. *Graph by forms (GBF)* provides for the definition of graphs from the database's data. With the help of simple commands, GBF describes a

relation's data in a graph that can be displayed in various forms (array, histogram, chart). Complete graph specificaton is therefore made possible by GBF.

5. *Applications by forms (ABF)* performs a more complex task, the creation and definition of application programs using visual programming. In particular, ABF allows one to develop applications with similar elements to those detailed above (QBF, RBF, and others). It has a simple language for defining menus and their functions. The various preceding products can be combined and synchronized using ABF. ABF has a procedural 4GL, called OSL, favoring the creation of complex applications. OSL integrates the screen functions with the SQL and QUEL languages. OSL enables structured programming by associating procedural blocks to the database attributes (triggers) or to the menu options.

4.5 INGRES/STAR

INGRES/STAR is the first commercial version of a DDBMS designed for heterogeneous environments. It provides transparent and simultaneous access from various DBMSs interconnected through a local or general network. INGRES/STAR achieves four primary objectives: location and replication transparency, performance, reliability, and open architecture framework.

Location and replication transparency allows the user to view a set of distributed and/or replicated relations as a single database. A global data dictionary records information about data location and replication and is used to translate a user transaction into transactions on local databases. Distributed transaction atomicity is guaranteed by a two-step commit protocol [Gray 78] and a distributed concurrency control algorithm with global deadlock detection.

As with Distributed INGRES, performance remains a primary goal. It is achieved by a distributed query optimization algorithm that exploits parallel processing, provided by data distribution and replication, and minimizes communication cost in case of a general network.

Reliability is enhanced by allowing data to be replicated. If the data at one site become unavailable after a failure, copies of them remain accessible at other sites. Therefore replication enhances data availability. Recovery after a media failure is fast since a database can be rapidly reconstructed by copying the useful replicated data from other sites.

An open architecture framework allows heterogeneous sites with different operating systems and/or different DBMSs to be integrated in a single database that can be accessed uniformly with the SQL language. This is probably the most powerful aspect of INGRES/STAR. The architecture of INGRES/STAR has a number of properties. First, the local DBMSs need not be changed. Second, security and integrity are managed by the local DBMSs. Third, the distributed database is the union of the local databases. Fourth, several distributed databases can be defined on the same set of local databases. Multiple updates of a distributed database can be handled concurrently or differed.

The architecture of INGRES/STAR is shown in Fig. 4.10 for a heterogeneous environment. The interface between the various machines is the standard SQL.INGRES/STAR works with two main components: INGRES/NET and Gateways. INGRES/NET is a distributed communication system that allows different operating systems, such as UNIX and MVS, to exchange information. A Gateway is a specific interface that converts SQL into the language of a particular DBMS — for example, DL/1 for the IMS system.

The INGRES/STAR open architecture supports many environments, including IBM, DEC, NCR, UNISYS, HP, DG, SUN, APOLLO mainframes, minicomputers, and microcomputers under the major operating systems: VM/CMS, MVS, VMS, UNIX, and MS-Dos. It provides access to the standard networks: DECNET, TCP/IP, SNA, and MAP.

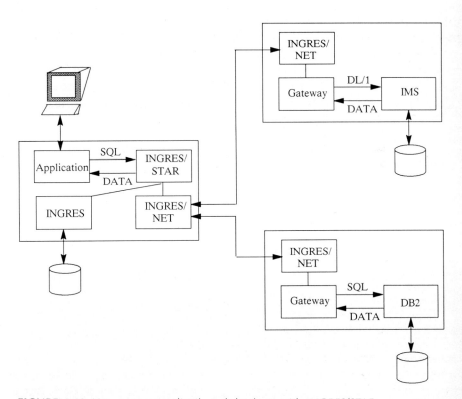

FIGURE 4.10 Heterogeneous distributed database with INGRES/STAR.

4.6 Conclusion

This chapter was devoted to the description of the INGRES systems. The INGRES prototype is an RDBMS functionally complete. The most significant contributions of INGRES were the design and specification of the QUEL non-procedural language, a good alternative to SQL, and the development of original solutions to query transformation, such as query modification and query decomposition. The work on a form-oriented language was also significant. The design of the prototype as an external layer of the UNIX system was a unique experience and enabled INGRES designers to validate the feasibility of an RDBMS with limited main memory. Distributed INGRES is an interesting DDBMS prototype whose primary objective was to increase performance by exploiting the parallel processing capability of multiple computers.

The INGRES product offers significant performance and functional enhancements over the prototype. The first measurements in monouser context [Bitton 83] have shown its excellent performance competitiveness. A complete set of form-oriented tools fully integrated with the DBMS simplifies and speeds up applications development. INGRES is currently implemented on a large number of operating systems and computers ranging from mainframes to minicomputers and microcomputers.

The most recent system built upon INGRES is the product INGRES/STAR, a heterogeneous DDBMS, which allows the cooperation of multiple DBMSs running on different computers interconnected through a local or general network. INGRES/STAR provides location and replication transparency, performance, reliability, and an open architecture framework.

References

[Allman 76] E. Allman, G. Held, M. Stonebraker, "Embedding a Data Manipulation Language in a General Purpose Programming Language," ACM SIGPLAN SIGMOD Conf. on Data Abstractions, Salt Lake City, March 1976.

[Bayer 72] R. Bayer, C. McCreight, "Organization and Maintenance of Large Ordered Indices," Acta Informatica, Vol. 1, No. 3, 1972.

[Bernstein 81] P. A. Bernstein, D. W. Chiu, "Using Semi-Joins to Solve Relational Queries," Journal of ACM, Vol. 28, No. 1, January 1981.

[Bitton 83] D. Bitton, D. J. DeWitt, C. Turbyfill, "Benchmarking Database Systems: A Systematic Approach," Int. Conf. on VLDB, Florence, Italy, September 1983.

[Blasgen 77] M. W. Blasgen, K. P. Eswaran, R. G. Casey, "Storage and Access in Relational Databases," IBM Systems Journal, Vol. 16, No. 4, 1977.

[Date 87] C. J. Date, *A Guide to INGRES,* Addison-Wesley Publishing Company, 1987.

[Epstein 78] R. Epstein, M. Stonebraker, E. Wong, "Query Processing in a Distributed Data Base System," ACM SIGMOD Int. Conf. on Management of Data, Austin, Texas, May 1987.

[Eswaran 76] K. P. Eswaran, J. N. Gray, R. A. Lorie, I. L. Traiger, "The Notions of

Consistency and Predicate Locks in a Database System," Comm. ACM, Vol. 19, No. 11, November 1976.

[Fagin 78] R. Fagin, "On an Authorization Mechanism," ACM TODS, Vol. 3, No. 3, December 1978.

[Fagin 79] R. Fagin, J. Nievergelt, N. Pippenger, H. R. Strong, "Extendible Hashing — A Fast Access Method for Dynamic Files," ACM TODS, Vol. 4, No. 3, September 1979.

[Go 75] A. Go, M. Stonebraker, C. Williams, "An Approach to Implementing a Geo-Data System," ACM SIGRAPH SIGMOD Conf. for Databases in Interactive Design, Waterloo, Canada, September 1975.

[Gray 76] J. N. Gray et al., "Granularity of Locks and Degrees of Consistency in a Shared Database," IFIP Working Conf. on Modelling of Database Management Systems, FreudenStadt (RFA), January 1976.

[Gray 78] J. N. Gray, "Notes on Database Operating Systems," in *Operating Systems: An Advanced Course,* Springer Verlag, 1978

[Held 75] G. D. Held, M. Stonebraker, E. Wong, "INGRES: A Relational Database Management System," AFIPS 1975 National Computers Conf., Montvale, N.J., 1975.

[Held 78] G. D. Held, M. Stonebraker, "B-trees Re-examined," Comm. ACM, Vol. 21, No. 2, February 1978.

[IBM 66] IBM Corp., *Planning for Enhanced VSAM under OS/VS,* IBM Corp., White Plains, N.Y., 1966.

[Knuth 73] D. Knuth, *The Art of Computer Programming: Sorting and Searching,* Addison-Wesley Publishing Company, Vol. 3, 1973.

[McDonald 75] N. McDonald, M. Stonebraker, "Cupid: The Friendly Query Language," ACM Pacific 75 Conf., San Francisco, April 1975.

[Ries 77] D. R. Ries, M. Stonebraker, "Effects of Locking Granularity in a Database Management System," ACM TODS, Vol. 2, No. 3, September 1977.

[Ries 79] D. R. Ries, M. Stonebraker, "Locking Granularity Revisited," ACM TODS, Vol. 4, No. 2, June 1979.

[Ritchie 74] D. M. Ritchie, K. Thompson, "The Unix Time-Sharing System," Comm. ACM, Vol. 17, No. 7, July 1974.

[Rowe 79] L. A. Rowe, K. A. Shoens, "Data Abstraction, Views and Updates in RIGUEL," ACM SIGMOD Int. Conf. on Management of Data, Boston, June 1979.

[Rowe 82] L. A. Rowe, K. A. Shoens, "A Form Application Development System," ACM SIGMOD Int. Conf. on Management of Data, Orlando, Fla., June 1982.

[RTI 83] RTI, *INGRES Reference Manual,* Relational Technology Inc., Berkeley, 1983.

[Schmidt 77] J. Schmidt, "Some High Level Language Constructs for Data of Type Relation," ACM TODS, Vol. 2, No. 3, September 1977.

[Shoshani 82] A. Shoshani, "Statistical Databases: Characteristics, Problems and Some Solutions," Int. Conf. on VLDB, Mexico, September 1982.

[Stonebraker 74] M. Stonebraker, E. Wong, "Access Control in a Relational Database Management System by Query Modification," ACM National Conf., San Diego, November 1974.

[Stonebraker 75] M. Stonebraker, "Implementation of Integrity Constraints and Views by Query Modification," ACM-SIGMOD Conf., San Jose, Cal., May 1975.

[Stonebraker 76a] M. Stonebraker, E. Wong, P. Kreps, G. Held, "The Design and Implementation of INGRES," ACM TODS, Vol. 1, No. 3, September 1976.

[Stonebraker 76b] M. Stonebraker, P. Rubinstein, "The INGRES Protection System," ACM National Conf., Houston, October 1976.

[Stonebraker 77] M. Stonebraker, E. Neuhold, "A Distributed Database Version of INGRES," 2d Berkeley Workshop on Distributed Data Management and Computer Networks, Lawrence Berkeley Laboratory, May 1977.

[Stonebraker 79] M. Stonebraker, "MUFFIN: A Distributed Database Machine," Conf. on Distributed Computing Systems, Huntsville, Ala., October 1979.

[Stonebraker 80] M. Stonebraker, "Retrospection on a Database System," ACM TODS, Vol. 5, No. 2, June 1980.

[Stonebraker 81] M. Stonebraker, "Operating System Support for Database Management," Comm. ACM, Vol. 24, No. 7, July 1981.

[Stonebraker 86] M. Stonebraker (ed.), *The INGRES Papers,* Addison-Wesley Publishing Company, 1986.

[Wong 76] E. Wong, K. Yousseffi, "Decomposition: A Strategy for Query Processing," ACM TODS, Vol. 1, No. 3, September 1976.

[Zook 76] W. Zook et al., *INGRES Reference Manual,* ERL Mem. NO-M585, U. of California, Berkeley, April 1976.

5
SABRINA

5.1 Introduction

SABRINA is an RDBMS developed in the SABRE project at INRIA, France, in cooperation with the MASI laboratory at the University of Paris 6. The SABRE project started in the early 1980s when the System R and INGRES projects were finishing. The objectives of the SABRE project were to attack problems not solved completely by those projects and to demonstrate their solutions in a prototype. More specifically, the initial objectives of the SABRE project were the following [Gardarin 83]:

1. *Develop an open DBMS kernel:* SABRINA end-user interfaces are built around an open kernel that provides a well-formalized interface based on tuple relational calculus extended with functions. Several interfaces have been developed and many others prototyped. This kernel can also be used to build a distributed DBMS.

2. *Improve performance:* SABRINA includes several techniques to minimize query response times and maximize system throughput. A multi-attribute clustering method allows the DBA to simply specify that data that are most often accessed together be clustered on disk. A filtering scheme has been developed to process efficiently an extended select operation that includes select, project, with arithmetic and aggregate functions on a large range of data types, including text. A large cache mem-

ory is managed by SABRINA to maintain the frequently accessed parts of relations and as many intermediate results as possible.

3. *Maintain extensively semantic data integrity:* Most RDBMSs are very restrictive in their support of semantic integrity control; in general, they support only domain and key uniqueness constraints. Hence most integrity controls must be embedded in application programs interfacing the DBMS. SABRINA can enforce a large range of integrity constraints, including referential integrity and quantified assertions, so that most integrity controls can be done by the DBMS rather than the application programs.

4. *Support efficiently transaction management:* In general, supporting transaction management is not efficient because the recovery mechanisms, which are designed independently of the storage model and the concurrency control algorithms, remain costly in terms of disk accesses. The storage model of SABRINA is based on a unique catalog that addresses all data pages. Transaction management is efficient because the reliability mechanism and the concurrency control algorithm are fully integrated with catalog management. In particular, there is no need for additional lock tables since the locks are stored in the catalog entries.

5. *Experiment with parallelism:* One important goal of the project was to define a functional RDBMS architecture that can be mapped efficiently in a multiprocessor environment. In this case, the RDBMS can be viewed as an efficient database machine that exploits parallelism. This database machine, designed in the SABRE project, is presented in Chapter 9. Original algorithms and techniques were developed to process relational algebra operations in parallel.

During the lifetime of the project, two new objectives were added [Gardarin 86] to extend the relational capabilities of SABRINA:

6. *Support abstract data types:* Current RDBMSs support a fixed set of data types. SABRINA extends these primitive data types by allowing user-defined abstract data types (ADTs) and associated operations. This capability allows SABRINA to be extended; the application developer may extend the basic data types of the DBMS with new types to support the application requirements.

7. *Support rule-defined relations:* Another important objective is to support virtual relations defined by complex programs of production rules. This capability makes SABRINA a deductive DBMS [Gallaire 84] able to support the emerging knowledge base applications.

SABRINA has achieved objectives 1 – 4 completely and 5 – 7 partially. A prototype now running fulfills most of the listed objectives.

Most of the solutions implemented in the prototype have been incorporated in a relational product marketed since 1986 by a group of three French companies (INFOSYS, EUROSOFT, and SAGEM). The product has been improved with form-oriented interfaces, application development facilities, and an efficient query optimization algorithm. The differences with the prototype reflect the fact that the product is targeted for many environments, including on-line applications and decision-support applications.

In this chapter, we present the current version of the SABRINA prototype with main emphasis on its relational capabilities, and the new functions of the SABRINA product. Since the product is very similar to the prototype, most of the chapter is devoted to the prototype. In Section 5.2, we give a description of the main end-user interfaces: FABRE (a flexible, nonprocedural language allowing the user to manipulate complex objects), SQL (the standard relational query language), PASREL (an embedding of relational queries in the Pascal language), UQBE (a universal relation based version of QBE), and UTILITIES (a set of utilities). In Section 5.3, we introduce the solutions to semantic data control, which include the support of views, integrity constraints, and authorizations. In Section 5.4, the original storage model of the system, based on a multiattribute clustering scheme with secondary indexes, and the query processing techniques are presented. In Section 5.5, an integrated solution to transaction management that combines concurrency control, catalog management, transaction atomicity, and workspace management is described. The SABRINA architecture is described in Section 5.6. The enhancements that can be found in the SABRINA product are given in Section 5.7.

5.2 User Interfaces

SABRINA provides a collection of user interfaces offered by a menu displayed to a logged in user in front of a terminal. The main menu of SABRINA is portrayed in Fig. 5.1.

The main interfaces are the following:

1. FABRE, a nonprocedural language, with flexible syntax, including facilities to manipulate complex objects.
2. SQL, the standard version of the SQL language.
3. UQBE, a two-dimensional language supported by a unique table that corresponds to the universal relation obtained by union of the attributes of a given set of relations.
4. PASREL, a programming language interface consisting of relational commands embedded in Pascal, similar to PASCAL/R [Schmidt 77].
5. UTILITIES, a set of utilities that includes a report generator, a relation editor, and save and restore facilities.

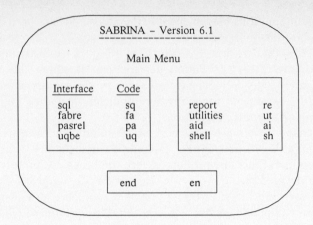

FIGURE 5.1 The SABRINA main menu.

5.2.1 FABRE Language

The SABRINA nonprocedural language, described in [Pasquer 84, Sabre 86], facilitates data definition, control, and manipulation. It is a first-order predicate calculus-based language that includes functions and aggregates. The language syntax is flexible in the sense that key words are parameterized and may be given by the DBA. The QUEL and SQL syntaxes are included in FABRE. In addition, the FABRE language allows the DBA to define complex domains (domains of relations that are composed of complex objects) as abstract data types and functions to manipulate these complex domains. These functions are defined using a LISP-like syntax and may be referred to within retrieval and update commands.

Data Definition with FABRE
The DEFINE command allows the DBA to specify complex object domains. First, the structure of the object must be defined as a LISP structure using basic domains — integer, real, and text. Then the functions related to the complex domain must be specified in a LISP-like syntax [Kiernan 87]. These functions may be used to express database queries.

The CREATE command enables one to create a new relation in a database with its attributes and domains, as well as the associated keys. For example, the creation of the DRINKER relation inside a database called WINES is defined as follows:

```
CREATE WINES.DRINKER (D#:integer, NAME:text, TYPE:text)
   (KEY1:D#);
```

A relation may be destroyed by an authorized user with the DESTROY command. One can also destroy a database (a set of relations) by specifying only the name of the database as a parameter of the DESTROY command.

The insertion of tuples in a relation may be done using the INSERT command. During the insertion, an optimized clustering of tuples on disk is generated. The physical clustering of a relation is requested by the CLUSTER command, which allows the DBA to specify an attribute hierarchy with the clustering criteria. To illustrate this command, let us consider the following relation:

DRINK (D#, W#, DATE, PLACE, QTY)

The relation will be clustered according to D# and then according to W# using the command:

CLUSTER WINES.DRINK USING
(D# MODULO 31), (W# HASHED ON 1);

It is also possible to define secondary indexes on nonclustering attributes for a given relation. This is done using the INDEX command. For example, an index may be created on attribute PLACE for the DRINK relation:

INDEX WINES.DRINK ON PLACE;

It is also possible to destroy existing indexes on a relation at any time.

The redefinition of a relation scheme is possible; one can either extend a relation with new attributes using the EXTEND command or suppress existing attributes of a relation using the RESTRICT command. The execution of such commands entails the automatic reorganization of the relation and its indexes if necessary. New attributes are filled up with null values.

The SABRINA schema is stored in a data dictionary organized as a database (metabase) so users can access schema data with the same relational language.

Data Manipulation with FABRE

FABRE is an interactive language based on tuple relational calculus. It encompasses a large number of capabilities of the QUEL and SQL languages and offers new extensions. FABRE is targeted for ad hoc queries and therefore supports decision-support applications. The language is simple and flexible; key words are adaptable to the user's native language because they are grouped into classes. The language parser [Pasquer 84] recognizes key word classes and executes an augmented transition network (ATN) [Woods 70] that supports syntaxes of type QUEL, SQL (without nested blocks), and hybrid. The user defines queries directly and is therefore not guided by the system but may be informed by a HELP facility on the language syntax. A query is analyzed one sentence after the other. When a syntactic or semantic error occurs, the user is informed of the type of error and the part of the sentence that is correct and accepted; he or she may either retype the incorrect part or switch to the text editor to correct the query.

The main query types are:

1. *Search* (SEARCH) qualified by a selection and/or join predicate (WHERE) with possible grouping on attribute (GROUP BY) and aggregate functions (MIN, MAX, COUNT, AVG) or arithmetic calculations. Sorting a relation is also possible (SORT BY) on a variable number of attributes, each in ascending or descending order. The formulation of a search query is also facilitated by various capacities such as the application of several functions to an attribute list — for example, MIN, MAX (VINTAGE, PERCENT). A search result may be saved in a temporary relation for further use. The saving may be specified during the query expression (SEARCH . . . INTO < temp >) or after evaluation of the result (SAVE INTO < temp >). The result of a query is automatically displayed in a table format on the screen. Result displaying may also be user controlled.

2. *Insertion* (INSERT) from the user terminal or from the result of a qualification including one or several relations. In the first case, user tuples are checked for syntactical validity (type control is performed).

3. *Suppression* (SUPPRESS) of a set of tuples in a relation defined by a qualification.

4. *Modification* (MODIFY) of a set of tuples in a relation based on the values of previously selected tuples or values given at the terminal.

All the update operations (query types 2, 3, and 4) may be controlled by displaying the modified data at query end; they are actually performed in the database at transaction end (commit time).

It is also possible to enter queries using the system text editor. Such predefined queries are identified by a name and stored in a specific file; they may include comments and parameters. A predefined query may be run by a specific command (EXECUTE) with parameter values. A set of predefined queries may be stored in a query file, which can be executed as a long transaction.

To illustrate the FABRE data manipulation language, we shall express the queries defined in Chapter 2 on the WINES database. We assume that the user is working on a single database WINES. This is specified to the system by the following statement:

BASE = WINES;

We also assume that variables have been declared inside the transaction as relation synonyms as follows:

VAR W = WINE, P = PRODUCER, H = HARVEST, D = DRINKER, R = DRINK

Thus the queries defined on the toy database may be expressed as follows (other equivalent syntaxes are possible):

(R1) SEARCH P.NAME
    WHERE W.VINEYARD = "Julienas"
    AND W.VINTAGE IN (1982, 1984)
    AND W.W# = H.W#
    AND H.P# = P.P#

(R2) SEARCH D.NAME
    WHERE D.D# = R.D#
    AND R.W# = W.W#
    AND W.VINEYARD - "C.*"
    AND W.PERCENT = NULL OR W.PERCENT BETWEEN 11 AND 12;

(R3) SEARCH WINE.VINEYARD, AVG(WINE.PERCENT)
    WHERE MIN(WINE.PERCENT GROUP BY WINE.VINEYARD) > 12.

(I1) INSERT IN DRINKER THE RESULT
    P.D#, P.NAME, NULL
    WHERE P.REGION = "Bourgogne"
    AND P.P# = H.P#
    AND H.W# = W.W#
    AND W.VINTAGE = 1983;

(M1) MODIFY H(QTY = H.QTY*1.1)
    WHERE H.W# = W.W#
    AND W.VINEYARD = "Julienas"
    AND W.VINTAGE = 1982;

Contrarily to most other RDBMSs, SABRINA does not restrict the access to a single database but is essentially multibase oriented. Multiple database relations may be referred to in the same query provided that the variable definitions are of the form < V = BASE.RELATION >. Since queries are expressed on relations, relations of different databases can be simply accessed.

In addition, FABRE allows the user to query complex objects using functions. These functions must be previously defined when the complex domain is specified. They are applied to the attributes of complex domains using the dot notation. Possible parameters may be added between parentheses. For example, let us assume that a complex domain TRIANGLE has been defined with the function PRESENT (color), which displays a triangle on the screen in a given color, and SURFACE, which computes the surface of a triangle. Let us assume the relation:

GEOMETRY (ID:TEXT, PICTURE:TRIANGLE)

The following query gives a red picture of all triangles of surface greater than 100:

SEARCH GEOMETRY.PICTURE.PRESENT(RED)
WHERE GEOMETRY.PICTURE.SURFACE > 100;

5.2.2 SQL Interface

SABRINA supports the standard SQL language for interactive use. The development of an SQL interface was facilitated by the relational completeness of FABRE, which is different from SQL only syntactically. In addition, control commands for creating access path and integrity constraints are supported in a syntax close to this of FABRE. Since SQL has been extensively illustrated in Chapter 3, we will not repeat its description here.

5.2.3 Universal Query by Example Interfaces

The UQBE (Universal Query By Example) query language [Sabre 86] presents to the end user a unique two-dimensional grid illustrating the universal relation derived from a specified set of relations. UQBE combines the advantages of QBE (user-friendly aspects) and the universal relation (there is no need to specify natural join predicates). With its graphic approach, UQBE offers a simple way to formulate queries. After the database and the set of relations have been chosen, a relation skeleton (the grid) that includes all the attributes of the specified relations is displayed on the screen. Two lines of the skeleton are reserved for the user to express queries. A query is expressed by entering in the columns of the skeleton the characteristics of the desired tuples.

Three types of elements may be used to express a query. Constants are used to give selection criteria, preceded by a logical comparison operator ($>$, $<$, $\geq$, $\leq$, $\neq$), equal being a default option. Question marks (?) are used to specify the projection criteria. Variables may be used to express certain joins that are not implicit or to express arithmetic calculations.

To simplify the user interface, natural joins on keys are implicit. When the skeleton is built, every attribute of the user-specified relations is placed into it; however, attributes of identical names that are keys or part of keys in several relations are not replicated. An implicit natural join is generated by SABRINA on key attributes. Therefore the user sees a unified relation where the key attributes appear only once. The joins on keys are then system generated when necessary. Thus, in general, the user does not have to specify joins, which become implicit. For example, when the keys of all relations have been specified, entity-relationship links are automatic. This advantage stems from the support of a universal relation interface.

During the formulation of a query, the user browses on the skeleton using keyboard functions. Thus the screen behaves as a window on the skeleton. This browsing capability is mandatory since, in general, a universal relation is too wide to fit on a screen. The current attribute is always the left-most on the screen; it is the column where the user can enter constants, question marks, variables, and expressions. A summary of all the already-filled columns appears on the last lines of the screen, allowing the user to remember the entire query. When the query is composed, it may be submitted to the DBMS; then it is processed, and the results are presented as a single table, which can then be manipulated by the UQBE language.

Let us illustrate the UQBE language using the WINES database. Assume the user has selected the three following relations whose keys are bold:

WINES (**W#**, VINEYARD, VINTAGE, PERCENT, PRICE)
DRINK (**D#, W#**, DATE, PLACE, QTY)
DRINKER (**D#**, NAME, TYPE)

The unified skeleton and the formulation of the query "Retrieve the name of each drinker in Paris or Austin, and the vineyards of the wines that they have drunk in a quantity more than 10" is illustrated in Fig. 5.2. The following joins are implicit:

WINE.W# = DRINK.W#, DRINK.D# = DRINKER.D#

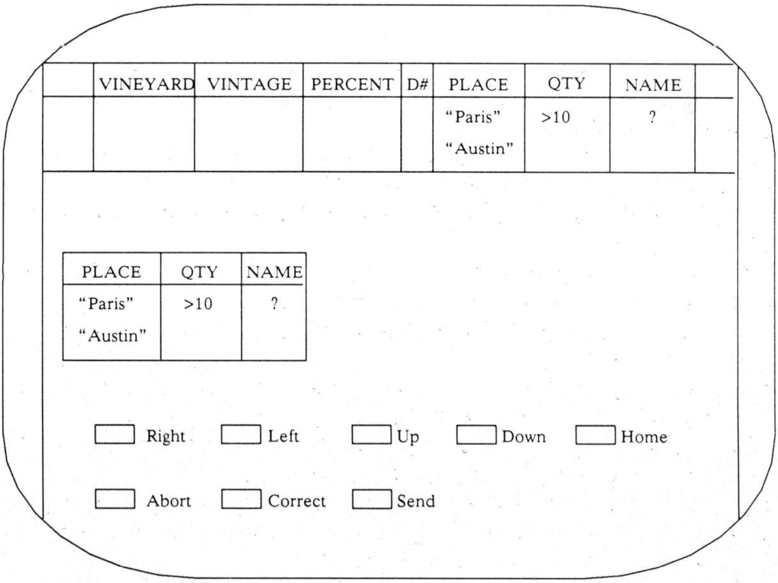

FIGURE 15.2 UQBE query example.

5.2.4 Relational Pascal

The relational Pascal (called PASREL) embeds the constructs of the FABRE data manipulation language into the Pascal programming language. This language is targeted for complex applications that require extensive database programming. More precisely, the objectives of the integrated language are to offer simple facilities to declare and manipulate a database in a Pascal program, to allow the system to guarantee database integrity in a programming environment, and to allow the sequential processing of sets of tuples that satisfy a given qualification. PASREL is therefore a database programming language embedding the capabilities of a database query language (FABRE) into a general-purpose programming language (Pascal).

Besides these objectives, the integration is designed so that the data manipulation language is kept as much as possible independent of Pascal. This constraint facilitates programming and debugging while not constraining the integration. Such independence is achieved by introducing in the source code a specific character at the beginning of each data manipulation command and a specific character at the beginning of each Pascal variable used in a data manipulation command. The following rules are observed:

- "*" is added at the beginning of each DML command.
- Inside a DML command, each Pascal variable is prefixed by "#".

These rules allow the PASREL precompiler to recognize the database instructions.

The data manipulation commands are classified into three types: commands that connect to the DBMS, commands that access and update data, and commands that manage transactions.

First, a PASREL program must be connected to the DBMS using the CONNECT command. This indicates that database interaction will follow. Disconnection, using a DISCONNECT command, is specified when database interaction in the program is finished. Databases and relations used in the program are defined using the BASE command. Derived relations computed under the control of the Pascal program may also be processed. The schema of derived relations must be defined using a CLICHE command. The derivation rule (the query to compute the tuples of a derived relation specified by a CLICHE command) is given using the RULE command. Finally, the database connection command set also includes the definition of variables. These variables, defined by the VAR . . . ENDVAR command, play a dual role: they correspond to database tuple variables representing any tuple of a relation, and they correspond to Pascal variables whose structure is a flat record similar to a relation schema. Thus variables are the central elements to map Pascal data structures into database data structures.

A second class of commands encompasses the database access primitives: the query commands. This includes the classical DML verbs FIND, INSERT,

DELETE, and MODIFY. Also a specific constructor, FOR EACH, allows the programmer to process sequentially a set of tuples satisfying a given qualification. It is an important feature for interfacing Pascal and the query language. Finally the EVALUATE statement performs the computation of the tuples corresponding to a declared derived relation (a cliche).

A third class of commands concerns transaction management. It includes the classical commands: BEGIN TRANSACTION, END TRANSACTION, and ABORT TRANSACTION.

Transaction nesting is not allowed. Also the WHENEVER statement allows the programmer to specify special procedures for error management.

A first example of a PASREL program is given in Fig. 5.3. It illustrates the use of a cliche relation QTYDRUNK that contains all the drinkers of name

```
Program EXAMPLE1;
{Pascal statements are bold}

{ Declaration of relations used }
* EXTERNAL SCHEMA = WINES (DRINKER, DRINK);
{ Definition of a cliche relation QTYDRUNK }
*CLICHE = QTYDRUNK (NAME:text, QTY:integer);
var readname:text
{ Definition of database variables }
*VAR D: WINES _ DRINKER;
      R: WINES _ DRINK;
      Q: CLICHE _ QTYDRUNK;
*ENDVAR;
{ Rule to compose the cliche QTYDRUNK }
*RULE OF QTYDRUNK
        IS D.NAME, SUM(R.QTY GROUP BY D.D#)
        WHERE D.NAME = readname AND D.D# = R.D#;

begin
        *CONNECT user; {Connection to SABRINA}
        *BEGIN TRANSACTION 1; {Begin transaction in inquiry mode}
        readln (readname);
        *EVALUATE Q: {Evaluation of the cliche relation}
        *FOR EACH Q DO BEGIN
                writeln (Q.NAME, Q.QTY);
        *ENDFOR;
        *COMMIT TRANSACTION;
        *DISCONNECT;
end.
```

FIGURE 5.3 A PASREL retrieval program.

<readname>, with the total amount of wine they have drunk. A second example is portrayed in Fig. 5.4, which modifies the prices of Julienas wines.

The approach to PASREL precompilation is somewhat similar to that of EQUEL precompilation (see Section 4.4.2). The PASREL precompiler transforms a PASREL program into a Pascal program by copying the Pascal statements and transforming the data manipulation commands into Pascal procedure calls, corresponding to entry points to SABRINA. Since SABRINA is written in Pascal, such a precompilation approach has been easy to develop. The resulting Pascal program is then compiled by the Pascal compiler and dynamically linked to the DBMS code. Therefore the object program may run efficiently.

```
Program EXAMPLE2;
{Pascal statements are bold}

{ Declaration of relations used }
* EXTERNAL SCHEMA = WINES (WINE);
var price:real;
*VAR W:WINES_WINE;
*ENDVAR;

begin
        *CONNECT USER; {Connection to SABRINA}
        *BEGIN TRANSACTION M; {Begin transaction in update mode}
        *FOR EACH W WHERE W.VINEYARD = "Julienas" DO BEGIN
        writeln (W.VINEYARD);
        if price < > 0 and W.PRICE < > pricen then
          begin
            W.PRICE : = price;
            *MODIFY W; {update the current tuple}
          end;
        if price = 0 then
            begin
              *DELETE W; {delete wines of price 0}
            end
        *ENDFOR;
        *COMMIT TRANSACTION;
        *DISCONNECT;
end.
```

FIGURE 5.4 A PASREL update program.

5.2.5 Utilities

A limited set of utilities has been included in the prototype, mainly to test the DBMS code and maintain the workload databases. They permit users to save a relation or a database in a file, to load a database or a relation from a file, to dump a relation or a database, or to edit a relation using a full screen mode. A special facility may also be used to recover from a media failure.

5.3 Semantic Data Control

5.3.1 Views

SABRINA provides the capability of defining derived relations, called *views,* from other relations. The view creator must have at least a read right on the relations from which the view is derived. The view creator becomes the derived relation's administrator who enjoys certain particular privileges. The view capability of SABRINA is quite general. Most RDBMSs limit the view definition to base relations (physically stored on disk). A view in SABRINA may be derived from base relations as well as other views. Furthermore it may be included in an existing database or a new one. Thus a view may be derived from different databases. This enables one to define a database network as shown in Fig. 5.5. The notion of database network provides a better adaptation to a complex environment than the classical solution of a unique database. It also provides a single transaction with the capability of accessing multiple databases.

A derived relation definition is specified as a search request by the CREATE AS command on base or derived relations, which may belong to different databases [Kerherve 86]. The derived relation JULIENAS-HARVEST is defined — for example, in the WINES database — by the following command:

```
VAR P = PRODUCER, H = HARVEST, W = WINE;
CREATE WINES.JULIENAS-HARVEST
(#P:INTEGER, NAME:TEXT, QTY:REAL)
AS P.P#, P.NAME, H.QTY
WHERE W.W# = H.W#
AND H.P# = P.P#
AND W.VINEYARD = "Julienas";
```

A view can be retrieved as any relation; however, updating is restricted to base relations. A derived relation query must be converted into a query on base relations. This is carried out by a method similar to query modification (see Section 4.2.3); derived relation definitions are merged with the query. The algorithm is more complex because a relation may be itself derived from derived relations.

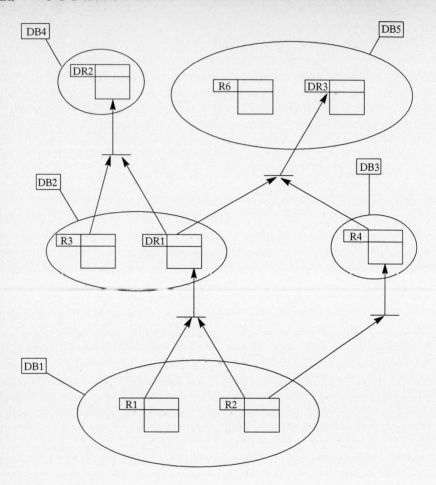

DRi – Derived relation i
Ri –   Base relation i

FIGURE 5.5 Example of database network.

5.3.2 Authorizations

SABRINA's authorization mechanism described in [Kerherve 86] provides decentralized data access control. The controlled objects are relations. A user may be endowed with either a unique right on a database, without distinction of individual relations, or multiple and different rights on different relations of a database.

The relation's creator becomes its administrator. The administrator has all authorizations for data manipulation (retrieval and update) as well as other privileges, in particular the administration privilege, and the capability of declaring integrity constraints on that relation or updating its schema. A user with the administration privilege may grant all authorizations on a relation using the AUTHORIZE command. In particular, the administration right may be granted. Inversely a relation administrator may deny the rights previously given with the PROHIBIT command.

The three types of rights, in increasing order of importance, are retrieval, update, and administration. Any user having a right on a relation may grant this right (or a less important right) to another user. For example, John may authorize Peter to modify the relation WINES.DRINKER, if he has at least that right, by the command:

AUTHORIZE PETER TO MODIFY WINES.DRINKER;

Peter may then grant another user the update or retrieval right for that relation.

Authorization enforcement differs depending on whether the query accesses schema information. In the first case, the user must be authorized to read (if the query is a retrieval) or modify (if the query is an update) the part of the metabase that contains the relevant schema information. Authorization is enforced by enriching the user query so that only the authorized subsets of the metabase relations are accessed. The technique used to enrich the query is similar to INGRES query modification. In the second case, the query invokes only derived or base relations. Authorization enforcement is easier here because the rights are granted on entire relations. Contrary to the first case, there is no need to restrict the access to subsets of relations. The query is accepted by the system if the user rights are compatible with the accessed relations.

5.3.3 Semantic Integrity

Semantic data integrity is ensured by enforcing integrity constraints when data are updated. SABRINA's integrity subsystem [Simon 84, Simon 86] is quite complete and based on efficient differential algorithms. An integrity constraint definition is expressed as a tuple relational calculus assertion or by a special sentence corresponding to predefined types of integrity constraints. The assertions or the predefined commands are translated by a constraint compiler into a set of assertions, each referring to a base relation for a particular type of update.

An integrity constraint can be declared with the ASSERT command. It leads to the verification of the constraint on existing data and to the constraint insertion in compiled form in the data dictionary if the constraint is satisfied. All integrity constraints that can be expressed in tuple relational calculus are accepted: domain, unique key, referential, temporal, and the others. Integrity constraints are defined on only physically implemented relations, since they are the only ones that can be updated. Taking into account the type of manipulation provides opportunities for precise integrity control, in which only a reduced subset of integrity constraints need be checked. The type of manipulation is chosen from insert, suppress, and modify. Certain assertions, which define conditions on an attribute's domain, refer only to tuples added to the database. Others, such as inclusion dependency, which specifies that the existence of tuples in a relation R1 is conditioned by the existence of tuples in a relation R2, must be checked when tuples are added to R1 as well as when tuples are suppressed from R2. The two following examples are an illustration of the specification of integrity constraints on the WINES database.

> *Domain constraint in suppression:*
> A harvest may be suppressed only if its quantity is equal to 0 or unknown.
> VAR H = HARVEST;
> ASSERT ON H IN SUPPRESSION
> H.QTY = 0 OR H.QTY = NULL;
>
> *Referential dependency:*
> A wine drunk at a reception must exist.
> VAR W = WINE, R = DRINK;
> ASSERT ON R IN INSERTION
> R.W# = W.W#;
> ASSERT ON W IN SUPPRESSION
> COUNT (W.W# WITH W.W# = R.W#) = 0;

The following more declarative expression is also possible, in which case the previous assertion is automatically generated by the integrity subsystem:

    ASSERT REFERENTIAL DEPENDENCY
    DRINK.W# FROM WINE.W#;

The integrity subsystem has control over the assertions by a method that prevents the introduction of inconsistencies in the database. Queries violating integrity constraints are rejected before data are updated in the database. This avoids undoing a transaction using the recovery mechanism. The integrity constraints are divided into three categories according to their enforcement cost and their complexity. An efficient enforcement algorithm is defined for each category:

1. Individual assertions, which include monorelation constraints such as domain and unique key.
2. Multirelation assertions such as referential dependencies.
3. Assertions with aggregates for which a particular processing for the aggregate values is required.

Theoretically integrity constraints should be verified at the end of each transaction because a transaction is an atomic unit of manipulation that guarantees database consistency. A SABRINA transaction can consist of several queries. The integrity constraint's taxonomy exhibits that certain assertions may be verified at query end (individual assertions), whereas others have to be verified at transaction end (multirelation assertions). In the latter case, it is possible to determine integrity enforcement points within a transaction. The method is based on the establishment of automatic save points, which make partial validation of a transaction's updates possible. However, in the current implementation of SABRINA, all constraints are checked at transaction end.

The integrity control algorithm's principle is to isolate tuples to be updated in two temporary relations called *differential relations*. One contains the tuples to delete, and the other contains the tuples to insert. The integrity assertions need to be checked against these differential relations, without being concerned with the base relations. This method is efficient, in particular compared to the query modification technique [Simon 84], and enables one to reject erroneous tuples with specific messages for each violated constraint. The valid tuples in temporary relations are inserted in the database at the end of the transaction by the transaction commit mechanism.

For an example, consider the referential integrity constraint above between relations DRINK and WINE. Suppose that the update is a deletion from WINE. The following FABRE-like sub-query is generated to enforce the integrity assertion:

```
VAR OLD = WINE⁻
VAR R = DRINK
SEARCH OLD.ALL
WHERE COUNT (R.W# GROUP BY OLD.W#
    WHERE R.W#=OLD.W#) = 0;
```

WINE⁻ is the differential relation that contains the wines to delete. The count aggregate function and the "GROUP BY" clause are used here to express the universal quantification of the variable R is a similar way to the QUEL language. The result of this retrieval will contain all the erroneous tuples, that is, all tuples that do not satisfy the integrity assertion.

5.4 Storage Model and Query Processing

Relational languages, such as SABRINA's interfaces, enable the expression of complex queries in a declarative style — for example, the selection of a set of tuples satisfying a complex predicate on several attributes. SABRINA's storage model is designed to accelerate data selection based on multiple criteria by restricting the search space to only relevant data. This method is based on a new data structure called *predicate tree* [Gardarin 84a, Valduriez 84a], which enables one to represent in a unified way different hashing functions applied to several attributes. A predicate tree may be viewed as a hierarchical method to divide a relation into smaller subrelations so as to locate data that satisfy the same criterion in the same subrelation. This structure fully adapts itself to dynamic data and may replace a large number of secondary indexes. SABRINA also supports secondary indexes [Cheiney 86a] but to a lesser extent than most other DBMSs. One advantage is that the additional cost of updating secondary indexes is significantly reduced. The storage structures and access paths are exploited by the query processing algorithm, particularly for optimizing the processing of join and select operations. In the rest of this section, we detail the storage model, the query optimization algorithm, and the join and select algorithms.

5.4.1 Predicate Trees

A *predicate tree,* associated with a relation, is defined as a balanced tree in which each level defines a logical partitioning of the relation according to a set of disjoined predicates. For example, a relation R may be first partitioned with a set of disjoined predicates P_1, P_2, . . . , P_n in n subrelations, each subrelation R_i containing tuples that verify the predicate P_i. Each subrelation may be itself partitioned with a list of disjoined predicates. To simplify the successive partitioning description, the same list of predicates is applied to all subrelations corresponding to a given level. Thus the vertices of the balanced tree at a given level are the roots of identical subtrees. Fig. 5.6 gives an example of a predicate tree for the WINE relation.

The definition of predicates of a level is constrained by certain restrictions, designed to lower the costs of processing and storage of predicate trees. A predicate tree's level is defined by only one attribute. Multiattribute predicates are specified with several levels. To facilitate predicate definition, predicates of a given level are generally of the form $\{H(A) = 0, H(A) = 1, . . . , H(A) = N\}$ where H is a hashing function taking values in $[O,N]$ and A is an attribute. This form allows the DBA to use hashing functions to define a set of disjoined predicates. The following level definitions are operational:

● Classical hashing with a MODULO function.
● Trie hashing, close to the function studied in [Litwin 81], based on the rank of the successive characters in the alphabet.
● Interpolation hashing [Burckard 83], which enables one to generate intervals by uniform partitioning of an attribute range.
● Enumeration of a domain's list of potential values, as shown by level 1 in Fig. 5.6.
● Interval enumeration, such as the definition of level 2 in Fig. 5.6.

This set of possible level definitions enables one to generalize a large number of dynamic hashing methods [Valduriez 84a]. The value of having a single storage

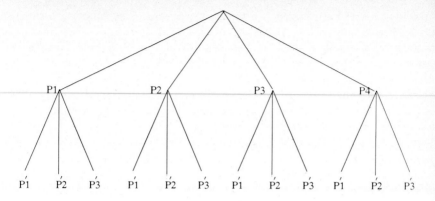

P1: VINEYARD="Beaujolais–Village"

P2: VINEYARD="Julienas"

P3: VINEYARD="Bordeaux"

P4: $\rceil$P1: $\wedge$ $\rceil$P2: $\wedge$ $\rceil$P3:

$P'1$: VINTAGE ≤ 1970

$P'2$: $1970 <$ VINTAGE ≤ 1980

$P'3$: VINTAGE > 1980

FIGURE 5.6 Example of predicate tree.

structure for all purposes is smaller code size and efficiency, particularly because of tight integration with transaction management (see Section 5.5).

Processing a retrieval query starts with comparing the query qualification (in general, a multiattribute predicate) with the predicate tree. Only subrelations that correspond to predicates that are not disjoined from those that constitute the qualification must be scanned. If the predicate tree is defined so that each subrelation corresponds to a frequent query, a large range of queries will be highly accelerated; for example, the query "retrieve the wines where vintage = 1982 and vineyard = Chablis" using the predicate tree depicted in Fig. 5.6 requires scanning only the right-most subrelation. The less precise query "retrieve the wines where vintage = 1970" requires scanning the four subrelations associated with predicate P'_1.

5.4.2 Clustering Using Predicate Trees

The primary value of predicate trees is the multidimensional clustering of the relation's tuples by placing subrelations in close physical spaces. Space allocation on disk is done by fixed-size units called pages. A page may be read in one disk access. It is a system parameter that can be anything between one sector and one track. The logical partitioning defined by the predicate tree is converted into a physical partitioning using logical addresses, called *signatures*. The signature of a node is represented by the concatenation of the branch numbers on the path from the root to that node. It is expressed as a chain of bits. For example, in Fig. 5.6, the leaf signature corresponding to the predicate ($P1$ and $P'2$) is 0001. The association of signatures with physical pages is stored in a unique catalog, implemented as a relation schema < relation number, signature, page address >, itself clustered according to a predefined predicate tree. The association of logical addresses with pages defines the relation's placement tree. An example of a placement tree in conformity with the predicate tree of Fig. 5.6 is given in Fig. 5.7.

The search in a relation is performed through the catalog. A search qualification is encoded by signature profiles (signatures having unknown parts), which are compared with the catalog's signatures using a filtering operator. The catalog is clustered by an efficient digital hashing method [Gardarin 84a] applied to the signature. This digital hashing method is specified as a predicate tree on the catalog using the relation number as first level and the successive bits of the signature as next levels. Thus the catalog is managed by the same tools (predicate trees). A search in the catalog gives the addresses of the pages that subsequently must be filtered to select the relevant tuples.

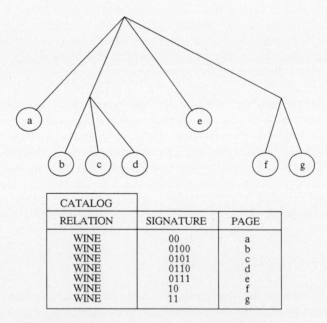

CATALOG		
RELATION	SIGNATURE	PAGE
WINE	00	a
WINE	0100	b
WINE	0101	c
WINE	0110	d
WINE	0111	e
WINE	10	f
WINE	11	g

FIGURE 5.7 Placement tree for the WINE relation.

5.4.3 Access Paths

Predicate trees enable one to represent a large number of access paths on different attributes in function of the application needs [Valduriez 84a]. As a particular case, a predicate tree in which each level uses the same attribute provides single key clustering. It may be ordered according to the key values by choosing digital hashing functions or may not be ordered using classical hashing functions. The main advantages of this single access method approach are simplicity and efficiency.

The definition of a new level for a predicate tree is not always recommended, particularly when the tree already has several levels. In that case and also when a secondary access path on a candidate key is desirable, secondary indexes should be used. A secondary index is implemented by a relation of schema < Relation-Id, Attribute-Id, Attribute-Value, Signature-profiles >, which associates a list of signature profiles to a secondary key value (the Attribute-Value). The signature logically profiles address tuples having the secondary key value. The use of profiles, as in the catalog, provides for some independence from the relation's content and avoids the need to update indexes when tuple updates occur. A secondary index may be placed according to a predicate tree defined on its attributes. When a search is performed using secondary indexes, signature profiles are found and composed with the profile given by the predicate tree of the searched relation. This greatly reduces the number of pages to scan [Cheiney 86a].

5.4.4 Query Optimization

The SABRINA query optimization algorithm converts a query into an optimized sequence of operations of an extended relational algebra (the operators actually implemented in the SABRINA's internal machine). The query is expressed in a normal conjunctive form. The method is recursive. At each recursion step, the pair of variables having the least join cost is selected if there are joins that stay in the part of the query to be processed. Then based on the simple heuristics of performing selections before joins, all the possible selections (restriction, projection) on relations that correspond to the selected variables are processed first. Finally the joins of the two relations reduced by the selections are successively executed.

In certain cases, the algorithm described above is not sufficient. For example, when two selections of different relations are connected by an "or," a union is required. Also, when an aggregate function (such as MINIMUM or AVERAGE) is specified in the query qualification, an aggregate function computation is required. In those cases, union or aggregate calculation is accomplished instead of the recursion step. Finally, recursion is no longer possible when the query is monovariable or incorrect. In the first case, the final result is calculated; in the second case, a semantic error is returned.

The selection of the variables to be joined requires estimating the join cost. This estimate takes into consideration the cardinality of the base relations, the size after selection, the join methods, and the access paths. Fig. 5.8 summarizes the query decomposition and optimization algorithm. A more detailed description of the algorithm can be found in [Gardarin 84b, Verlaine 86].

The approach to query optimization developed in the SABRINA prototype is similar to the dynamic approach used in INGRES (see Section 4.2.5). It is very cost-effective for ad hoc queries that are executed only once. Furthermore unlike System R's static optimization approach, costly statistics need not be maintained by the system since exact cardinalities are known at run time. This approach is not appropriate for predefined queries that must be executed many times.

5.4.5 Join and Selection Processing

The optimization algorithm dynamically constructs a tree specifying the order of extended relational algebra operations. These operations are selection (restriction and projection without duplicate elimination), join, sort, duplicate elimination, union difference, functions, and arithmetic calculations. Most of the complex operations that require repeated processing on relations, such as union and difference, are handled by sorting. The important and most frequent operations, join and selection, are processed by efficient algorithms.

A local optimization is made to choose a join algorithm between two according to the tuple ordering, the cardinality of operand relations, and the storage size allocated to the operation. Taking into account the lowering of main memory costs, this parameter is important. Relations that are to be joined may be fully contained in main memory. Also two join algorithms are available, each being optimal according to critical performance parameters [Valduriez 84b].

The first algorithm is the sort-merge join algorithm (see Section 3.2.5). This method is systematically chosen when both operand relations are too large to be contained in main memory or when the relations are already sorted.

The second algorithm combines hashing techniques and bit tables [Valduriez 84b] and makes best use of the memory space allocated to the operation [Verlaine 86]. The method consists of dividing two relations that are to be joined into two hashed files on the joined attribute and in joining the buckets of the same number two at a time by the nested-loop join method. Hashing is not necessary because the relation predicate tree includes a hashing on the join attribute. The algorithm's main parameter is the number of buckets on which hashing is applied. It is a function of the available main memory size and the relation sizes. To eliminate useless tuples as soon as possible, a bit table is used. It is built during

ALGORITHM DECOMP (Query);
Begin

    {Reduction of query by selections and joins}
    if there exists a couple of join variables **then**
        begin
            Select couple (X,Y) of minimum cost;
            Apply selections to X;
            Apply selections to Y;
            Perform join of X and Y relations;
            Replace X and Y by the resulting temporary relation;
            DECOMP (Modified Query);
        end;

    {Reduction of query by union}
    if union is possible **then**
        begin
            Apply union;
            Replace variables by the resulting temporary relation;
            DECOMP (Modified Query);
        end;

    {Reduction of query by aggregates}
    if aggregate is possible **then**
        begin
            Perform aggregate computation;
            Replace variables by the resulting temporary relation;
            DECOMP (Modified Query);
        end;

    {Computation of monovariable query}
    if query is monovariable **then**
        begin
            Perform selection;
            Exit DECOMP:
        end;

    {Exit for incorrect queries}
        Error DECOMP;

end

FIGURE 5.8 Query decomposition algorithm.

the hashing of the smallest relation by marking with the value 1 the existence of a join attribute hashing value. During hashing of the second relation, tuples that do not correspond to a 1 bit in the bit array are deleted. Evaluations of this algorithm show that its costs are generally proportional to the size of the operand relations and result. It is less efficient than the preceding algorithm only when the relations are already sorted or when the ratio of the sum of sizes of relations to be joined onto the storage size is more than 4. This algorithm, with no distribution phase, also processes inequi-joins.

The selection of tuples that satisfy a search qualification in a relation is first converted, using the corresponding predicate tree, to a selection of a relevant subset of the relation. This subset is a list of pages on disk. The selection in a page is performed by a filtering operator that encodes the search qualification. Currently this operator is carried out in main memory by a program. Placed between the disk controller and the disk unit, a filtering processor with a local memory would avoid transferring irrelevant data into main memory. It would also perform filtering in parallel with data transfer from disk into main memory. Such a processor may be a fast microprocessor or a specialized VLSI [Faudemay 85]. In summary, the multidimensional access method based on predicate trees and the join and selection algorithms provides efficient associative memory management.

5.5 Transaction Management

Transaction management contributes to the maintenance of database integrity by supporting two main functions: synchronizing the concurrent accesses to shared objects (that is, concurrency control) and recovering a consistent database state after failure of a transaction, system, or media (disk) (that is, reliability). The first function involves synchronization mechanisms based on serializability theory. The second function is based on the transaction concept whose main feature is atomicity: either all the transaction's updates are integrated in the database or none are.

The SABRINA approach to transaction management is based on tailoring the concurrency control and reliability techniques to the peculiarity of the storage model, which has a unique catalog. The rationale for this approach is that an integrated solution to transaction and catalog management will lead to increased performance. This solution, detailed in [Viemont 86, Michel 87], is a variant of the shadow page mechanism [Lorie 77] fully integrated with a two-phase locking algorithm and a two-step commit protocol. The integration of a transaction's updates in the database is actually done at commit time.

The shadow page mechanism works as follows. When a data page is updated, it is not updated "in-place" in the database; instead, two versions of the updated page are maintained while the transaction is active: the page image before update, called *shadow page,* and the version of the page after update, called *current page.* To commit the transaction, current pages must logically replace the shadow pages by atomically updating the page table. One advantage of this approach is that the set of current pages constitutes a user private workspace; the user can read or write the data not yet committed without interfering with other users.

5.5.1 Concurrency Control

The concurrency control algorithm, based on page locking/unlocking, distinguishes between data pages and catalog pages. The access to data pages is controlled by a basic two-phase locking algorithm with deadlock detection. As read/write operations on the catalog are permutable, catalog pages are locked only for the duration of a read/write operation. This significantly increases the multiprocessing level for active transactions.

The overhead due to concurrency control is minimized by integrating the lock tables with the catalog entries. With this approach, transaction synchronization for accessing data pages is achieved by locking the catalog entries that correspond to the accessed data pages. Before updating a data page, a transaction must hold a lock in exclusive mode (write lock) on the catalog entry referring to the accessed page. Data pages that need not be updated are locked in shared mode (read lock). Transactions may concurrently read the catalog but must wait or be aborted if they attempt to lock a catalog entry already locked by another transaction in incompatible mode (read/write or write/write).

The transaction locks are recorded with catalog entries of the lowest level by an indirection mechanism. Each such entry contains two additional attributes: a bit table that indicates the accessing transactions and the associated locking mode. Thus the catalog entries at the lowest level have the format < relation number, signature, page address, transaction bit table, locking mode >. Fig. 5.9 illustrates the implementation of lock tables at the catalog entry level. Managing the locks at the lowest level of the catalog entries, which must be accessed anyway to map signatures to page addresses, avoids the extra accesses of a traditional lock table.

By default, the locking granule is the page. If, however, a transaction requires locking all the pages of a relation, perhaps to modify schema data, the locking granule becomes the relation that can be logically locked at the data dictionary (metabase) level. In this case, no physical locking of all the corresponding catalog entries is needed.

The concurrency control algorithm is the two-phase locking algorithm. When a data page lock cannot be obtained because of a conflict, the requesting transaction, say T_i, is deactivated and waits. This is implemented by adding an arc from T_i to the waiting transaction, say T_j, in the waiting graph. If updating the graph entails the creation of a cycle (deadlock), transaction T_i is aborted. Deadlock detection is done systematically each time a transaction must wait. The

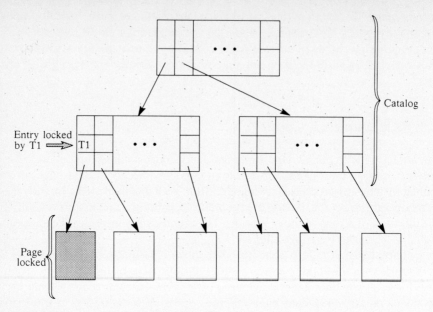

FIGURE 5.9 Lock entries in the catalog.

deadlock detection algorithm consists of recursively traversing the waiting graph and looking for a cycle (T_i, T_j). This recursive procedure is illustrated in Fig. 5.10.

5.5.2 Reliability

The reliability mechanism is based on shadow paging. The virtue of this technique is that transaction updates need not be undone in case of transaction abort or system failure. The principle of shadow paging is to save on stable memory (disk) the page images after update (the current pages) in new locations so shadow pages are still available. At commit time, the integration of the current pages in the database is done atomically by updating the catalog. Since it is never necessary to undo or redo a transaction to recover from a transaction or system failure, this mechanism belongs to the class of "no-undo/no-redo" algorithms [Bernstein 83]. Redoing a transaction is still required for recovering from a media failure.

Updates to the lowest level of the catalog occur because of overflowing data pages and shadow paging. To avoid the threat of "lost updates," which can stem from concurrent accesses to the catalog, each transaction is associated with a private differential catalog. The differential catalog records the updates to be made to the lowest level of the catalog. These updates consist of catalog entry

Procedure DEADLOCK (waited-tran, waiting-tran);
   Begin
        origin := 0;
        target := 0;
        {search if waited-trans is waiting}
        while (origin < number-of-waiting-trans) and (target=0) do
            begin
                origin := origin + 1
            if (WAIT[origin].waiting-trans = waited-trans)
            then target := origin;
            end;
        if target =0 then DEADLOCK := false
        else   {the waited-trans is waiting}
            if (Wait[origin].waited-trans = waiting-trans)
            then DEADLOCk := true
            else DEADLOCK:=DEADLOCK(waiting-trans,
                WAIT[origin].waited-trans);
   End.

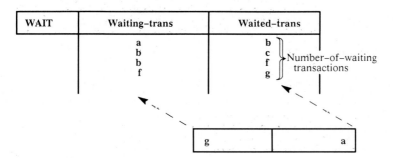

FIGURE 5.10 Deadlock detection algorithm.

deletions, followed by insertions of new entries. The entries to be deleted refer to shadow pages, while the entries to be inserted point to the current pages that will be integrated according to the shadow paging mechanism and the signature generation algorithm. The catalog is updated based on the transaction's differential catalog at transaction commit time. Fig. 5.11 illustrates the case where an updated page A (shadow page) must be split into two new pages B and C (current pages). The differential catalog records a deletion request for the A entry and insertion requests for the B and C entries.

Transaction atomicity is achieved by a two-step commit protocol [Gray 78]. This protocol has been chosen because it will enable SABRINA to be run in a parallel environment, such as multiprocessor computer or distributed database system. A transaction has three distinct phases:

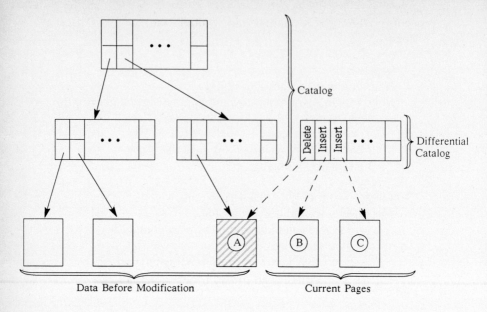

FIGURE 5.11 Differential catalog and shadow paging.

1. During the update phase, the updates are done through shadow pages, and the updates to the lowest level of the catalog are recorded in a differential catalog.
2. During the precommit phase (first step of the protocol), the current data pages are forced to disk, and the differential catalog is recorded in the log. The transaction becomes "ready to commit."
3. The commit phase (second step of the protocol), executed in critical section, updates the catalog from the differential catalog. The effect of updating the catalog is to integrate the current pages of the transaction in the database.

The catalog update recursively applies the digital hashing method, used to place the catalog, to the different catalog levels by shadow paging. Thus each catalog page affected by an update is updated through shadow paging by writing to disk a new catalog page. At the last step of recursion, a new root page is created in main memory. The atomicity of the procedure is achieved by writing the new root page to disk, which then replaces the shadow root page. This procedure is illustrated in Fig. 5.12. At the end of the commit phase, the transaction is terminated by releasing its locks and freeing the disk spaces containing shadow pages. As shown in Fig. 5.13, a transaction gets committed as soon as the new root

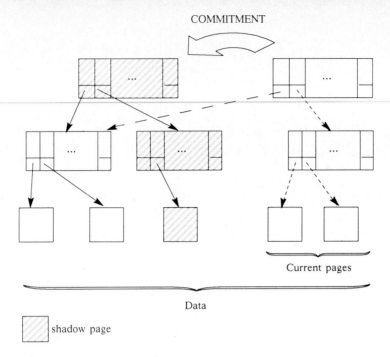

FIGURE 5.12 Execution of commit.

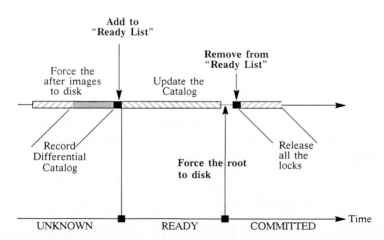

FIGURE 5.13 Various states of a SABRINA transaction.

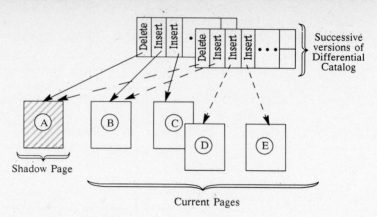

FIGURE 5.14 Private workspace management.

page is written on disk. The recovery procedure after system failure consists of committing the ready transactions that are not yet committed.

Recovery after media failure is based on the classical solution of periodic backup copies, checkpoints, and a log of page images after updates.

5.5.3 Transaction Workspace Management

The support of a private workspace for each active transaction enables the user to see the effects of a transaction's updates that are not yet integrated in the database. Let C be the set of committed database data accessible to transaction T, D be the set of data deleted by T, and I be the set of data inserted by T. The management of a private workspace for T enables T to read or update the data set defined as $(C \cup I) - D$.

The management of a differential catalog per active transaction allows a simple implementation of private workspaces. The management of the private workspace requires a transaction to access or update data through its differential catalog so that only the current pages are visible. Fig. 5.14 shows the various states of the differential catalog after two subsequent updates: the first update relates to page A, which splits into pages B and C; the second update relates to page C, which splits into pages D and E. At commit time, pages B, D, and E are integrated in the database.

5.6 System Architecture

The SABRINA functional system architecture is divided into three layers, called machines. Each machine includes several modules. The most external machine is the *interface machine:* it is composed of various interface modules, each corresponding to a specific language. The intermediate machine is the *assertional machine*. It receives tuple relational calculus (with functions) commands expressed in an internal form, called *data manipulation protocol* (DMP), performs semantic data controls, and transforms each command in a sequence of relational algebra operations, using the query optimization algorithm. The internal machine is the *algebraic machine,* which executes extended relational algebra commands using the predicate tree physical organization. The functional architecture is based on the unique interface model with the DMP as single system entry point. In the sequel, we detail the modules that constitute each machine (Fig. 5.15).

The interface machine includes the *FABRE module,* the *SQL module,* the *PASREL module,* and the *UTILITIES module.* Each of these preprocessors performs the parsing of the external commands and the translation of these commands into the data manipulation protocol. The interface machine also includes the authorization module that performs access rights management and control.

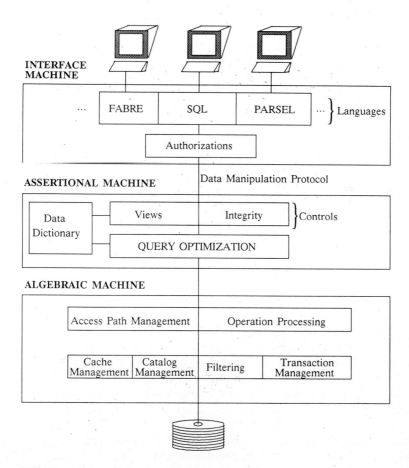

FIGURE 5.15 SABRINA functional architecture.

The assertional machine, which receives the commands corresponding to the data manipulation protocol, is composed of four modules. The *integrity module* executes the semantic integrity controls at each update end, using a differential algorithm. The *view module* converts view interrogations into interrogations on base relations, using a variation of the query modification algorithm. The *data dictionary module* manages the metabase of SABRINA. The metabase is the set of relations that describes the data relations, with their access paths, integrity constraints, and so forth. The *query optimization module* performs query decomposition and optimization and generates calls to the algebraic machine.

The algebraic machine is composed of two sets of modules. The most external set manages access paths (predicate trees, indexes) and performs join and aggregate computations. It is composed of two modules: the *access path management module,* which determines the logical addresses (signatures) of pages to access to execute a query on a relation, and the *operation module,* which performs join, sort, and duplicate eliminations and aggregate computations. The most internal set of modules manages physical pages for access and control. It includes four modules: *the catalog management module,* which accesses pages on disk from the logical addresses, allocates disk space, and stores new pages on disk; the *filter module,* which executes selections inside pages; the *cache management module,* which stores and retrieves temporary results in main memory (or on disk if not enough main memory is available); and the *transaction management* module, which performs commit processing and concurrency control.

From the process point of view, SABRINA implements the process model. To each user is attached a host process that executes the chosen language analyzer as well as authorization management. Each user query in internal format (data manipulation protocol) is handled by a separate DBMS process that runs all the software modules of the algebraic and assertional machines.

SABRINA's layering into functional modules provides high independence with regard to the hardware machine. Adaptation to a parallel architecture is possible, as illustrated in Chapter 9. Indeed the attribution of modules to real processors enables one to increase the degree of parallellism and to improve SABRINA's performance. Most of the crucial algorithms have therefore been designed to exploit a multiprocessor environment.

5.7 The SABRINA Product

Around 1985, the company INFOSYS was started up by several key members of the SABRE research group so as to develop and market the first French RDBMS product. The development of the product was done as a joint venture with two other French companies: EUROSOFT, a software house, and SAGEM, a computer manufacturer. The SABRINA product runs on all UNIX-based mainframes, minicomputers, and microcomputers. The product is targeted to many different environments, including decision-support applications that are retrieval intensive and on-line applications that are update intensive. The product is similar to the prototype and includes most of its code; however, there have been improvements in usability and performance. The main improvements concern data manipulation, storage model and query processing, and additional tools.

5.7.1 Data Manipulation

SABRINA's main query language is the standard SQL, enriched with the powerful data definition and semantic data control facilities of FABRE. The SQL key words may be tailored to different user languages. SQL can be used in two modes: in a direct mode, in which SQL commands are entered at the dot-prompt, or in a menu-based mode. With the latter mode, the user is assisted by pull-down menus of options, with which all SQL commands can be used, and various forms displaying on the screen the context of use (schema, current command, result, and so forth). This mode facilitates user interaction and minimizes the probability of user error. It provides some capabilities found in other form-oriented database languages such as QBE and QBF. The menu-based mode therefore enables one to define complex transactions, for which default screens are automatically generated.

To permit the development of complex applications, SQL may be embedded in various programming languages such as C, Pascal, or COBOL, using a multi-language interface. This interface has four primitive commands: CONNECT, which connects the application program to DBMS; SABRINA, which executes any SQL command; READ, which reads one tuple of a temporary result produced by a retrieval command; and DISCONNECT, which disconnects the application program. A precompiler that recognizes the multilanguage interface commands is necessary for each host programming language. The precompilation approach is similar to that of System R.

5.7.2 Storage Model and Query Processing

Most RDBMSs, whose functional architecture is based on the uniform interface model, generally implement a simple conceptual-physical mapping by storing each conceptual relation in a separate file. DB2, INGRES, and the SABRINA prototype use that approach. When conceptual relations are normalized (for example, in third normal form), this approach is quite inefficient for complex queries because they require many natural joins, a time-consuming operation. The SABRINA product solves that problem by providing the DBA with the capability of defining a physical relation as the natural join of several conceptual relations. A physical relation is essentially a nonnormalized relation implemented in a file using a compression scheme. Therefore many join operations may be avoided. The user may still deal with normalized relations, the mapping to physical relations being entirely controlled by SABRINA.

The query optimization of the prototype consisted of dynamically generating the execution plan for each query. Although very effective for ad hoc queries, this interpretation approach is not appropriate for predefined queries that are executed many times because optimization is repeated at each query execution. To support efficiently both ad hoc and predefined queries, the SABRINA product supplements the dynamic algorithm with a static query optimization algorithm that compiles a query into an execution plan of relational algebra operators. The algorithm has similarities to the System R algorithm. In particular, it selects the best join ordering based on statistical information and formulas for estimating intermediate result sizes. However, the solution space is significantly reduced by the use of heuristics. The main heuristic is the one that pushes selections before joins. This heuristic has proved to be very practical and favors the use of the efficient main memory hash-based join algorithm.

5.7.3 Additional Tools

SABRINA provides a set of integrated tools to speed the development of complex applications. The main tools are a powerful report generator and a screen manager. The report generator enables the definition of complex reports for result presentation. The specification of a report is done in a menu-based interaction. The report parameters include the report presentation characteristics (headers, footers, groups and subgroups, titles) and the content definitions (result specification, grouping attributes). All parameters have default values so the developer task is minimized. The report generator enables report edition, creation, and deletion and the execution of a report with SQL queries defining the results.

The screen generator allows one to define, edit, and use custom screens for data manipulation. The custom screens may be derived from default screens produced by transaction definitions. A screen definition includes the screen presentation characteristics and the predefined transaction names, which may be used to produce results on the screen. Within a screen, the user can enter and edit data and execute the predefined transactions by giving the actual parameter values.

5.8 Conclusion

In this chapter, we have described SABRINA, the system built in the SABRE project. Most of the chapter has described the SABRINA prototype, of which most solutions have been incorporated in a French relational product. The distinguishing features of the SABRINA system are complete and efficient semantic integrity control, a single storage structure called predicate tree with which many kinds of hashing methods can be specified, an efficient hash-based join algorithm that exploits large main memories, and an original integrated solution to transaction management. The SABRINA product is available on UNIX-based environments, including mainframes, minicomputers, and microcomputers.

Currently the prototype (and ultimately the product) is extended toward a future-generation DBMS. Four main activities aiming at the design of such a system are in process:

1. Support of abstract data type objects. This extension is required for multimedia data management (text, graphics, or pictures). A first approach is already included in the FABRE language. The goal is to generalize these facilities.
2. Development of a production rule-based system including data manipulation language production rule catalogs and an inference subsystem. This extension is necessary to obtain an intelligent tool to support future expert systems. A prototype of the inference subsystem is operational [Gardarin 86, DeMaindreville 85].
3. Adjunction of an automatic designer of database schemas from a description in a high-level language [Bouzeghoub 85, 86]. A prototype of such a design tool has been written in PROLOG and has been interfaced with SABRINA. Such a tool is a useful aid for DBAs.
4. Development of a parallel algebraic machine to increase the system's throughput. Several studies have been made in this direction [Valduriez 85, Cheiney 86b].

These four new functions as well as their integration in the current SABRINA system provide an ambitious research project, which should make SABRINA a DBMS of the future.

References

[Bernstein 83] P. A. Bernstein, N. Goodman, V. Hadzilacos, "Recovery Algorithms for Database Systems," Proc. IFIP 9th World Computer Congress, pp. 799–807, North-Holland, Paris, September 1983.
[Bouzeghoub 85] Bouzeghoub M., Gardarin G., Metais E., "Database Design Tools: An Expert System Approach," Int. Conf. on VLDB, Stockholm, 1985.
[Bouzeghoub 86] Bouzeghoub M., Gardarin G., *Tools for Database Design and Programming — A New Perspective,* Infotech State of the Art Report, Pergamon Press, 1986.
[Burckard 83] Burckard W., "Interpolation Based Index Maintenance," ACM Symposium on PODS, Atlanta, March 1983.
[Cheiney 86a] Cheiney J. P., Faudemay P., Michel R., "A Reliable Parallel Backend Using Multi-attribute Clustering and Select-Join Operator," Int. Conf. on VLDB, Kyoto, August 1986.
[Cheiney 86b] Cheiney J. P., Faudemay P., Michel R., "An Extension of Access Paths to Improve Joins and Selections," Int. Conf. on Data Engineering, Los Angeles, February 1986.
[DeMaindreville 85] DeMaindreville, C., Gardarin G., Simon E., "Extending a Relational DBMS towards a Rule-Based System: An Approach Using Predicate Transition

Nets," Crete Workshop on DB & AI, June 1985, to appear in Springer-Verlag book, Thanos and Schmidt Ed.

[Faudemay 85] Faudemay P., Valduriez P., "Design and Analysis of a Direct Filter Using Parallel Comparators," Int. Workshop on Database Machines, Grand Bahamas Island, Lecture Notes in Computer Sciences, Springer-Verlag, 1985.

[Gallaire 84] Gallaire H., Minker J., Nicolas J. M., "Logic and Database: A Deductive Approach," ACM Computing Surveys, Vol. 16, No. 2, June 1984.

[Gardarin 83] Gardarin G., Bernadat P., Temmerman N., Valduriez P., Viemont Y., "Design of a Multiprocessor Relational Database System," IFIP 83 World Congress, Paris, September 1983.

[Gardarin 84a] Gardarin G., Valduriez P., Viemont Y., "Predicate Trees: A Way for Optimizing Relational Queries," Int. Conf. on Data Engineering, Los Angeles, April 1984.

[Gardarin 84b] Gardarin G., Simon E., Verlaine L., "Querying Real Time Data Bases," Int. Conf. on Communications, Amsterdam, May 1984.

[Gardarin 86] Gardarin G., Abiteboul S., Scholl M., Simon E., "Towards DBMSs for Supporting New Applications," Int. Conf. on VLDB, Kyoto, August 1986.

[Gray 78] Gray J. N., "Notes on Database Operating Systems," in *Operating Systems, An Advanced Course,* Springer-Verlag, 1978.

[Kerherve 86] Kerherve B., "Relational Views in Centralized and Distributed DBMSs" (in French), Ph.D. thesis, University of Paris 6, March 1986.

[Kiernan 87] Kiernan G., Le Maoult T., Pasquer F., "The Support of Complex Domains in a Relational DBMS: An Approach by Integration of a LISP Interpreter," BD3 Workshop, INRIA Ed., May 1987.

[Litwin 81] Litwin W., "Trie Hasching," ACM SIGMOD Int. Conf. on Management of Data, Ann Arbor, Mich., 1981.

[Lorie 77] Lorie, R. A. "Physical Integrity in a Large Segmented Database," ACM TODS, Vol. 2, No. 1, March 1977.

[Michel 87] R. Michel, "Concurrency Control and Reliability in a Uniprocessor and Multiprocessor Architecture" (in French), Ph.D. thesis, University of Paris 6, May 1987.

[Pasquer 84] Pasquer F., "Design and Implementation of an Assertional Database Language" (in French), Ph.D. thesis, University of Paris, May 1984.

[Sabre 86] Gardarin G. et al., "SABRINA: A Relational DBMS Derived from Research," Technology and Science of Informatics, Dunod Ed., Vol. 5, No. 6, 1986.

[Schmidt 77] Schmidt J. W., "Some High Level Language Constructs for Data of Type Relation," ACM TODS, Vol. 2, No. 3, September 1977.

[Simon 84] Simon E., Valduriez P., "Design and Implementation of an Extendible Integrity Subsystem," ACM SIGMOD Int. Conf. on Management of Data, Boston, June 1984.

[Simon 86] Simon E., "Design, Analysis and Implementation of a Relational Integrity Subsystem" (in French), Ph.D. thesis, University of Paris 6, June 1986.

[Valduriez 84a] Valduriez P., Viemont Y., "A Multikey Hashing Scheme Using Predicate Trees," ACM SIGMOD Int. Conf. on Management of Data, Boston, June 1984.

[Valduriez 84b] Valduriez P., Gardarin G., "Join and Semi-Join Algorithms for a Multiprocessor Database Machine," ACM TODS, Vol. 9, No. 1, March 1984.

[Valduriez 85] Valduriez P., "Relational Algebra Operation Processing in a Database Machine" (in French), es science doctorate (Doctorat d'état) thesis, University of Paris 6, December 1985.

[Verlaine 86] Verlaine L., "Query Optimization in a Database Machine" (in French), Ph.D. thesis, University of Paris 6, June 1986.

[Viemont 82] Viemont Y, Gardarin G., "A Distributed Concurrency Control Algorithm Based on Transaction Commit Ordering," 12th Fault Tolerant Computer Symposium (FTCS), Santa Monica, Cal., June 1982.

[Viemont 86] Viemont Y., "The SABRE Parallel, Concurrent and Reliable Algebraic Machine" (in French), Ph.D. thesis, University of Paris 6, November 1986.

[Woods 70] Woods M., "Transition Network Grammar for Natural Language Analysis," Comm. of ACM, Vol. 3, No. 10, October 1970.

6
SUPRA

6.1 Introduction

A distinction should be drawn between RDBMSs with homogeneous data structures, built to support the relational model concepts, and those with heterogeneous structured systems, supporting varied and sometimes preexisting internal data structures. The former category stems from a top-down design approach and the latter from a bottom-up design approach. SUPRA [Cincom 85a] from Cincom is an example of a heterogeneous system. Although it has a heterogeneous structure, SUPRA can be considered as a relational DBMS.

In this chapter, we shall examine the basic functions and environment of the SUPRA system. SUPRA supports relational views, including the concepts of relation, attribute, and domain. It also provides built-in referential and entity integrity enforcement. Furthermore SUPRA boasts a high-level nonprocedural language, SPECTRA, and other application development tools, including a 4GL programming language, MANTIS. Relational database design is automated using NORMAL, a third normal form relation design tool. This tool generates a normalized conceptual schema from user views, which is then implemented, either directly or after optimization, in the form of files of varying structures. Existing files can also be retrieved; in this case, the mapping from conceptual level to internal level is left to the administrator.

SUPRA, targeted for IBM mainframes, is at the heart of an information system architecture called TIS/XA. Illustrated in Fig. 6.1, this architecture also

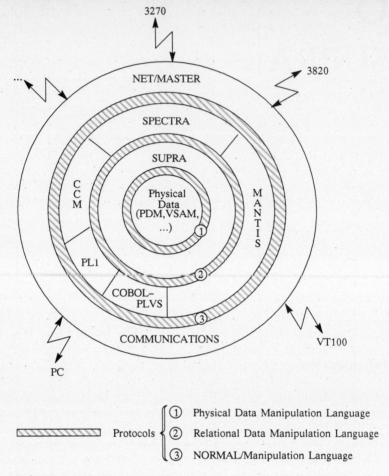

FIGURE 6.1 TIS/XA architecture.

includes a network manager, NET/MASTER, and a production control package, CONTROL CONE MANUFACTURING (CCM). A version of SUPRA, called ULTRA, is available for the DEC VAX computers.

In Section 6.2, we present an overview of the main functions of SUPRA from the data definition point of view. SUPRA is built around an In-Line Directory, and we shall detail its components. We shall also look at NORMAL, the integrated design tool. In Section 6.3 comes an investigation of the main data manipulation languages provided by SUPRA, with a detailed look at the least conventional ones (SPECTRA and MANTIS). In Section 6.4, we move on to the features of the SUPRA system: the relational data manager (RDM) and the physical data manager (PDM). Finally, we shall outline the system architecture in Section 6.5.

6.2 Data Definition

6.2.1 Definition Levels

SUPRA supports heterogeneous physical structures. It implements relational views in various internal files that can be accessed using multiple languages. A user view is therefore an external-level relational table, the columns of which are attributes, characterized by a name and accessible by one or more users.

Mapping user views to files is done by logical views that usually correspond to normalized relations, that is, the conceptual schema. A logical view relation is thus a relation representing a real world object that ensures the mapping from user views to internal files. Although, in theory, a user view is initially translated into conceptual relations by the DBMS, users can be offered conceptual relations directly. Consequently user views and logical views are often confounded and referred to as *views* or *relational views*.

The physical structures, or internal files, supported by SUPRA are numerous, including specific structures and other conventional structures such as those of VSAM, TOTAL, and IMS. SUPRA authorizes the integration of existing data, with the possibility of choosing the optimal structure for new data. The description of the rules for moving from relational view level to file level is automated by the system (using NORMAL) or controlled by the DBA by means of the access description concept.

SUPRA also ensures view manipulation to internal file access transformation. This transformation, carried out using the data access path navigation, is transparent for the user and automated and optimized by SUPRA. Hence SUPRA ensures automatic navigation; in other words, relational view tuples are built one at a time by navigating through file records, in random, sequential, or indexed access modes.

In summary, SUPRA offers three data description levels: the external schema (user views), the conceptual schema (logical views), and the internal schema (internal files). Besides these schemas, the administrator must also define the navigation rules for moving from the relational views to the internal files. This is achieved by access description. Fig. 6.2 illustrates the three schema levels. It should be recalled that the primary advantage of support for three schema levels by a DBMS is to ensure complete data independence. More specifically the external schemas ensure logical independence of programs from other users and provide a particular and simplified view of the conceptual schema. The internal schema allows integration of different types of physical files (VSAM, TOTAL, DL1, and others) and changes to physical characteristics of the files (indexing,

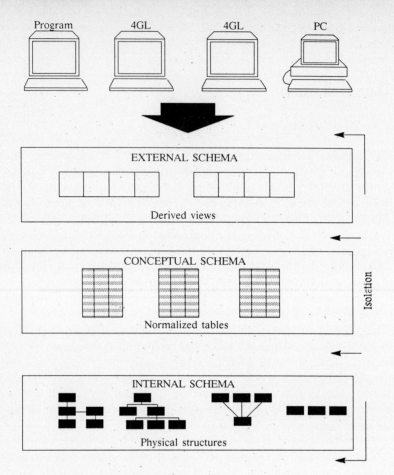

FIGURE 6.2 Data description levels.

chaining, copying, grouping) without changing the programs. In an environment integrating preexisting applications and heterogeneous physical structures, there is virtually no alternative to the three schema level support, despite the complexity of the approach.

6.2.2 In-Line Directory

Organized around an integrated In-Line Directory, SUPRA offers a rational and optimized database schema design. The In-Line Directory houses the set of files containing the definition of the user views, logical views, internal files, and access descriptions in a format specific to the system. It is the central source of control of the entire system. Its contents continuously drive the execution of all SUPRA components. In this way, the directory actively controls data type transformations, semantics checks, physical accesses, access authorizations, and the optimizations to be done. For this purpose, it contains the description of the external views, the conceptual schema, the physical files and their contents, including indexes, and secondary keys, as well as the relationships among the schemas. It contains all operational and user requirements data. The directory is divided into five parts.

External schema data contain the description of the logical views and external fields. This information tells the system how the data will appear to the user and application programs. Constraints related to data security and internal schema relationships are also included at this level. Fig. 6.3 shows the main descriptive entities and their relationships specifying the external schema level.

Conceptual schema data contain relational definitions of the logical global database. Included here are:

- Attribute domains, containing validation options and type characteristics.
- Relations made up of a collection of attributes taking values from previously defined domains.
- Primary keys for each of the relations composed of one or more attributes.
- Foreign keys that identify the attributes in one relation that must appear as the key in another relation.
- Navigation primitives for building each relation from the physical data.

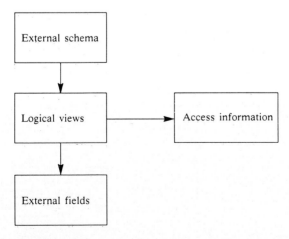

FIGURE 6.3 External schema.

Fig. 6.4 illustrates the main entities that appear in the conceptual schema and their relationships.

Internal schema data contain the physical representation of the database. This information is used to access the physical data. A link is made at this level with external views and conceptual relations in such a way that each external or logical view is connected to one or more internal schemas containing:

- An environment description, describing the type of file (PDM, VSAM, and so on) and its operating environment, including logging and security options.
- A description of the buffers required for IO operations.
- A description of the file, including name, logical record size, and block size.
- A description of the file records.
- A description of the physical fields of each database element.
- A description of the secondary keys and related index type files.

Fig. 6.5 illustrates these descriptive entities and their relationships.

System data describe the operating environment considerations that are independent of any schema data. Included here are the execution options for directory maintenance, edit masks for the directory, conversion tables, and utilities. User data describe all system users, as well as the procedures they have defined for database accesses. The directory has several related tools. The main one is Directory Maintenance, used for directory creation and modification; it operates in interactive or batch mode. Numerous commands (add, change, and others),

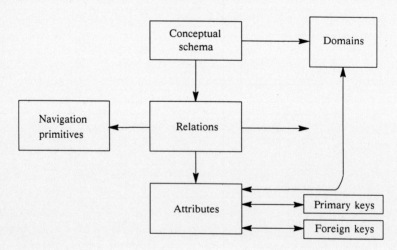

FIGURE 6.4 Conceptual schema.

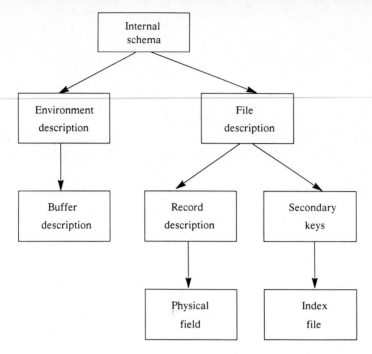

FIGURE 6.5 Internal schema.

illustrated in Fig. 6.6, can be used on most entities in the directory, as shown in Fig. 6.7.

Different types of reports to help monitor the system can also be generated. These reports offer directory structure checking and database optimization facilities. Finally it is worth noting that the DBAID utility may be used for logical view generation and testing.

6.2.3 NORMAL: A Conceptual Schema Generation Tool

NORMAL is an integrated tool in the SUPRA DBMS. It generates a conceptual schema in third normal form using user views and their associated descriptions. Thus it supports a database design process that integrates user views in order to make up a schema in third normal form. An integrated model of the application data is developed in the form of atomic values, which are represented by tables. This model is stored in the data dictionary. It can be implemented directly or linked in a more complex manner, better suited to an internal schema describing different types of files, using the access descriptions. More specifically NORMAL

```
SELECT CATEGORY      TIS/XA DIRECTORY MAINTENANCE

ENTER CATEGORY

AS    ACCESS SET                      NP    NAVIGATION PRIMITIVE
AT    ATTRIBUTE                       PF    PHYSICAL FIELD
BP    BUFFER POOL                     PR    PROCEDURE
CS    CONCEPTUAL SCHEMA               QC    QUERY COMPONENT DESC
DC    DIRECTORY COMPONENT DSC         RE    RELATION
DM    DOMAIN                          RW    RESERVED WORD
ED    ENVIRONMENT DESCRIPTION         SC    SCHEMA
EE    EXPRESSION EQUATION             SK    SECONDARY KEY
EM    EDIT MASK                       SS    LOGICAL VIEW
FI    FILE                            TA    TABLES
FK    FOREIGN KEY                     UC    UTILITIES COMPONENT DSC
IR    INTERNAL RECORD                 US    USER
KC    KEY CODE                        XF    EXTERNAL FIELD
LG    LOG GROUP
LV    LOGICAL VIEW



ACTIVE SC:            ACTIVE ED:         MAINTENANCE PERMITTED:
```

FIGURE 6.6 Selecting a directory entity category.

is a design tool that enables the four stages required for relational database design under SUPRA to be carried out:

1. Functional analysis that provides the external schema for each group of users.
2. Data analysis that allows the conceptual schema to be built.
3. Semantics analysis that enables the conceptual schema to be enriched, especially with the interrelation constraints and links.

```
INTREC COMMANDS              TIS/XA DIRECTORY MAINTENANCE


AD    ADD                        SD    STRU DSPLY
CG    CHANGE                     SE    SHORT EDIT
CK    CHECK                      ST    SHORT TEXT
DE    DELETE
DI    DISPLAY
LE    LONG EDIT
LT    LONG TEXT
RN    RENAME



ENTER SELECTION CODE:            SUBCATEGORY CODE:

ENTER NAMING DATA:
SCHEMA:
FILE:
INTERNAL RECORD:
```

FIGURE 6.7 Selecting a command.

4. Base generation that enables the internal schema to be built and the different views to be implemented.

Only the first stage of functional analysis is left to the designer. View normalization, semantics, analysis and database generation are fully and automatically carried out by NORMAL. The rest of this section presents the NORMAL environment and then specifies, function by function, how the design process is carried out.

NORMAL is an interactive design tool that interacts with the user through a chaining of screens and menus. The main menu in NORMAL (Fig. 6.8) offers several choices for carrying out the four stages of the design method. During these stages, NORMAL uses a "scratch-pad" area that offers progressive design realization. This area contains the objects being designed through to the final stage, called *generation,* which implements the database and three schemas. The schemas are stored in the scratch pad in the form of hierarchical entities.

These entities are manipulated using the facilities proposed in the main menu, either directly by selection "Scratch Pad Editing" (PF1) or indirectly via the design stages of the other choices. Only the "Scratch Pad Editing" facility selection authorizes operation at all entity levels. The following facilities operate on relations and enable a specific relation to be manipulated in a given conceptual schema.

"Create Relation from an Existing Data View" (PF2 key) allows the definition of relations of a conceptual schema that are to be normalized and implemented during future stages. This comprises two phases. The first phase aims to


```
                        DESIGN FACILITIES                    86/07/10
                                                             15:30:04

   OPTION   PF KEY                    FACILITY

      1      PF1        SCRATCH PAD EDITING
      2      PF2        CREATE RELATION FROM AN EXISTING DATA VIEW
     *3      PF3        DESIGN A CONCEPTUAL SCHEMA
      4      PF4        COPY A RELATION
     *5      PF5        LOAD A CONCEPTUAL SCHEMA
     *6      PF6        AUTHORIZE A CONCEPTUAL SCHEMA




   ENTER OPTION NUMBER OR
   PRESS CORRESPONDING PF KEY : 1 :

   * ENTER CS NAME:                         :



                                          PA1=CLEAR   PA2=EXIT
```

FIGURE 6.8 NORMAL main menu.

make each basic data item in an external schema view correspond to a unique attribute in the relation being created in a conceptual schema. The second phase determines the key attributes and the attribute domains of the relation. In the first phase, the designer specifies four names: the name of the relation to be created, the name of the conceptual schema containing the relation and the names of the external schema, and the generating view. In the second phase, a window displays a comprehensive list of all the attributes defined for this relation. Each attribute is allocated a domain, which, by default, has the same name as the attribute. NORMAL flags unknown names on screen with an asterisk. The designer can then associate an existing domain to the attribute or define a new domain by returning to option 1 (scratch-pad editing). Another function of this window is to allow the designer to define the attributes that make up the primary key of the relation. To summarize, facility PF2 in the menu defines the relations that are the starting point for conceptual schema specification. These relations are normalized by the following facility.

The design of a conceptual schema (PF3 key) covers end of data analysis by normalizing the conceptual schema and semantics analysis by specifying the type of foreign keys detected by NORMAL. With this facility, the status of the schemas obtained can be checked at any time, and, if appropriate, it is possible to modify what has already been done. A relation of conceptual level can be constructed by normalizing and then defining the type of its foreign keys. NORMAL also offers the possibility of updating the attributes of the relation ("Edit Relation") and reviewing the operations carried out on the relation. Relation update is carried out in a window that displays all the attributes. The designer can add (AD), delete (DE), or replace (RP) an attribute and review (RV) or change (CG) the characteristics of this attribute. A special screen is reserved for attribute characteristics and contains the name, references, domain, type, and editing specifications of the attribute. The characteristics of all of its attributes must be defined for a relation to be normalized.

Relation normalization is also carried out in interactive mode using a window in which all the attributes of the relation are displayed. The designer must confirm the primary keys, specify which attributes are part of repeating groups, and define where the dependencies are (on partial or other keys). Once the relations are normalized, NORMAL proposes regrouping the relations in third normal form in the same conceptual schema having a common primary key. The designer decides whether to regroup. Following normalization and relation grouping, the data analysis state is terminated. The conceptual schema is therefore defined.

Finally to carry out semantics analysis, NORMAL identifies all foreign keys existing in the conceptual schema by specifying the names of the attributes that they contain and the names of the referenced relations. Before generating the three schemas, the designer can check the consistency of the result obtained by using the check function, which summarizes the specification and history of the relation.

When all the relations of a conceptual schema have been normalized, analyzed, and checked, the conceptual schema loading process (PF5 key) is undertaken. The internal schema is constituted, and the designer can load the conceptual schema relations, one by one, by specifying the average number of tuples that they contain. By using facility 4 (Copy a Relation: PF4 key), the designer can undertake the denormalization process often required to obtain good performance. External view acceptance and recording in the in-line dictionary is also carried out automatically by NORMAL during this state.

The final facility (PF6 key) consists of authorizing the use of a conceptual schema. There are three types of access, depending on the public, private, or system nature of a relation:

1. ALL: All users may access this public relation.
2. INCLUDE: Only users identified by the letter Y in the authorization window may access this private relation.
3. EXCLUDE: No user but the administrator may access this system relation.

The specification of these access authorizations allows the definition of the protection modes for the database where the relations and three schemas are implemented.

6.3 Data Manipulation

6.3.1 Overview

Cincom offers a wide variety of high-level application development tools to use with SUPRA for fast program writing and specification and for reducing maintenance and upgrade costs. Access to SUPRA is via the Relational Data Manipulation Language (RDML) standard access primitives. The query language is called SPECTRA [Cincom 85b]. The most elaborated tool is MANTIS, a fourth-generation interactive application development language. Cincom also offers access via COBOL and PL/I, full screen relation editors, and a report editor. We shall investigate SPECTRA and MANTIS here.

6.3.2 SPECTRA, the Query Language

SPECTRA is a nonprocedural query language for data retrieval and update, with report writing capabilities. It provides SQL-type nonprocedural constructions and is as powerful as SQL. This means it offers project, select, join, arithmetical calculation, and aggregate functions. It also supports complex updates. The constructions, usually slightly less compact than those in SQL, can be abbreviated by using the function keys, thus providing SPECTRA with a push-button mode. This utilization mode, which allows requests to be stored as internal procedures, is particularly effective.

As is the case with the other products in the SUPRA environment, the first contact with SPECTRA is through a menu, offering the user four facilities (CENTRAL FILES, PERSONAL FILES, PROCESSES, AND USER'S GUIDE). The user guide provides easy-to-understand on-line documentation. We shall illustrate the main SPECTRA capabilities using example queries from the WINES database defined in Chapter 2. This will include query types (R1), (R2), (R3), (I1), and (M1).

(E1) Output the wine number and the alcohol content of all Jurancon vintages for 1962:
GET ALL
FROM WINE
WHERE VINEYARD = "Jurancon" AND VINTAGE = 1962
PRINT W#, PERCENT

(E2) Output the name of drinkers having tasted anything, without duplicates:
GET D#, NAME
FROM DRINKER
GET D#
FROM DRINK
WHERE SAME D#
PRINT NAME
ORDER DISTINCT NAME

(R1) Give the names of producers of Julienas 1982 or 1984:
GET P#, NAME
FROM PRODUCER
GET P#, W#
FROM HARVEST
GET W#
FROM WINE
WHERE SAME P# AND SAME W#
AND VINEYARD = "JULIENAS" AND (YEAR = 1982 OR
    YEAR = 1984)
PRINT NAME

(R2) Give the drinkers of wines of vintages beginning with "C" and where the alcohol percent is unknown or between 11 and 13 degrees:
GET ALL
FROM DRINKER
GET D#, W#
FROM DRINK

```
        GET W#
        FROM WINE
        WHERE SAME D# AND SAME W#
        AND (PERCENT BETWEEN 11 AND 13 OR PERCENT = '''')
        PRINT ALL
```

(R3) Calculate the average alcohol content for all wines where the minimum percentage is greater than 12 degrees:

```
        PRINT VINTAGE, AVE (PERCENT)
        FROM WINE
        WHERE MIN(PERCENT) > 12
```

(E3) Output the numbers of drinkers who have tasted Jurancon or Montbazillac wines:

```
        GET nv_ju = W#
        FROM WINE
        WHERE VINEYARD = ''Jurancon''
        GET nv_mon = W#
        FROM WINE
        WHERE VINEYARD = ''Montbazillac''
        GET D#
        FROM DRINK
        WHERE W# = nu_ju
        OR W# = nv_mon
        PRINT D#
```

(E4) Output the number of drinkers who have tasted Jurancon and Montbazillac wines:

```
        GET D#, W#
        FROM DRINK
        GET W#
        FROM WINE
        WHERE SAME W#
        AND VINEYARD = ''Jurancon''
        PUT D# INTO NEW temp
        WHEN FINISHED
                (GET D#
                FROM temp
                GET D#, W#
                FROM DRINK
                WHERE SAME D#
                GET VINEYARD, W#
                FROM WINE
                WHERE SAME W#
                AND VINEYARD = ''Montazillac''
                PRINT D#)
```

(I1) Insert as drinkers Bourgogne producers who harvested a 1983 wine:
GET ALL
FROM PRODUCER
WHERE REGION = ''Bourgogne''
GET HARVEST
WHERE SAME P#
GET WINE
WHERE SAME W#
AND VINTAGE = 1983
INSERT P#, NAME INTO DRINKER

(M1) Increase the harvested quantities of 1982 Julienas by 10 percent:
GET ALL
FROM HARVEST
GET W#
FROM WINE
WHERE SAME W# AND VINEYARD = ''Julienas'' AND VINTAGE
= 1982
INCREASE QTY BY 10%

These examples provide an introduction to the nonprocedural language SPECTRA. This comprehensive language also integrates, in addition to functions similar to those in SQL, an easy-to-use full screen editor. Given the influence of nonprocedural language standardization, however, it is likely that Cincom will support SQL syntax from SPECTRA. There appear to be no major difficulties in moving from SPECTRA to SQL.

6.3.3 MANTIS, a 4GL

Generating an application is a complex business involving the handling of various entities, such as screen definitions, database views, external files, and programs. In order to design, develop, and implement applications that are easily accessible to nonspecialists, MANTIS provides interactive tools that simplify the definition, prototyping, testing, and integration of MANTIS entities. MANTIS can be regarded as a working tool in the SUPRA environment. Data managed by SUPRA can be retrieved and updated using four commands: GET, INSERT, UPDATE, and DELETE. Access is via an external view. In order to simplify the relation between the different applicative objects, especially between database views and screens, MANTIS ensures automatic move between logical fields with the same name.

In addition to the principles detailed above, MANTIS offers a four-stage applications development methodology:

1. Application prototyping, for installing entities, except programs, and specifying possible chaining scenarios.

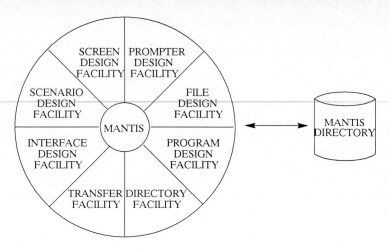

FIGURE 6.9 MANTIS main facilities.

2. Program design, the development stage for programmed modules. They may be written in a specific structured language or in COBOL, PL/I, FORTRAN, or Assembler.
3. Testing, used for application debugging.
4. Application implementation.

Fig. 6.9 summarizes the various facilities MANTIS offers. These facilities are integrated around the MANTIS directory, which contains the MANTIS entities, as well as a report history file. When logging onto MANTIS, these facilities are displayed in menu form, as shown in Fig. 6.10. As a rule, operation under MANTIS is carried out using menus of this type.

MANTIS

RUN A PROGRAM BY NAME.................1	SIGN ON AS ANOTHER USER.........11
DISPLAY A PROMPTER..........................2	MANTIS RUN SYSTEM.....................12
DESIGN A PROGRAM............................3	RUN A SCENARIO 13
„ SCREEN...............................4	DIRECTORY FACILITY.....................14
„ FILE.....................................5	TRANSFER FACILITY......................15
„ PROMPTER..........................6	
„ INTERFACE..........................7	
„ TOTAL FILE VIEW..............8	
„ EXTERNAL FILE VIEW.......9	
„ SCENARIO..........................10	

TERMINATE..PA2

: 3 :

FIGURE 6.10 Initial facility selection menu.

6.4 Management of Relational Databases

6.4.1 Relational Data Manager Main Functions

The Relation Data Manager (RDM) [Cincom 85c] is the relational kernel of the SUPRA DBMS. It provides definition and maintenance of the relational views offered to all user facilities (COBOL, PL/I, MANTIS, SPECTRA) through access primitives. The latter forms a simplified manipulation language, RDML (Relational Data Manipulation Language). The RDM ensures the logical and physical independence of programs from data using two levels of manipulation and data transformations: conceptual decomposition allows user view access to be transformed into conceptual table (logical view) access, and physical decomposition ensures the mappings from conceptual to internal schema. Furthermore the RDM carries out semantics checks on the data, including access authorization verification and domain, key, and referential integrity enforcement.

The main advantages offered by the RDM are as follows:

1. Insulation of application programmers and external users vis-à-vis physical data implementation-related problems.
2. Possibility of changing and restructuring the database without rewriting or recompiling application programs.
3. Availability to programmers of a simplified data manipulation language (RDML) for database modification and interrogation.
4. Database integrity and security controls.
5. Support for base relation structures (relations, integrity contraints, and so on) and associated operators (select, project, and so on) from data located in multiple and various files.

Below we shall describe how RDM offers these advantages and carries out the corresponding procedures.

6.4.2 Defining Logical Views

The DBA defines the conceptual schema relations making up the first-level logical views. This entails storing the definition on the directory. It is recommended to use NORMAL to obtain third normal form logical views; however, nonnormal views can also be defined, for example, for reporting. A logical view is defined by specifying the attributes that it contains (name, characteristics, and properties) and by defining the physical file access in order to make up the view. A logical view that can be accessed for update must contain the keys of the participating entities. The RDM user can use all or some of these logical views to make up user views. Thus the user accesses the database through the user views. Fig. 6.11 illustrates these principles.

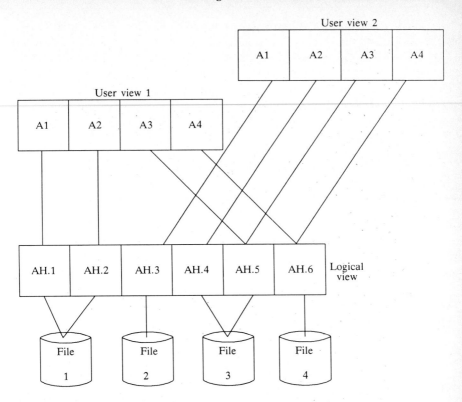

FIGURE 6.11 User and logical views.

The Access Set Description (ASD) can be carried out directly using the DBAID utility or Directory Maintenance or indirectly using NORMAL. This description contains the specification of all the attributes of the logical view. For each attribute, the names of the physical components must be specified, as well as the essential characteristics (nonnullity, constant value, key participation). More precisely attribute definition is carried out using the command:

```
REQ
[UNIQUE] CONST [attribute=] field1 [=fieldn] . . . [constant]
[NONUNIQUE] KEY
```

REQ, CONST, and KEY indicate, respectively, that the attribute is required, has a constant value optionally unique, or is key (optionally with other attributes) in the view. The attribute name in the view must be specified; otherwise the name of the first associated physical field will be used as attribute name. A constant can be specified if the attribute is constant in the view (view constructed by file selection).

Furthermore the DBA must define how the physical files containing the fields comprising the view are to be accessed so that the tuples of this relational view can be built. This is done using the ACCESS command, the format of which depends on the access methods used. The usual format supported by the RDM, which determines the appropriate access paths (primary index, secondary index, or sequential scanning), is as follows:

```
ACCESS filename(item-code . . . )
[ONCE]
WHERE field1 = value[AND fieldn = value]
[GIVING attribute1[attributen] . . . ]
[ALLOW [SHARED] [ALL] [INSERT] [DELETE] [UPDATE]]
```

6.4.3 Data Retrieval

An ASD specifies the attributes and file access. The RDM carries out the internal database navigation for the users. The tuples of a logical view can be accessed one by one using the command:

$$
\text{GET} \left\{ \begin{array}{l} \text{NEXT} \\ \text{LAST} \\ \text{SAME} \\ \text{FIRST} \\ \text{PRIOR} \end{array} \right. \quad \text{viewname [FOR UPDATE]} \quad \left\{ \begin{array}{l} \text{AT MARK} \\ \\ \text{USING val}_1 \text{ [val}_n] \end{array} \right.
$$

When a relation (or logical view) requires access to one or more files, three methods can be used for accessing (the methods may be combined):

1. Penetration consists of direct access based on a key value to a file, followed by access to other files. This is used each time the search criterion includes the access key to a file, which in turn contains the access key to another file, and so on, from file to file.
2. Indexing achieves access via an index by selecting the first index entry that meets the primary access criterion and then the following entries successively.
3. Scanning is used when no primary or secondary key has been specified; it implies moving to the next (or prior) item that meets the access conditions.

The relations between files are thus made on each access either directly by the key values specified by the user or found in the files or by the item position in the index considered or the file. The RDM optimizes navigation in the files by accounting for mandatory keys and fields.

6.4.4 Data Modification

Modification of data supporting a logical view is mainly carried out by insert, delete, or update operations. Modifications trigger the integrity control procedure described below. Because referential integrity is maintained by the system, modifications require that entities and relationships be distinguished. Updating an entity usually entails updating the corresponding relationships according to the integrity constraints declared. We shall describe below the main update commands that can be applied to a logical view.

The insert command allows a tuple to be added to a relation described in the form of a logical view. The syntax is:

$$
\text{INSERT}
\left\{
\begin{array}{l}
\text{NEXT} \\
\text{LAST} \\
\text{FIRST} \\
\text{PRIOR}
\end{array}
\right\}
\quad \text{viewname [MASS]}
$$

Inserting one or more logical tuples (MASS option) is carried out in the files supporting the view. The view must contain the keys of the accessed files since this guarantees the bijective transformation of the view items into file items. The relative position in the logical view specified by the user can be modified by the logical view to file transformation commands (ACCESS).

The delete command enables the last tuple searched for or all tuples in a view to be deleted. The command syntax is:

DELETE [ALL] viewname

Deleting a tuple from a relationship can be carried out without constraint (that is, at any time), whereas deletion of a tuple in an entity usually requires prior deletion of all the tuples in the relationships in which the entity participates.

The update command can modify entity or attribute values and change relationships. The command syntax is:

UPDATE viewname [attribute = value] . . .

A GET command must always be run before an UPDATE command. The last tuple accessed is then modified according to the command; the tuple keys must not be modified. Relationship modifications are handled by the RDM, which checks integrity constraints.

6.4.5 Integrity Controls

In addition to the unique key value controls for each relation, the RDM supports referential integrity constraints. A referential constraint implies specifying a foreign key. A foreign key is an attribute of a relation that must contain only the values in the primary key of another relation. This concept enables entity-relationship relations to be captured. The RDM allows foreign keys to be defined at the internal file level using NORMAL. Manual definition during logical view specification is also possible by specifying entity and relationship key redundancy at entity logical view level and access to the entity via the relationship. The referenced file represents the entity, whereas the dependent file corresponds to the relationship.

The RDM supports two referential integrity rules:

1. A foreign key value in the dependent file must have been found as primary key value in the referenced file.
2. A foreign key may not have a null value.

The RDM controls the referential integrity constraints during modifications as follows:

1. On insertion or update of a dependent file item containing a foreign key. The value of this key must appear in the referenced file.
2. On deletion in the referenced file. The deletion cannot be accepted while the value of the primary key appears as foreign key in the dependent file.

6.4.6 Access Controls

The RDM controls user access rights at the physical file level. When the view is defined, the administrator specifies rights in the ACCESS clause using the key word ALLOW. The following options are available: DELETE, allowing deletions in the file; INSERT, allowing insertions in the file; UPDATE, allowing updates; SHARED, allowing logical views to be shared; and ALL, allowing all forms of update.

6.4.7 Maintenance of the RDM Kernel

View maintenance is mainly carried out using the DBAID utility. In addition, performance optimization is possible. Views can be opened at system initialization (global view support); others can be linked to user programs (logical view binding). The RDM can also be run in reentry mode or not. Finally the RDM provides statistics that can be used for view and system optimization.

6.4.8 File Structure

The physical data manager (PDM) ensures optimized access to SUPRA internal data structures. This is primarily based on indexing. The tables generated by

NORMAL or by the administrator are stored in the VSAM files indexed on the primary key. Direct or chained BDAM files can also be used. Secondary index files are automatically created on foreign keys, as well as on request by the administrator (dynamic indexing). In addition to indexing, the PDM provides support for direct, chained, and sequential file access, with possible grouping of several types of items in the same file. Finally SUPRA supports direct access to preexisting TOTAL or VSAM files. This means SUPRA provides efficient file accesses and offers a broad opening to any physical data structure, especially preexisting data.

6.4.9 Transaction Environment Management

From system environment data, the PDM manages buffers used for saving disk accesses. Buffer management is optimized by anticipated reading for sequential navigation and by using access statistics. The buffers can be shared by user procedures. The transaction concept is taken into account on option, thereby ensuring global validation of updates. A modified buffer lock guarantees that no transaction may access data modified by noncommitted transactions (a transaction is committed by a COMMIT command). In the event of an access attempt, a transaction is put in a holding queue. Deadlocks are prevented by examining holding queues.

The PDM can operate in several operating modes in a batch environment and/or on line. It can be attached exclusively to a batch program or shared in attached or central mode.

6.4.10 Recovery Procedures

The PDM supports a warm recovery procedure that cancels noncommitted transactions. This procedure can be invoked by the programmer in the event of program error or by the system to roll back a transaction. A centralized control procedure cancels one or all noncommitted transactions in the event of system failure without loss of secondary memory. This guarantees physical data integrity in the event of system failure without loss of secondary memory.

In case of media failure, a cold recovery procedure allows data to be reloaded from the last backup and supplies transactions that have been completed since the last backup to roll forward to the last committed transaction.

6.5 SUPRA Architecture

SUPRA's functional architecture is organized around the RDM, which, from the files stored in different formats, supplies the physical data relational views. The tables provided by the RDM have no direct physical existence; they correspond to the external relations. The RDM carries out a logical decomposition into three layers corresponding to the external to conceptual mapping modules and the modules accessing to the different types of files supported. Support is provided for VSAM, TOTAL, and IMS files, as well as PDM specific files. This list is indeed open.

The RDM naturally uses the data directory, which contains all data descriptions, including external views, conceptual schema, and internal schema. This directory is generated by a design tool, such as NORMAL, that can normalize and integrate external views in a third normal form relational conceptual schema. This tool can also generate standard internal schemas. The directory contains the structures for moves from one schema layer to another. It can be modified di-

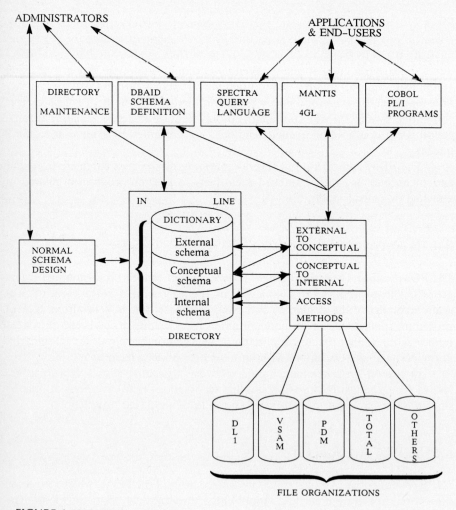

FIGURE 6.12 SUPRA architecture.

rectly (for example, to group physical files or add dynamic indexes) using the directory maintenance tool. It can also be interrogated by data administrators and by authorized users. Finally it should be noted that the directory is accessed via a control module (In-Line Directory) that ensures data security.

A third aspect of SUPRA is the wide variety of interfaces offered to users and application programs. The data manipulation language, with facilities similar to an SQL-type nonprocedural language, is SPECTRA. The 4GL, offering fast development of interactive applications, is MANTIS. Simple interfaces can be accessed from COBOL, FORTRAN, and PL/I. Fig. 6.12 summarizes the functional architecture of SUPRA, which is based on the separate interface model. SUPRA implements the process model, with one user process and one DBMS process per active user.

6.6 Conclusion

SUPRA is an RDBMS supporting multiple and heterogeneous data structures, integrated via the relational model. Although the system includes a full range of functions, extensions are already planned. At the RDM level, further support for integrity constraints enabling domain validity testing is planned. New types of domain are also being considered, as well as format conversions. In order to optimize access, the possibility of materializing virtual fields, such as sum and average, should be supported. To improve data directory management, the directory should in time be organized as a SUPRA database, thereby constituting a true metabase. Following this extension, successive schema versions will be accepted and managed by the system.

At the file level, accesses to DL1 and SQL are planned to be supported directly. Thus the RDM will be able to generate SQL accesses. In time, this should allow support for database machines offering SQL. In order to recover existing programs accessing VSAM files without rewriting, VSAM transparency should be ensured; a VSAM-type access to a logical view will be accepted by the RDM, which will translate this access into, for example, access to PDM files. Finally new languages and application development tools are being developed, including an SQL interface and specialized modeling and decision-making assistance tools for certain application domains (financial control and the aerospace industry, among others).

References

[Cincom 85a] Cincom Systems, "SUPRA: The Advanced Relational Database Management System," SUPRA Digest, Cincinnati, 1985.
[Cincom 85b] Cincom Systems, "SPECTRA: User's Guide," Cincinnati, 1985.
[Cincom 85c] Cincom Systems, "SUPRA: RDM Administrator's Guide," Cincinnati, 1985.

7
SIX OTHER
RELATIONAL SYSTEMS

7.1 Introduction

This chapter describes six interesting relational DBMS. It completes the comparative introduction to relational systems of Chapter 2 and the detailed presentation of four relational systems in Chapters 3 – 6. Each system is described according to the standard plan specified in Section 2.2. The data manipulation languages are introduced using the queries on the toy database of Section 2.3. For obvious reasons, each system presentation is briefer than those of the four preceding systems. For instance, the architecture of each system is only briefly described since most architectures are similar and correspond to those detailed in the previous chapters. And the terminology and the concepts used throughout this chapter have been extensively detailed and illustrated in the previous chapters. Information regarding these six systems has been obtained directly from the corresponding designers and vendors listed in the Appendix. Therefore references are omitted. Sections 7.2 to 7.7 present, respectively, the following sytems, in alphabetical order: DATACOM/DB, FOCUS, NOMAD, ORACLE, SYBASE, and UNIFY.

7.2 DATACOM/DB

DATACOM/DB was introduced to the market in the early 1970s as an advanced inverted-list DBMS. It was already fully multithreaded and was designed for efficient on-line transaction processing. DATACOM/DB was acquired by Applied Data Research (ADR) in 1979, which proceeded to improve the product with relational and distributed database capabilities.

DATACOM/DB has become a powerful RDBMS that supports SQL and comes with several other tools: DATAQUERY for end user query and reporting; IDEAL, a powerful 4GL system, and POWERPACK, a COBOL generator, for application development; IDEAL-ESCORT for PC LAN departmental applications; DEPICTOR, a CASE product for database design and process design; and InfoReach, a distributed database facility. These products are uniquely targeted for IBM operating environments.

7.2.1 Data Definition

The DBA defines the database data in relational terms (areas, tables, rows, fields, keys, and so on) and in terms of *dataviews*. The interactive dictionary, DATADICTIONARY, is the heart of all ADR products. All use the same definitions of data (stored in the DATACOM/DB databases). Thus DBAs have a unique and centralized entry point in the whole DBMS and development environment. New users, views, relations, and so on can be introduced at any time. Interactive or batch routines are used to update the dictionary. IDEAL is based on an application model maintained in the dictionary that contains all information on subsystems, programs, reports, dataviews, and users of IDEAL. The dictionary, automatically updated by IDEAL to reflect development, is active and dynamic. Database schema design can be aided by the data dictionary.

7.2.2 Data Manipulation

Data manipulation can be performed in various ways. IDEAL programs can be executed from traditional programming languages such as COBOL, PL/1, RPG, and assembly language using a CALL interface. Data can be directly accessed from COBOL with the POWERPACK language that uses the METACOBOL preprocessor and interfaces with the dictionary to retrieve data definitions. The database can also be manipulated directly with ADR/DATAQUERY, a user-oriented data manipulation language that can be used interactively or in batch with graphic presentation on color terminals, and with ADR/DATAREPORTER, a batch report writer.

IDEAL supports two relational data manipulation languages: an algebraic language based on a FOR construct and SQL. The following example queries on the WINES database illustrate the algebraic language; here the user must specify the ordering of the relational operators. For readability, FOR EACH and FOR ALL may be used interchangeably. In addition, DATACOM/DB supports the "FOR THE FIRST n" and "FOR ANY n" syntax, which can be used to limit the size of the selected set. Null values are not supported. The view definition example, which cannot be expressed with the algebraic language, is given in SQL.

```
(R1)  FOR ALL WINE
            WHERE VINEYARD = 'Julienas' AND
            (VINTAGE = 1982 OR 1984)
            FOR EACH HARVEST
                WHERE W# = WINE.W#
                FOR ALL PRODUCER
                      WHERE P# = HARVEST.P#
                      PRODUCE REPORT
                ENDFOR
          ENDFOR
      ENDFOR
```

In query R2, the percentage sign acts as a wild-card character. The unknown value is supposed to be coded as 0:

```
(R2)  FOR ALL WINE
            WHERE VINEYARD CONTAINS 'C%'
            AND ((PERCENT = 0) OR (PERCENT BETWEEN 11 AND 13))
            FOR EACH DRINK
                WHERE W# = WINE.W#
                FOR ALL DRINKER
                      WHERE D# = DRINK.D#
                      PRODUCE REPORT
                ENDFOR
          ENDFOR
      ENDFOR
```

In query R3, computing the average percentage by vintage can be easily accomplished by selecting a parameter in the definition of REPORT:

```
(R3)  FOR ALL WINE
            WHERE PERCENT > 12
            PRODUCE REPORT
      ENDFOR
```

In query I1, the **FOR NEW** construct is used to insert data:

```
(I1)  FOR ALL PRODUCER WHERE REGION = 'Bourgogne'
            FOR EACH HARVEST WHERE P# = PRODUCER.P#
                FOR ALL WINE
                      WHERE W# = HARVEST.W# AND VINTAGE = 1983
                      FOR NEW DRINKER
```

```
                          SET D# = PRODUCER.P#
                          SET NAME = PRODUCER.NAME
                          SET TYPE = ' '
                    ENDFOR
                 ENDFOR
              ENDFOR
           ENDFOR

   (M1)  FOR ALL WINE
              WHERE VINEYARD = 'Julienas' AND VINTAGE = 1983
              FOR EACH HARVEST
                 WHERE W# = WINE.W#
                 SET QTY = QTY * 1.1
              ENDFOR
           ENDFOR
```

A multirelation view can be defined using SQL or fill-in-the-blank forms.
The SQL syntax is as follows:

```
   (V1)  CREATE VIEW JULIENAS-HARVEST
              AS SELECT PRODUCER.P#, NAME, QTY
                 FROM WINE, HARVEST, PRODUCER
                 WHERE VINEYARD = 'Julienas'
                    AND HARVEST.W# = WINE.W#
                    AND PRODUCER.P# = HARVEST.P#
```

7.2.3 Semantic Data Control

With **DATADICTIONARY**, all authorizations can be controlled in a centralized
way. Users may access programs and data only if they have the correct privileges
recorded by the administrator in the dictionary.

Relational multirelation views, called *dataviews,* are supported. Only the
views that are derived from a single relation by selection-projection can
be updated.

Semantic integrity control is limited to domain and unique key controls.
However, sophisticated control procedures written by the user can be stored in
the dictionary and executed when the referenced data are updated.

7.2.4 Transaction Management

DATACOM/DB provides complete and efficient transaction management. Two
transaction environments can be simultaneously supported: single user and multi-

user. Single-user mode is the more efficient for dedicated applications that only retrieve data since the overhead of concurrency control is avoided. Concurrency control is provided for the multiuser environment in different modes (batch, interactive, and distributed) through a two-phase locking algorithm with deadlock detection. The concurrency control granularity is the record. Logging, backup copy, and checkpoint facilities are used for recovery after system or media failures. The commitment or abortion of a transaction can be decided inside the transaction (CHECKPOINT and BACKOUT).

7.2.5 Query Processing and Storage Model

The storage model is based on a compound relational index architecture. Instead of using a separate index per key or base relation, DATACOM/DB uses a database-level index. This index has the advantage of eliminating the need to store synonym key occurrences redundantly across many indexes. Most significant, the compound index relates multiple relations and tuples, thus allowing the system to process joins with minimal index probing. The compound index is organized as modified B+-trees, which contain a fine granularity of data population statistics at multiple levels of the tree.

DATACOM/DB employs an optimizer, which optimizes join processing and uses expert rules to handle complex AND and OR selections. The optimizer can select execution strategies where multiple indexes are used in parallel to triangulate the data before resorting to data sequential scan. The optimizer employs a phase-binding approach with which static decisions made at compile time can be refined at run time based on more accurate information. The optimization process is controlled by cost formulas that include the cost of optimization itself. A statistical population counting technique is used to determine an optimal access path by probing the highest levels of the index. With this evolving cost-saving estimate, the optimizer can decide to defer a portion of the optimization to run time when it determines that the advantage of this deferral will greatly outweigh its cost. This phase-binding approach provides the advantage of increasing the accuracy of the access plan and automatically adjusting to the dynamics of keys, data access patterns, and query parameters. In addition, the optimizer employs heuristics.

Population statistics are tracked automatically and heuristically, and the optimizer automatically saves complex access plans so as to be able to track and refine access performance over time.

Data encryption for increased security and data compression are supported. Bulk data transfer algorithms are used for pipelining disk accesses, as well as for packetizing interregion communications. Several data placement options are available to the DBA to suit application requirements. They include relation and tuple-level clustering, random placement, and wrap-around placement.

7.2.6 Architectures

IDEAL is a complete fourth-generation application development system. It provides an integrated workstation environment, an active data dictionary, a source library facility, a powerful 4GL, and screen painting and report generating tools for addressing the entire application life cycle. It also provides an integrated utility subsystem for operating a large database shop. Utility functions include data loading, unloading, extraction, and reformatting; restart and recovery; statistics, diagnostics, and tuning reports; and security and accounting maintenance.

ADR also provides a set of migration softwares called Transparencies. Transparency for VSAM, TOTAL, and DL/I allows files based on old access technologies to be ported to the RDBMS environment. Existing applications continue to execute without change. And the organization is able to provide end user access, develop new applications using 4GLs, and cross-reference data without the problems of disparate technology.

7.2.7 Additional Tools

The DATACOM/DB functional architecture is based on the separate interface model, with the data dictionary as the DBA entry point and SQL and IDEAL as major end user entry points.

The process architecture is based on the multiple server model. In the multiuser mode, the DBMS occupies its own address space (or partition) in the operating system. Concurrent transactions (CICS, IMS/DC) and batch jobs are serviced in a fully multithreaded and multitasked manner. Multitasking allows DATACOM/DB to leverage N-way processors by automatically balancing the DBMS workload across all processors. Buffers are shared by all tasks to ensure minimal disk accesses. A hashing algorithm is used to handle very large buffer pools for large database operations.

A single-user mode is available for running dedicated applications without the overhead of multiuser management.

For VM shops operating both VSE and CMS, the Multi Guest Sharing Option (MGSO) allows VSE and CMS users to share data transparently. The MGSO uses the IBM Inter User Communications Vehicle (IUCV) to support concurrent multithreaded read/write access.

7.2.8 Distributed Database Management

DATACOM comes with InfoReach, a homogeneous distributed database facility. InfoReach provides data location and data replication transparency, data partitioning, and multisite updates. A two-phase commit protocol is employed to ensure distributed transaction atomicity. All information about distribution is contained in DATADICTIONARY, which can be centralized or decentralized.

The Distributed Data Manager component of InfoReach, part of the multi-user nucleus, is also used to support the Teradata DBC/1012 database machine. In this way, data may be ported between IBM DASD and the DBC/1012 transparently, providing users with cost-effective storage options.

7.2.9 Operating Environments

DATACOM and IDEAL operate on IBM 370, 4300, 3000, and 9370 and compatible computers under DOS/VSE, VSE/SP, MVS/SP, MVS/XA, and VM/CMS. ADR software takes advantage of the latest IBM operating systems. For example, DATACOM/DB runs in MVS/XA above the 16 megabyte line and supports the Multiple Address Spaces of VSE/SP2 and VSE/SP3.

7.3 FOCUS

Marketed by Information Builders Inc. (IBI), FOCUS is a popular system that includes a fourth-generation system and a database system. The DBMS combines the respective advantages of the relational and hierarchical models. Although not advertised as relational, FOCUS can be used as a pure RDBMS. FOCUS includes a complete set of 4GL tools that provide many capabilities, including English query language, report writer, graphics, spread sheet, statistical analysis, and powerful application development.

The complete FOCUS configuration includes the 4GL components and the DBMS. A smaller configuration, FOCUS For SQL, includes only the 4GL components, which can be used on top of a different SQL-based RDBMS such as DB2, SQL/DS, or the Teradata DBC/1012 database machine.

Read/write interface facilities enable users to read and update external files (VSAM) or databases (IMS, DB2, SQL/DS) within the FOCUS environment. These facilities are the basis for IBI's Universal Access Strategy, which allows users to access and update combinations of files residing on any hardware in any format. FOCUS is available on several operating environments, including IBM mainframes, DEC VAX and Wang VS computers, and personal computers.

7.3.1 Data Definition

A database is defined by a text editor or window-driven front end. Relations constitute segments that can be organized as a hierarchy inside a file. For each relation of a FOCUS file (that is, a hierarchy of relations), the relation attributes with their name, alias, type, default value, and, possibly, an index can be defined. In addition, all DBMS-required descriptors for fields, keys, and definitions of field-level input validation, predefined calculations, and report column headings can be included in the file definition. The joins that cross-reference the multiple relations within a file must also be declared as part of the file description. The description of a file can be directly stored in source or encrypted form in secondary storage. The file description can be modified using specific statements that generate the automatic file reconstruction. Nonprofessional users can also define the file schema by interacting with the schema manager through a menu-driven interface.

All data definitions are stored in an interactive and dynamic data dictionary, MASTER. The dictionary can be accessed through a menu-based language. It provides on-line facilities for schema storage, analysis, and auditing, and it can maintain resource utilization statistics for optimizing FOCUS procedures.

7.3.2 Data Manipulation

Data manipulation can be done interactively with a 4GL. This nonprocedural language, like most other 4GLs, is based on relational algebra extended with algorithmic and editing capabilities. It offers the following statements: join, selection (IF), projection and report writing (TABLE, PRINT, LIST), sort (BY), arithmetic operations (SUM, ADD), and aggregate functions (MAX, MIN, TOT, PCT). Navigation in hierarchies and sequential access (NEXT) is possible. Join is allowed only if one relation (the outer one) has an index on the join attribute; however, any complex join can be programmed (by the user) with the statement MATCH. Operations on various source files (IMS, ADABAS, VSAM, DB2) can be expressed within the same procedure; however, updates of relations from several sources must be done with procedures in several steps. Null values are fully supported and can be specified in a query with the key word MISSING.

FOCUS's 4GL statements can be embedded in programming languages such as COBOL, PL/I, FORTRAN, and others using a CALL interface. Furthermore a COBOL file definition translator enables automatically to translate COBOL file definitions into FOCUS relation definitions.

To illustrate data manipulation with the 4GL, we express the queries introduced in Chapter 2 on the WINES database.

```
(R1)   JOIN P# IN PRODUCER TO ALL P# IN HARVEST AS JOIN1
       JOIN W# IN PRODUCER TO ALL W# IN WINE AS JOIN2
       TABLE FILE PRODUCER
           PRINT NAME VINEYARD VINTAGE
           IF VINEYARD CONTAINS 'Julienas'
           IF VINTAGE IS 1982 OR 1984
       END
```

(R2)   JOIN D# IN DRINKER TO ALL D# IN DRINK AS JOIN1
       JOIN W# IN DRINKER TO ALL W# IN WINE AS JOIN2
       TABLE FILE DRINKER
          PRINT NAME
          IF VINEYARD IS 'C$*'
          IF PERCENT IS MISSING OR (GE 11 AND LE 13)
       END

(R3)   TABLE FILE WINE
       WRITE MIN.PERCENT NOPRINT AVE.PERCENT BY VINEYARD
       IF TOTAL MIN.PERCENT GE 12
       END

(I1)   JOIN P# IN PRODUCER TO ALL P# IN HARVEST AS JOIN1
       JOIN W# IN PRODUCER TO ALL W# IN WINE AS JOIN2
       TABLE FILE PRODUCER
          PRINT NAME BY P#
          IF REGION CONTAINS 'Bourgogne'
          IF VINTAGE IS 1983
       ON TABLE HOLD
       END
       MODIFY FILE DRINKER
       FIXFORM D# NAME
       DATA ON HOLD
       END

(M1)   JOIN W# IN HARVEST TO ALL W# IN WINE AS JOIN1
       TABLE FILE HARVEST
          PRINT W# QTY BY P#
          IF VINEYARD CONTAINS 'Julienas'
          IF VINTAGE EQ 1983
       ON TABLE HOLD
       END
       MODIFY FILE HARVEST
       FIXFORM FROM HOLD
       MATCH P# W#
            ON MATCH COMPUTE
                   QTY = D.QTY * 1.1;
            ON MATCH UPDATE QTY
            ON NOMATCH REJECT
       DATA ON HOLD
       END

FOCUS does not support relational views, and thus the view V1 cannot be expressed.

7.3.3 Semantic Data Control

FOCUS does not support complete relational views. It is possible, however, to define virtual relations composed of several relations residing in segments of hierarchies. A useful capability is the inversion of hierarchies, which allows the user to view a file structure from a different angle. Virtual relations can be updated provided that the update rules have been fully specified by the DBA.

Access privileges are granted to the users at file description time by the administrator of the file. Authorizations are granted by the DBA to programs, files, relations, attributes, or even values within attributes. The authorizations are: no access, read-only access, update-only access, write-only access, and read/write access. Privileges can be dynamically modified by the administrator.

When a file is defined, domain and unique key constraints can be specified. All other complex integrity constraints must be defined in application programs. These constraints can also be introduced as complex security conditions stored in FOCUS procedures.

7.3.4 Transaction Management

A FOCUS transaction can be seen as a procedure that is the expression of a complex query. Concurrency control is applied during updates by comparing the versions of records read by a transaction with those in the database. When n records have been updated (for instance, $n = 100$), a system checkpoint can be recorded. FOCUS supports system and media recovery using an after- and before-image log. The reliability mechanism is based on shadow paging.

7.3.5 Storage Model and Query Processing

The basic data storage model used for records is the BDAM hierarchical storage structure, which stores in 4K-byte pages relations linked by hierarchies in which the links are materialized by pointers. The indexes can be organized as hashed files or B-trees. Data can be stored in fully or partially encrypted files for increased security.

The operations specified in a FOCUS query are optimized when they are executed in the order of relation references with the application of selection before join. Selections are performed using existing indexes or by sequential scan. The join algorithm is the nested-loop join algorithm where the inner relation is directly accessed by index for the JOIN statement and sequentially for the MATCH statement. The hierarchical storage of several relations avoids the need to perform joins over these relations. However, this storage model remains complex, so database reorganization is difficult.

7.3.6 Additional Tools

FOCUS offers a large number of fourth-generation tools, in particular:

- An English-query language available on the PC version of FOCUS combines menu-based and natural language capabilities for end user data manipulation,
- A screen manager enables the definition of menus and data entry screens for rapidly developing complex applications,
- An automatic application generator, ModifyTalk, permits the generation of complete applications for data maintenance, including input/output and processing logic.
- A graphic capability enables users to produce results as various high-resolution graphics (histograms, bar charts, diagrams, pie charts, and others).
- A statistical analyzer gives detailed information on the query results (variance, regression, series, correlation, and so on).
- A spread-sheet option provides advanced features for manipulating spread sheets populated from FOCUS files.
- A project management system provides project managers with facilities to define and analyze complex projects.
- A read/write facility interfaces FOCUS with external files (VSAM, QSAM, ADABAS, and others), thereby allowing uniform access to various external sources.

FOCUS For SQL is a version of FOCUS that includes only the 4GL tools and works on SQL-based systems, such as DB2 and SQL/DS, and the Britton Lee IDM and Teradata DBC/1012 database machines. FOCUS For SQL provides transparency from the underlying RDBMS so that the same FOCUS application can be ported on different RDBMSs. FOCUS converts the 4GL commands into SQL statements, which can be processed by the underlying RDBMS. FOCUS data descriptions can also be automatically converted into SQL-based data definitions.

In addition, the PC version of FOCUS provides interfaces to various microcomputer DBMSs such as dBASE III and spread-sheet programs such as Lotus.

7.3.7 Architectures

FOCUS's architecture is based on the separate interface model, with multiple entry points. FOCUS is organized around a kernel that enables access to the data dictionary MASTER, the temporary files (HOLD), and the permanent data files (FOCUS files). The kernel also includes facilities to access nonstandard data files, such as IMS, IDMS, TOTAL, ADABAS, QSAM, VSAM, and ISAM. The kernel is interfaced with the 4GL and other utilities. The process architecture of FOCUS is based on the process model. For each active user, there is one process running the 4GL tools and one process running the FOCUS DBMS.

7.3.8 Distributed Database Management

FOCUS does not support distributed database management; however, a limited form of remote database access is provided by a workstation-server interface. The workstations, which should run the microcomputer version PC/FOCUS, can transfer data from or to the mainframe server running FOCUS.

7.3.9 Operating Environments

FOCUS is available on all IBM systems/370 and compatible computers under MVS, MVS/XA, and VM/CMS; DEC VAX computers under VAX/VMS; Wang computers under VS; and IBM RT PC, Pyramid, NCR, and AT&T 3B series computers running under AT&T UNIX. The microversion PC/FOCUS is available on IBM PC and compatibles under PC-DOS or MS-DOS.

7.4 NOMAD

Marketed by MUST Software International, NOMAD is a system that integrates a complete set of 4GL-based tools with relational database management capabilities. Similar to FOCUS, relations can be organized as hierarchies. The 4GL-based system provides facilities for statistical analysis, graphics, report generation, ad hoc query, window management, and application development.

The 4GL system can be separated from the NOMAD DBMS and used with SQL/DS, DB2, or the Teradata DBC/1012 database machine through an interface that permits users to read, write, and create SQL data. In addition, there are many interfaces to other popular file or database systems, such as VSAM, ISAM, and IMS/VS.

NOMAD is available only on IBM operating environments. It is written in IBM assembly language in order to exploit fully the IBM virtual machine environment (such as memory management). A microversion, PC-NOMAD, is available on IBM personal computers and compatibles.

7.4.1 Data Definition

A NOMAD database is defined as a set of masters, which can be arranged as relations or segment hierarchies inside files. Thus the database structure can be relational, hierarchical, or hybrid. Except for common attributes, the attributes names in a database must be unique. Schema definition is done in a file, which is compiled. Schema definition includes relation, attribute, and hierarchy definitions. Access protections, integrity constraints, and data evaluation rules can also be specified. Furthermore the internal data structures can be specified or not. If they are not, the system takes the default structure. An interactive data dictionary is provided and is useful for database schema design. Schema updates are dynamic: they do not require the recompilation of the database schema. Relation schema modifications (for example, addition of an attribute) are managed by the system, which propagates the necessary reorganizations on data.

7.4.2 Data Manipulation

NOMAD supports a procedural language for querying and updating data and a powerful algebraic language restricted to inquiry (no updates). The procedural language is a high-level programming language with procedural database access routines (FIRST, NEXT, and so on). All data manipulations are possible (arithmetic operations, byte string manipulation, and others). The key word NAV is supplied for denoting null values. Several commands can be combined in a procedure with control instructions (if, while, and so on) and be precompiled for repetitive usage. The procedural language can also be embedded in any programming language with the CALL interface.

The algebraic language is a powerful report generator, which allows users to access multiple bases. It also provides various join types. A number of joins can be nested in the same command if the join attributes are the common attribute. Otherwise intermediate relations must be generated. IBM COBOL, FORTRAN, and PL/I routines can be called directly from NOMAD programs.

To avoid the specification of frequent join predicates, NOMAD can define in a relation virtual attributes coming from different relations based on the equality of a common attribute. This is different from the concept of view because virtual attributes remain real and visible in their source relation.

The queries defined in Chapter 2 have been expressed using this *virtual join* capability. The attributes of relations DRINKER and WINE have been made virtual in relation DRINK, and the attributes of relations PRODUCER and WINE have been made virtual in relation HARVEST. To illustrate this powerful feature, the schema definition of the WINES database precedes the expression of the queries in the algebraic language.

```
MASTER DRINKER KEYED DNO;
        DNO AS 99; DNAME AS NAME 'F L' ;
        TYPE DOCUMENT AS A1 LIMITS('H', 'A', 'L')
            DOCUMENT 'HEAVY, AVERAGE, OR LIGHT DRINKER';
```

MASTER WINE KEYED WNO;
    WNO AS 99; VINEYARD AS A20; VINTAGE AS A4;
    PERCENT AS 99%; PRICE AS 99.99;

MASTER PRODUCER KEYED PNO;
    PNO AS 99; PNAME AS NAME 'F L' ; REGION AS A20;

MASTER PARTY KEYED DNO, WNO, WHEN, PLACE;
    DNO AS MEMBER 'DRINKER'; WNO AS MEMBER 'WINE';
    WHEN AS DATE; PLACE AS A30; QTY AS 999;
    DEFINE PVINEYARD AS
        EXTRACT 'VINEYARD FROM WINE KEY WNO' ;
    DEFINE PPERCENT AS EXTRACT 'PERCENT FROM WINE KEY
        WNO';
    DEFINE PNAME AS EXTRACT 'DNAME FROM DRINKER KEY
        DNO';

MASTER HARVEST KEYED PNO, WNO;
    PNO AS MEMBER 'PRODUCER'; WNO AS MEMBER 'WINE' ;
    QTY AS 999;
    DEFINE HVINEYARD AS
        EXTRACT 'VINEYARD FROM WINE KEY WNO';
    DEFINE HVINTAGE AS EXTRACT 'VINTAGE FROM WINE KEY
        WNO' ;
    DEFINE HNAME AS EXTRACT 'PNAME FROM PRODUCER KEY
        PNO' ;
    DEFINE HREGION AS
        EXTRACT 'REGION FROM PRODUCER KEY PNO' ;

(R1)   LIST BY HNAME WHERE HVINEYARD CONTAINS ('Julienas')
        AND HVINTAGE AMONG ('1982', '1984');

(R2)   LIST BY PNAME WHERE SUBSTR(PVINEYARD,1,1) EQ 'C'
        AND (PPERCENT = &NAV OR PPERCENT BTWN (11,13));

(R3)   LIST BY VINEYARD MIN(PERCENT) NOPRINT SET &X
        AVG (PERCENT)
        OUTPUT WHERE &X > 12;

(I1)   FOR EACH HARVEST
        IF HVINTAGE EQ '1983' AND HREGION EQ 'Bourgogne'
        THEN
            INSERT DRINKER.DNO = HARVEST.PNO DNAME =
            HNAME;

(M1)   FROM HARVEST CHANGE ALL QTY=QTY*1.1
             WHERE HVINTAGE='1983'
             AND HVINEYARD EQ 'Julienas' OTW;

(V1) NOMAD can support only static views with the CREATE command:

    CREATE FROM HARVEST BY PNO HNAME QTY
            WHERE HVINTAGE = '1982' ;
            ON JULIENAS-HARVEST ;

7.4.3 Semantic Data Control

Subschemas can be specified on a database schema only with selection-projection operations. Updates through subschema are directly supported. These subschemas can be associated with access authorizations specified by passwords. Also databases can be created as static views (snapshots) by applying complex operators (for example, join) to other databases. These static views do not reflect subsequent updates to the base relations.

Access privileges to the database constituents are controlled by a multilevel password mechanism. The access privileges can be combined with procedures stored in the schema. An encryption system controlled by passwords is also provided.

Semantic integrity includes the support for domain (LIMIT, MASK) and referential integrity constraints. Complete referential integrity is ensured through RULE statements stored in the data dictionary. Other integrity constraints should be specified as procedures stored in the data dictionary and triggered on updates.

7.4.4 Transaction Management

NOMAD maintains database consistency in the presence of concurrent accesses and all types of failures (transaction, system, and media). A transaction is a set of NOMAD statements. By default, there is no concurrency control, thereby avoiding control overhead for read-only transactions. Also the user can be informed of the state of a concurrency granule (being read, being modified, and so on) and can have the resposibility for concurrency control. The user can also lock the masters he or she wants to access in exclusive mode. With this strong control, there is no possibility of deadlock.

A before-log is used for undoing transactions. An after-image log (AUDIT) and system checkpoints are also managed for system and media recovery. Recovery after media failure can be selective (some transactions can be ignored).

7.4.5 Storage Model and Query Processing

Masters (relations and hierarchies) are stored in BDAM files, based on a single or multiple key. The hierarchical clustering of child segments with the parent segment avoids the need to perform join operations for the majority of data access. Large and dynamic files can be organized as B-trees. Secondary indexes are supported.

The ordering of operation execution is the one given in the program. Data access is optimized using data structures and access paths. For supporting navigational access, records are chained through logical pointers. Furthermore NOMAD optimizes dynamically the user space management according to the user needs and the workload.

7.4.6 Additional Tools

NOMAD includes an integrated set of fourth-generation tools such as report generator, graphics, statistics, application generator, screen manager, and text manager. The subsystems are combined with the DBMS. NOMAD also provides the capability to access external files as valid databases. Three kinds of access are available: a read/write/extract interface for SQL/DS, DB2, and DBC/1012 databases; a read/extract interface for VSAM, QSAM, ISAM files, and IMS, IDMS databases; and a generalized interface for other files. These interfaces and a schema generator enable users to access existing data of a format different from NOMAD databases.

7.4.7 Architecture

NOMAD's functional architecture is based on the separate interface model, with multiple entry points. The process architecture of FOCUS is based on the process model. For each active user, there is one process running the 4GL system and one process running the NOMAD DBMS. NOMAD has been designed specifically for the IBM virtual machine (VM) environments such as VM/CMS. The main advantage is that the system takes full advantage of the operating system; NOMAD manages the virtual memory of the database users, thereby providing optimal sharing of resources. The drawback to this optimized Assembly language base is the low portability of the system to non-IBM hardware.

7.4.8 Distributed Database Management

NOMAD does not support distributed database management; however, remote database access between workstations running PC NOMAD and a server running

NOMAD is supported through an import/export facility with which data can be exchanged.

7.4.9 Operating Environments

Originally designed for the IBM virtual machine environment, NOMAD is available for IBM and compatible systems running MVS, MVS/XA, MVS outside TSO, and VM/CMS. A microversion is available on IBM and compatible microcomputers running PC-DOS, MS-DOS, and OS/2. A DEC VAX version has been announced for delivery in 1988.

7.5 ORACLE

Marketed by Oracle Corporation since 1979, ORACLE is a popular RDBMS that supports the SQL language as unique entry point for end users and administrators. ORACLE optimizes the execution of relational operations using efficient storage structures, in particular, multirelation clustering.

ORACLE comes with a set of 4GL tools that interface the RDBMS through SQL. Included are a 4GL, a form-oriented application generator, a report writer, a database design help, a color graphics facility, and an easy-to-learn spread sheet. ORACLE supports relational distributed database management.

An initial objective in designing the system was portability. As a result, ORACLE is available on a large variety of operating environments, including mainframes, minicomputers, and microcomputers.

7.5.1 Data Definition

Data definition, data control, and data manipulation are uniformly handled with a unique entry point: the SQL language. The explicit notion of database is not supported. Rather relations are the basic units users manipulate. A statement enables the creation of a relation at any time with the list of attributes and their type. The types supported are numerical, text, and date. Users can insert actual tuples in the relation using either SQL or a load facility converting a file into the relation. Information about relations, attributes, views, integrity constraints, access privileges, and indexes is stored in a data dictionary, organized as a metabase. This dictionary is dynamic since it can be updated at any time, even while running other transactions, and propagates schema modifications on affected data automatically. The schema of a relation may be dynamically modified by addition of new attributes. It is also possible to add a secondary index at any time, which implies its immediate creation.

7.5.2 Data Manipulation

Oracle's SQL language is a nonprocedural language fully compatible with DB2's SQL and ANSI SQL. It has the power of relational calculus enhanced with capabilities of sorting, aggregate, and arithmetic functions, and others. Null values are handled by the system and can be manipulated with the key word NULL in select criteria.

ORACLE data can be accessed within standard programming languages using two types of programmatic interfaces: precompiler and subroutine CALL interface. With the precompiler approach, SQL statements, embedded in a program, are translated into the appropriate programming language source code by a precompiler. The source code can then be compiled into efficient object code. There is one such precompiler per host programming language. With the subroutine CALL interface, SQL statements can be integrated in the program as ORACLE subroutine calls and passed to the RDBMS for interpretation at run time. This approach is more flexible but less efficient than the precompiler approach.

Oracle's SQL is illustrated by the expression of following queries defined in Chapter 2.

```
(R1)   SELECT DISTINCT NAME
       FROM PRODUCER P, WINE W, HARVEST.H
       WHERE P.P# = H.P#
             AND H.W# = W.W#
             AND VINEYARD LIKE 'Julienas%'
             AND VINTAGE IN (1982,1984)

(R2)   SELECT NAME
       FROM DRINKER D, WINE W, DRINK R
       WHERE D.D# = R.D#
             AND R.W# = W.W#
             AND VINEYARD LIKE 'C%'
             AND (PERCENT BETWEEN 11 AND 12
                 OR PERCENT IS NULL)

(R3)   SELECT VINEYARD, ROUND (AVG (PERCENT,2))
       FROM WINE
       GROUP BY VINEYARD
       HAVING MIN (PERCENT) > 12

(I1)   INSERT INTO DRINKER (D#,NAME)
       SELECT P.P#, P.NAME
       FROM PRODUCER P, HARVEST H, WINE W
       WHERE REGION = 'Bourgogne'
```

```
          AND P.P# = H.P#
          AND H.W# = W.W#
          AND VINTAGE = 1983

(M1)  UPDATE HARVEST
          SET QTY = QTY * 1.1
          WHERE W# =
              (SELECT W.W#
              FROM WINE W, HARVEST H
              WHERE H.W# = W.W#
                    AND VINEYARD EQ 'Julienas'
                    AND VINTAGE = 1983)

(V1)  CREATE VIEW JULIENAS-HARVEST
          SELECT H.P#, P.NAME, H.QTY
            FROM WINE W, PRODUCER P, HARVEST H
            WHERE H.W# = W.W#
              AND H.P# = P.P#
              AND VINEYARD = 'Julienas'
```

7.5.3 Semantic Data Control

ORACLE fully supports relational views, which can be specified by assigning the viewname with a possibly multirelation retrieval query (see example query V1). Updates through views are possible only if they can be propagated without ambiguity on the base relations. Thus only single-relation views defined with select-project can be updated.

The authorization control is decentralized. This is also a reason for the absence of database notion. The creator of a relation or a view is its administrator and can grant or deny selected access privileges (insert, query, update, and so on) on it. The administrator can also grant administration privilege. This authorization mechanism enables centralized, decentralized, or hybrid control. Furthermore increased protection of the various database objects (relations, attributes, sets of tuples) can be achieved through a powerful password mechanism.

Semantic integrity constraints can be defined as assertions and stored in the data dictionary. Integrity control is restricted to key and domain control.

7.5.4 Transaction Management

A transaction is defined as a set of SQL statements. The concurrency control granularity is variable. By default, it is the tuple. However, a whole relation can be locked and unlocked by the user. The concurrency control algorithm is based on two-phase locking with deadlock detection. When a deadlock is found, the youngest transaction is aborted and restarted (by the system).

Transaction commitment or abortion must be specified (COMMIT or ROLLBACK) within a transaction. Several COMMIT statements may be specified within the same long transaction, thereby creating a multistep transaction. A before-image log is managed by the system. It is useful for transaction abortions or warm restart after system failure. The DBMS also supports an after-image log, backup copies, and checkpoints for media recovery.

7.5.5 Query Processing and Storage Model

Relations are stored in files organized as B+-trees, which favor random and indexed access. Data can be compacted on disk to increase disk utilization and performance. Relations can be clustered or indexed on one or more attributes. An important feature for optimizing joins is *multirelation clustering,* which allows the storing together (in the same disk pages) of tuples of different relations based on the equality of a common attribute. This clustering method is actually hierarchical and therefore avoids the processing of join operations at the expense of more complex update processing.

ORACLE implements a complex query optimization algorithm based on the static choice of the best access plan at compile time. Access paths to the data (primary or secondary indexes) are used as much as possible for selection operations. The estimation of intermediate results of relational algebra operations enables the ordering of these operations by increasing order of complexity and estimated cost.

7.5.6 Additional Tools

ORACLE includes several 4GL tools for improving application development and result presentation. These tools allow the combination of SQL statements. Interactive application generators enable developers to build form-based applications using a menu-based language and a screen painter and to design custom menu-driven interfaces for user applications. An SQL-based 4GL combines the power of SQL with powerful report writing and data transfer capabilities. A report writer allows the preparation of complex reports, including results of SQL queries and text. A design help facility permits the automatic generation of relation definitions for new applications.

Furthermore ORACLE includes several simple end user interfaces. A menu-based language allows casual users to build SQL queries, reports, and graphs. A color graphics facility permits query results to be presented in full-color graphs, such as pies, and bar or line charts. Finally an easy-to-learn spread-sheet program can be used with ORACLE data.

7.5.7 Architectures

ORACLE functional architecture is based on the uniform interface model. The system is functionally divided into three components: application and end user products; the SQL interface, the unique system entry point; and the ORACLE kernel, including the data dicionary, which executes user queries. ORACLE implements the process model, with one application process and one DBMS process per user. The ORACLE buffer manager employs the least recently used (LRU) replacement strategy.

7.5.8 Distributed Database Management

ORACLE supports a homogeneous distributed databasc capability, SQL*Star. SQL*Star provides full location transparency and some DBMS independence by allowing the remote connection of ORACLE systems with different RDBMSs, such as SQL/DS and DB2. Distributed transactions are managed using a two-phase locking algorithm with global deadlock detection and a two-step commit protocol. Distributed query optimization is also provided.

7.5.9 Operating Environments

ORACLE runs on a large variety of computing environments, including IBM 370 and 43XX mainframes under MVS, MVS/XA, and UTS; AT&T 3B series computers under UNIX; DEC VAX computers under VMS and Ultrix; Honeywell computers under GCOS, HUS, and UNIX; IBM 9370 under MVS and VM/SP; Prime computers under PRIMOS and UNIX; and Sequent machines under DYNIX. ORACLE is also available on many microcomputers such as IBM PC and compatibles under PC-DOS and MS-DOS, DEC Microvax computers under MicroVMS, and most UNIX-based microcomputers.

7.6 SYBASE

Marketed by Sybase Inc., SYBASE is the newest SQL-based RDBMS. It is targeted for on-line data processing applications, which are typically update-oriented and require high multiuser performance. SYBASE consists of two subsystems: the DataToolSet and the DataServer. The DataToolSet provides data definition, data manipulation, extensive semantic data control, ad hoc query, and application development facilities accessible through window and menu-based interfaces. The DataServer is based on a multithreaded architecture and provides high-performance database management functions, including query optimization and high availability.

SYBASE supports distributed database management and makes optimal use of multiprocessor configurations such as VAXcluster. SYBASE is primarily available on DEC VAX and SUN environments under VMS and UNIX.

7.6.1 Data Definition

Data definition, as well as data manipulation and data control, are uniformly supported by TRANSACT-SQL, an extended version of SQL. The central concept is that of a database, which is a set of relations.

The type of an attribute may be system defined (there are eleven such types, including MONEY and DATETIME) or user defined. A user-defined type associates a type name with a type definition, using system-defined types, and additional constraints (such as not null). User-defined types are stored in the data dictionary. An attribute may be allowed to be null or may have a default value; for example, "the default percent of a wine is 12."

Once created, a relation definition may be modified by the addition of new attributes. Tuples may be inserted into a relation using a TRANSACT-SQL transaction or a facility that loads the relation from a file. All schema and data control information is stored in a central data dictionary. This data dictionary may be concurrently accessed and modified by multiple transactions. The updates to the data dictionary are systematically propagated to the data so they become visible to the users. Primary and secondary indexes may be defined on any relation's attribute. The definition of an index triggers its creation.

7.6.2 Data Manipulation

The language TRANSACT-SQL supplements SQL with algorithmic capabilities (IF_ELSE, GOTO, WHILE), user-defined messages (PRINT, RAISERROR), and clock time–based actions (WAITFOR). Therefore TRANSACT-SQL is a powerful 4GL based on relational calculus.

Most RDBMSs embed their query language into a programming language via a precompiler. SYBASE uses a different approach by providing a unique programming language interface, DB-LIBRARY, which manages the communication between any front-end process and the DataServer. DB-LIBRARY provides database access to programs written in C, COBOL, or FORTRAN. The advantages of such an approach are better independence of applications, better error control, and simpler preprocessors. TRANSACT-SQL is illustrated by the following queries on the WINES database.

```
(R1)   SELECT PRODUCER.NAME
       FROM      PRODUCER, WINE, HARVEST
       WHERE   PRODUCER.P# = HARVEST.P# AND
```

```
          WINE.W# = HARVEST.W# AND
          VINEYARD LIKE 'Julienas%'
          AND VINTAGE IN (1982,1984)

(R2)  SELECT DRINKER.NAME, DRINKER.SURNAME
      FROM   DRINKER, WINE, DRINK
      WHERE DRINKER.D# = DRINK.D# AND
          WINE.W# = DRINK.W# AND
          VINEYARD LIKE 'C%' AND
          (PERCENT IS NULL OR PERCENT BETWEEN 11 AND 13)

(R3)  SELECT VINEYARD, AVG (PERCENT)
      FROM  WINE
      GROUP BY VINEYARD
      HAVING MIN (PERCENT) > 12

(I1)  INSERT INTO DRINKER (D#, NAME)
          SELECT PRODUCER.P#, PRODUCER.NAME
          FROM PRODUCER, WINE, HARVEST
          WHERE REGION LIKE 'Bourgogne%' AND
              PRODUCER.P# = HARVEST.P# AND
              WINE.W# = HARVEST.W# AND
              VINTAGE = 1983

(M1)  UPDATE HARVEST
      SET QTY = QTY * 1.1
      WHERE HARVEST.W# IN
              (SELECT WINE.W#
              FROM WINE, HARVEST
              WHERE WINE.W# = HARVEST.W# AND
                  VINEYARD = 'Julienas *' AND
                  VINTAGE = 1983)

(V1)  CREATE VIEW JULIENAS-HARVEST
      AS SELECT HARVEST.P#, PRODUCER.NAME, HARVEST.QTY
          FROM WINE W, PRODUCER P, HARVEST H
          WHERE H.W# = W.W#
          AND H.P# = P.P#
          AND V.VINEYARD = 'Julienas'
```

7.6.3 Semantic Data Control

Comprehensive data control is provided by view management, authorization control, and outstanding semantic integrity control.

Relational views may be multirelation. A multirelation view may be updated if the attributes subject to update belong to the same relation.

The authorization control is decentralized. There is only one DBA per database, and authorizations on database objects (view, relation, attribute) and procedures can be granted only by the DBA. The protection system recognizes a hierarchy of users, each with a different status: the system administrator, the DBAs (one per database), the owners of database objects, and others.

SYBASE extensively supports semantic integrity control by its emphasis on on-line applications, which are update intensive. Unique key, referential integrity, and domain constraints are supported. Furthermore a stored procedure, a set of SQL statements identified by a name, may be defined as a trigger that will be executed automatically when a specified update operation occurs. Stored procedures and triggers enable the DBA to specify complete integrity checking with various alternatives (for example, abort transaction or issue warning).

7.6.4 Transaction Management

A transaction may be a single insert, update, or delete or a set of data retrieval and modification statements delimited by TRANSACT-SQL's BEGIN TRANsaction and COMMIT TRANsaction commands. Other transaction control syntax includes: SAVE TRANsaction, which is used to set a savepoint within a user-defined transaction, and ROLLBACK TRANsaction, which is used to roll a user-defined transaction back to the last savepoint in the transaction or to the beginning of the transaction. Therefore multistep transactions are supported.

SYBASE supports automatic locking at the page level with deadlock detection. Both repeatable reads and nonrepeatable reads (incurring lower overhead) are supported. The DataServer allows concurrent access for reads as well as updates through the data and indexes. Data are locked at the page level, and indexes are locked using a proprietary technique that allows concurrent reading and changing of the index. Page-level locking, together with SYBASE's clustered indexes, provides a high level of concurrency with minimal overhead. Deadlock detection is general purpose, covering logical locks, resource locks, and any resource that would cause a deadlock if a process goes to sleep.

Reliability is achieved by the on-line maintenance of a physical log, which contains before- and after-images, and periodic backup copies, which are done concurrently with running transactions. SYBASE provides system and media recovery facilities.

7.6.5 Query Processing and Storage Model

A relation is stored in a file clustered according to a B-tree index. In addition to clustered indexes, secondary (nonclustered) indexes are supported. Clustered and nonclustered indexes are used for random and range queries. Data in main memory are managed by the least recently used (LRU) buffering algorithm.

SYBASE implements a query optimization algorithm designed to handle large, complicated SQL statements with many choices of access paths. Optimization is static and based on cost estimates according to statistical knowledge of the size and distribution of the data. Joins are performed by nested loop with existing or dynamically created indexes. The execution plans produced by optimization are saved for subsequent use.

7.6.6 Additional Tools

The DataToolSet is a complete set of tools for developing and maintaining on-line applications. Most tools are window based and exploit the capabilities of the new generation bit-mapped workstations. The DataToolSet contains three components: DB-LIBRARY, APT-FORMS, and Data Workbench. DB-LIBRARY is a library of commands for interfacing programming languages, such as C, COBOL, and FORTRAN. APT-FORMS is an application development tool based on visual programming for generating forms and menus. Data Workbench is a set of window-based tools for application development, data manipulation, and report writing. It includes TRANSACT-SQL and VQL, a visual and menu-based version of SQL.

7.6.7 Architecture

SYBASE's functional architecture is based on the uniform interface model with SQL as single entry point. The architecture is functionally divided between the application functions (DataToolSet) and the database management functions (DataServer). The simple interface to the DataServer is TRANSACT-SQL, on top of which the DataToolSet is built.

SYBASE's process architecture follows the single-server model, with one-server process managed in a fully multithreaded way. SYBASE has a requester/server multithreaded architecture in which multiple DBMS server threads process the application transactions (the requesters). Each requester process, one per user, runs the DataToolSet; the unique server process runs the DataServer. The correspondence requester/server thread is neither one-to-one nor many-to-one, as in most other DBMSs, but many-to-many. This architecture enables the parallel processing of a request by multiple server threads while minimizing operating system overhead.

7.6.8 Distributed Database Management

SYBASE can be configured as a distributed DBMS where the database is distributed on multiple heterogeneous computers, each running the DataToolSet and/or the DataServer. SYBASE's approach to distributed database management is unique. Instead of adding another distributed database product that would run as a separate process, the DataServer is extended with distributed database capabilities so there is direct communication between remote server processes. This approach removes the traditional communication overhead between DBMS and DDBMS processes and allows efficient database management on multiprocessor configurations such as VAXclusters.

SYBASE is a homogeneous DDBMS with location transparency. It does not yet support replication transparency and distributed query optimization. For distributed database management, a two-step commit protocol is provided to guarantee, despite hardware or software failures, the atomicity of a transaction executed as multiple subtransactions. SYBASE soon will be able to support complete and heterogeneous distributed database management.

7.6.9 Operating Environments

SYBASE was designed primarily for DEC VAX computers under VMS and UNIX and SUN computers. It should run on the major DEC, IBM, and UNIX environments. The front end, DataToolSet, will be available on many computers, including the IBM PC.

7.7 UNIFY

Marketed by Unify Corporation, UNIFY is a high-performance RDBMS uniquely targeted for on-line transaction processing applications in the UNIX environments. UNIFY is available on all UNIX-based operating environments. High performance is attained by exploiting the features of the most recent versions of UNIX, such as shared memory for lock management, and bypassing UNIX functions, such as the file subsystem, which are inefficient for database support. UNIFY's access model includes four access methods, each optimized for a specific access type: hashing for random access, multiple attribute B-trees for range queries and wild-card search, links for joins, and buffered sequential access for efficient scan.

UNIFY comes with a number of form-oriented tools for data management, which access uniformly the DBMS through a unique low-level interface. UNIFY can be part of an integrated development environment, ACCEL, which combines the capabilities of application generators, windowing interfaces, 4GLs, and relational database management.

7.7.1 Data Definition

Database schema description can be entered through predefined screen formats where relations and attributes are introduced. UNIFY includes a capability to specify explicit links between the key of a relation and an attribute (foreign key) in another relation. This facilitates referential integrity control and increases the performance of join operations.

Schema modification (for example, addition of a relation or an attribute) can be done with the same screen format and may imply database restructuring. The main reason is that UNIFY stores the relation occurrences (tuples) in fixed-size disk areas for optimizing search time and storage utilization. Thus the empty slots left by deleting tuples in a relation are immediately reused. Variable-length text for documents and other textual data, and binary files, for video images and other bit-mapped data, are also supported. These are stored separately from the fixed-length tuples. Storage management algorithms reclaim space freed as a result of changes in field lengths.

A data dictionary, itself managed as a UNIFY database, keeps track of relations, attributes, links, users with their associated privileges, screen masks, menus, and programs.

7.7.2 Data Manipulation

UNIFY contains four data manipulation interfaces that access the DBMS through a uniform low-level interface composed of database interface routines:

1. At the lowest level, database interface routines can be directly called from C or RM/COBOL programs. These database interface routines are internal forms of nonprocedural statements.
2. A restricted version of SQL is supported for interactive use. The use of the UNIX shell language and a text editor enables the user to store parametric SQL or LST commands. The value of the parameters is given at run time. SQL is not embedded in host programming languages.
3. UNIFY allows the use of database access and SQL primitives from interrogation screens with two products: QUERY-BY-FORMS and SQL-BY-FORMS. Users describe the fields useful for selection. They do not need to be aware of the database schema.
4. An interrogation language, LST, enables users to select records that satisfy a multirelation predicate.

The queries defined in Chapter 2 can be expressed using UNIFY's SQL as follows. Note that all SQL statements must end with "/".

```
(R1)  SELECT PRODUCER.NAME
      FROM PRODUCER, WINE, HARVEST
      WHERE PRODUCER.P# = HARVEST.P# AND
            WINE.W# = HARVEST.W# AND
            VINEYARD = 'Julienas*'
            AND VINTAGE IN < 1982,1984 >/
```

```
(R2)  SELECT DRINKER.NAME
      FROM DRINKER, WINE, HARVEST
      WHERE DRINKER.D# = DRINK.D# AND
            WINE.W# = DRINK.W# AND
            VINEYARD = 'C*' AND
            [PERCENT = 0 OR PERCENT BETWEEN 11 AND 13]/
```

```
(R3)  SELECT VINEYARD, AVE (PERCENT)
      FROM  WINE
      GROUP BY VINEYARD
      HAVING MIN (PERCENT) > 12/
```

```
(I1)  INSERT INTO DRINKER (D#, NAME)
          SELECT PRODUCER.P#, PRODUCER.NAME
          FROM PRODUCER, WINE, HARVEST
          WHERE REGION = 'Bourgogne *' AND
                PRODUCER.P# = HARVEST.P# AND
                WINE.W# = HARVEST.W# AND
                VINTAGE = 1983/
```

```
(M1)  UPDATE HARVEST
      SET QTY = QTY * 1.1
      WHERE W# =
          SELECT WINE.W#
          FROM WINE, HARVEST
          WHERE WINE.W# = HARVEST.W# AND
                VINEYARD = 'Julienas *' AND
                VINTAGE = 1983/
```

(V1) UNIFY does not support relational views.

7.7.3 Semantic Data Control

Access authorizations are controlled in a centralized way. The DBA controls the users and specifies the screen masks that they can use (QBF, SQL BY FORM, data input masks). The administrator may restrict the manipulation rights by these screen masks and specify the programs that users can execute. In addition, a multilevel password-based protection mechanism is provided. User passwords can be given to individuals or groups of users. Datebase objects may be protected using authorizations associated with read and write access passwords.

The semantic integrity control is powerful. Domain constraints for predefined types (numerical of length n, string of p characters, data, time, amount in dollars, and so on), unique key constraints, and explicit links (referential constraints) can be specified.

7.7.4 Transaction Management

The explicit notion of transaction exists for application programs written in C or RM/COBOL. With QBF or SQL, the notion of transaction, which is limited to a single SQL query, is implicit. UNIFY applies a two-phase locking algorithm with deadlock prevention. UNIFY supports multiple levels of locking (relation, set of tuples, and tuple) for maximum concurrency.

UNIFY supports recovery after system or media failure via roll-forward recovery. A transaction log records the start and end of logical transactions, as well as the operations performed. To recover from a media failure, one restores the database from a backup tape and uses the REPLAY program to apply the after-images contained in the log.

7.7.5 Query Processing and Storage Model

The storage model supported by UNIFY provides four access methods: hashing, B-trees, links, and sequential access. Hashing is the most efficient way to organize data that must be randomly accessed. Multiple attribute B-trees are most efficient for range queries and wild-card search and are also good for random access. Links connecting relations on a join attribute are implemented by explicit pointers and provide fast processing of joins and efficient referential integrity control. Buffered sequential access performs fast sequential scan using a large buffer for read-ahead.

The access methods are used by the optimizer for efficiently performing database access routines, particularly selection and join operations. Buffered sequential scan is systematically chosen for queries with poor selectivity (returning a large result). If access methods are not available, the optimizer may decide to build them dynamically for speeding up expensive joins. The optimization does not include the ordering of operations within an SQL statement; rather, they are interpreted in the bottom-up order.

7.7.6 Additional Tools

UNIFY has a limited set of products for application development: different languages (QBF, SQL, LST), menu and screen manager (MENUH, SFORM, ENTER), and report generator (REPORT, RPT). All of these tools are accessible in a uniform way through the menu system. Although this set of tools provides some 4GL capabilities, it lacks completeness and power to allow the development of complex applications without having to write COBOL or C programs.

To remedy this deficiency, Unify Corp. has recently introduced ACCEL, a powerful development environment integrating the UNIFY RDBMS, a visually oriented application generator, a 4GL, and a windowing manager. UNIFY has been improved to support efficiently ACCEL. The application generator, highly interactive, allows the developer to paint and modify screen forms, define screen windows, specify data access, create default menus, and define the synchronization of forms. The 4GL is a nonprocedural database language with control logic. It complements and understands the application generator. The window manager provides the ability to design end user interfaces of overlapping windows rather than the menus generated by MENUH.

7.7.7 Architectures

The functional architecture of UNIFY is based on the uniform interface model, with database access routines as single entry point for all data manipulation interfaces. The system is implemented on UNIX and written in C language, as is UNIX. The process organization of UNIFY is based on the process model. In most cases, there are two UNIX processes running per active user: the menu handler, which presents the user with a series of options; and a UNIFY program, such as ENTER, SQL, or LST, which performs database operations.

To attain performance, UNIFY exploits the operating system capabilities when possible. The shared memory feature of UNIX System V is used for fast interprocess communication. Furthermore UNIFY bypasses the UNIX file management system, optimized for small text files, and directly manages disk access and file allocation by exploiting the UNIX RAW device capability. As a result, one level of interface between UNIFY and UNIX is eliminated. Another advantage is that large files can be efficiently managed by UNIFY and span up to eight disks.

7.7.8 Operating Environments

Because it runs efficiently on UNIX, a successful operating system, UNIFY is available on well over one-hundred different computers.

7.8 Conclusion

In this chapter, we have presented six relational database systems — DATACOM/DB, FOCUS, SYBASE, NOMAD, ORACLE, and UNIFY. With DB2, INGRES, SABRINA, and SUPRA, they constitute the set of products summarized and compared in Chapter 2.

8
RDBMSs for MICROCOMPUTERS

8.1 Introduction

Database management is one of the most important areas of software for micro-computers. A large and increasing number of database management systems are available on microcomputers. These systems are used primarily in business applications, such as accounting, inventory control, and client billing. They range from simple file systems to relational database systems. None is fully relational according to the definition given in Chapter 1, but many exhibit powerful relational features.

The growth of relational systems for microcomputers stems from two trends. The first is the development of software programs specifically designed for running on microcomputers. These programs are constantly evolving to exploit the increasing power of microcomputers and to satisfy requirements of a larger number of users. The second trend is the adaptation of database systems designed for mainframes to run on microcomputers. The rapid progress in hardware (microprocessors, main memories, hard disks) has led to the development of microcomputers performing more than 1 million instructions per second (1 MIPS) and having one or more megabytes of main memory. Some microcomputers today are more powerful than minicomputers were several years ago. Therefore RDBMSs designed for mainframes and minicomputers, such as most of those introduced in Chapter 2, have been adapted to run on microcomputers. DATACOM/DB, FOCUS, INGRES, ORACLE, SYBASE and UNIFY are examples of systems of which a microversion, much simpler than the mainframe version, exists.

Database management systems for microcomputers offer less functionality and less performance then those designed for mainframes. There are five main differences. First, there are important size limitations, such as number of relations, relation sizes, and number of open relations. These limitations reflect the hardware capabilities (main memory, hard disk) and the implementation choices of the DBMS. Second, they generally provide limited data control facilities, such as view management, protection, and semantic integrity control. Third, the database language is rarely embedded in other programming languages such as C or COBOL; however, results of database programs can be stored as files to be converted in a format suitable for another programming language. Fourth, transaction management functions, such as concurrency control and recovery management, are generally limited. One reason is that microcomputers are often single user, which precludes the need for concurrency control. Those that are multiuser can handle only a few users. Another reason is that recovery management is hard to implement on small computers and would make the system too inefficient. Fifth, physical access methods and internal algorithms are generally poor. Data structures are often flat files with indexes. Also query optimization is limited.

Database management systems for microcomputers have at least two strong advantages. First, their price is about one hundred times less than that of DBMSs on larger computers. Therefore their potential market is very large. Second, they offer sophisticated and user friendly interfaces, which use forms and graphics to manipulate the schema and data. They have good screen and report management facilities. They often include an application generator. Sometimes they can be interfaced with spread-sheet programs that offer many built-in functions for data analysis (such as financial, arithmetic, and trigonometric functions). Also many spread-sheet programs now include a relational database capability for storing and retrieving data.

In this chapter, we present four representatives of "relational" database management systems for microcomputers. We first detail two successful systems, dBASE III PLUS and KNOWLEDGEMAN/2, according to the following plan: (1) main features, (2) data description (manipulation of schema, indexes, and so on), (3) data control (data protection, semantic integrity control, and view management), (4) data manipulation (opening of database, data entry, data retrieval, updates, copy, sort and join, calculations), (5) report generation (management of reports and other forms), (6) application development (tools for programming and generating database applications), and (7) interfaces with other systems (network, spread sheet, and so on). Then we describe two other successful DBMSs: R:BASE 5000 for the IBM PC and compatibles and EXCEL for the Macintosh. Although these two systems are interesting and powerful, we provide a description shorter than those for dBASE III PLUS and KNOWLEDGE-MAN/2 since they have many features in common. R:BASE 5000 is a rather complete RDBMS. EXCEL does not provide full database capabilities. Rather it is a work-sheet package integrating several functions such as spread sheet, main memory database, and graphics. We include it in this chapter because it is representative of the current trend of integrated programs for microcomputers.

8.2 dBASE III PLUS

dBASE III PLUS is the most recent version of the dBASE systems (dBASE II and dBASE III) marketed by Ashton Tate. The dBASE systems are among the most popular database management systems available on PC-DOS and MS-DOS environments.

dBASE III PLUS exhibits several relational features. In particular, it supports views, an interactive language and its own programming language, indexed files, a multiuser version for use in a network environment, a screen manager, and an application generator. Up to ten relations can be used simultaneously and joined on a common field. With all these features, dBASE III PLUS is a powerful and simple tool suitable for small business applications.

Some relational features are missing. A relation's keys cannot be specified by the user; a sequential number is assigned to each tuple by the system. One advantage is that tuple uniqueness is automatically enforced. There is, however, no additional capability to specify user-defined key constraints. Finally dBASE III PLUS does not support referential integrity.

More complete presentation of the dBASE systems can be found in [Kruglinski 83, McCharen 84, Simpson 86].

8.2.1 Main Features

A dBASE III PLUS database is a single relation. The domains can be fixed-length character string, numerical, Boolean, date, and variable-length character string (of up to 5K bytes). The notions of database, relation, and file are synonymous. Therefore *tuple* and *record* are also synonymous terms. The maximum size of a record is 65535 bytes.

The maximum size of a file is limited by the disk size. A database (a relation) is stored in a unique file. Up to ten relations can be simultaneously opened and linked using common attributes that define relationships. Two relations can be joined on any attribute to produce a third relation. Views derived by join and projection are supported in retrieval mode.

A file can have up to seven (secondary) indexes. Accessing a relation can be done by sequential scan or via index. The indexes currently opened are automatically updated.

dBASE III PLUS offers two types of interface: an interactive language for data manipulation and a programming language for developing dBASE applications. The interactive language can be used in two modes: through the assistance of pull-down menus or directly by the dot-prompt method. With the first mode, the user is assisted by a menu of options with which all the dBASE commands can be used. The main menu has eight options, including set up, create, and update. When one of these options is highlighted, the corresponding submenu pulls down. This assisted mode relieves the user of having to remember command syntax. Pressing the ESC key from the main menu makes the menu disappear and returns to the second mode, where commands may be typed directly at the dot prompt. This mode is faster but requires a good knowledge of the interactive language.

The interactive language is based on commands of the form <Verb> [<Scope>] [<Attributes>] . . . [<Condition>]. *Verb* indicates the action to be done on the opened relation. *Scope* defines a subset of tuples affected by the action (for instance, the first ten tuples). The *attributes* indicate the relevant data items. *Condition* specifies selection of relevant tuples.

The programming language is a structured language with data manipulation primitives, constructors such as DO WHILE, DO CASE, and IF, dialogue and editing capabilities, and a large number of built-in functions.

dBASE III PLUS can run in a local area network (LAN) environment. Several PCs can be interconnected such that one PC is the file server and the others are workstations that can access the file server. The file server must use the multiuser version of dBASE III PLUS.

Finally, dBASE III Plus comes with a number of built-in functions for aiding application development: screen manager, report generator, and application generator.

8.2.2 Data Description

The definition of a relation (also called database or file) is done with the command CREATE <file_name>. Then the following message asks the user to specify the relation schema:

> Field Name   Type Width Decimal
> **1.**

Field numbers like 1 above are automatically generated. For each attribute, the user must enter its name, its domain (C = character, N = numerical, D = date, M = memo or variable-length string, L = logical or Boolean), its maximum width, and the number of decimal places for numerical attributes. Once all attributes have been defined, it is possible to switch to data entry mode.

Information about an existing relation can be displayed by the command DISPLAY STRUCTURE <file_name>. The schema of a relation can be modified by the command MODIFY STRUCTURE <file_name>, which is followed by three actions. First, the system copies the specified relation into a backup file and deletes the relation. Second, the user interacts with the system to provide the new relation schema. Third, the backup file is read into the new relation by copying only the attributes whose name has not changed. New attributes are initialized to a default value.

A relation is stored in a sequential file. Secondary indexes can be defined with the command INDEX ON <Attribute(s)> TO <index name>, which creates an index on the opened relation. An index is a file of records [attribute(s), tuple number] ordered on attribute(s). Indexes must be active (open) in order to be updated automatically. When several indexes are open, the first selected one determines the ordering for data display.

8.2.3 Data Manipulation

In order to be used, a relation must first be opened by the command USE <file_name> INDEX <index_list>, where the list of indexes is defined on file_name. Up to ten relations can be simultaneously open. The distinction between different open relations is done using the SELECT command with the letters A through J or the numbers 1 through 10. For instance, the opening of relations HARVEST and WINE of the WINES database of Chapter 2 could be specified as:

```
SELECT A
USE WINE INDEX WINDEX1
SELECT B
USE HARVEST
```

In subsequent commands, A → and B → refer, respectively, to tuple variables of relations WINE and HARVEST.

The addition of tuples at the end of a relation requires the use of the APPEND command. This command opens the EDIT mode to insert the next tuple. The EDIT mode can be opened in two other cases: after a relation has been created and with the command EDIT <record_number>, which selects an existing tuple for subsequent modification. In the EDIT mode, the relation schema and the attribute values of the current tuple are vertically displayed on the screen. Control keys permit movement of the cursor within the record attributes and movement back and forward one record. New data values can be entered in front of attribute names. A specific record can be made current by the commands GOTO <record_number>, GO TOP (go to relation beginning), and GO BOTTOM (go to relation end).

The manipulation of relation tuples can also be done with the Browse option, which allows the user to scroll through the relation displayed as a two-dimension table horizontally and vertically to manipulate tuples.

The selection of tuples in a relation can be specified with qualifications of the form [<scope>] [<attribute>] . . . [FOR <Condition>]. *Scope* defines the scope of the selection (all tuples, NEXT N tuples after the current record, RECORD N). Some attributes of the attribute list can be calculated; that is, they are the result of arithmetic or aggregate functions applied to the relation's attributes. The *condition* is a logical formula with union, intersection, and/or negation of simple single-attribute predicates. This type of qualification can be used by several commands. Examples of the LIST command applied to the WINE relation are:

```
LIST ALL
LIST VINEYARD VINTAGE FOR PERCENT > 12 .AND. PERCENT > 13

LIST NEXT 2 VINEYARDS
```

The results are displayed on the screen.

Selective update commands (CHANGE, DELETE, REPLACE, and others) also employ qualifications. Examples of selective updates of the WINE relation are:

```
CHANGE ALL FIELD PERCENT FOR VINEYARD = "Volnay"
DELETE NEXT 5 FOR PERCENT > 12
REPLACE ALL VINTAGE WITH 1982, PERCENT WITH 12
```

In the first example, the new values of PERCENT will be asked of the user. The delete command marks the tuples relevant for deletion. Then the user can review those tuples and suppress them with the PACK command.

In order to be used in the same command, relationships between relations must be established. A relationship is specified between two relations with the SET RELATION command by giving the name of the joining attribute. This name must be identical in both relations. Therefore join predicates do not have to be given in the subsequent commands that retrieve data from several relations. The following example illustrates a complex query on the WINES database introduced in Chapter 2: "List the vineyards, with their quantity and producer name for the vintage 1982":

```
SELECT A
USE HARVEST
SELECT B
USE WINE
SELECT C
USE PRODUCER
SELECT A
SET RELATION TO W# INTO WINE
SET RELATION TO P# INTO PRODUCER
LIST B→ VINEYARD, QTY, C→ NAME FOR B→VINTAGE = 1982
```

dBASE III PLUS also includes a JOIN command for joining two relations based on a more complex condition. Two other commands permit the creation of a new relation from an existing one: COPY and SORT. The COPY routine copies a subset of a relation (by projection and restriction) in a target file for which the format is specified. For example, the copy of attributes VINEYARD and PERCENT for the wines of 1982 will be done by:

COPY TO WINE1 ALL VINEYARD, PERCENT FOR VINTAGE = 1982

The SORT command produces a sorted file from a base relation according to one or more attributes, each in increasing or decreasing order. The SORT command exploits the available indexes (implemented as sorted files) when possible.

8.2.4 Data Control

dBASE III PLUS includes some features for view management, data protection for the network environment, and type checking on data entry.

A view can be defined on two relations by join and projection. The relations must have a common joining attribute of identical name. Views can be queried as relations for retrieval but cannot be updated. Many different views can be defined on the same relations.

dBASE III PLUS provides security facilities when it is used on a network system, where several workstations may access the same file server via the network. Three levels of protection are available. First, users must be identified and authenticated through the log-in security system (user name and password). Second, access privileges can be granted by the network administrator. Privileges (Extend, Delete, Read, Change) are specified over tuples or even some attributes. Third, data on disk can be encrypted, thereby becoming unintelligible to unauthorized users.

Semantic integrity control is restricted to checking that the types of entered data agree with those defined in the relation schema (characters, numerical, date, Boolean, and variable-length strings).

8.2.5 Report Generation

dBASE III PLUS contains a report generator that produces tables with titles, totals, and subtotals from data retrieved from the database. A report format can be specified with the following command: REPORT FORM <report_name> [<scope>] [FOR <condition>] [TO PRINT] [PLAIN].

Like most other dBASE commands, report definition can be helped by the menu assistant. The definition of a report requires the specification of print options, titles, subtitles, totals, subtotals and subsubtotals, and so on. The report format is saved in a file and can be subsequently modified. A report can be printed by specifying parameter values for scope and condition. Therefore different reports of the same format can be generated from the same database. A predefined report format exists for mailing labels; thus custom mailing labels can be defined easily. Furthermore labels can be printed in sorted order using existing indexes.

8.2.6 Application Development

Applications can be developed with the screen manager or the application generator or by writing programs in the dBASE programming language.

The screen manager allows the definition of custom screens for adding and editing data. It provides an alternative to the default screen format of the EDIT mode. Screens can be specified simply by drawing boxes. dBASE III PLUS handles multipage screens. Furthermore with a color monitor, screens can be colored so that data editing is easier. Screen formats are saved for future use or modification.

The application generator allows the user to specify simple applications easily. An application can be defined by giving the name of the relations, indexes, screen formats, report formats, label formats, and their dependencies. From the application definition, the application generator produces the corresponding application program automatically in dBASE programming language.

The development of more complex applications must be done with the dBASE structured programming language. An application is programmed using command files < file _ name > .CMD, which can be run by entering the command DO < file _ name > . CMD. A command file can also have DO commands, which permit several programs to be called (considered as subprograms) with one. The RETURN command in a program returns to the calling command file. A command file also includes four types of commands:

1. Data manipulation commands as presented in Section 8.2.3.
2. Variable management commands to pass parameters between various commands and subprograms.
3. Commands for controlling the program structure.
4. Commands for managing the dialogues and outputs.

Up to 256 variables can be used in a program. Variables must be typed between numerical, character string, Boolean, and so on and assigned a value. Assigning a variable can be done in two ways: (1) with the instruction STORE < expression > TO < variable >, where *expression* is built from attributes of the current tuple by applying calculations, and (2) with aggregate functions (COUNT, SUM, and so on) applied to tuple attributes and postfixed by TO < variable >. The control commands — DO WHILE, DO CASE, and IF ELSE — permit programs to be structured.

Many commands for managing the dialogues and outputs are available. Parameters and options can be set with the SET command. Possible parameters include report titles (Heading), margins, and date; the options specify whether to use the console, the printer, or a trace on a file (ALTERNATE). Input commands are INPUT, ACCEPT, and WAIT TO <variable>. The output command is @ m,n SAY < parameter >, which prints parameter at position (m,n) on the screen.

Finally, dBASE III PLUS includes a number of basic math functions and string functions.

To illustrate application programming with dBASE III PLUS, Fig. 8.1 presents a program simulating a bar offering wines stored in the WINE relation. The choice is indicated by the wine number. If the wine does not exist, the message "SORRY! I DON'T HAVE THIS WINE" is displayed. If the wine exists, the user is asked to specify the quantity. If the wine is available in sufficient quantity, the message "ENJOY" is displayed. Otherwise the message "SORRY: I HAVE NOT ENOUGH OF xxx yyy" is displayed (*xxx* is the vineyard and *yyy* the vintage). The program iterates while the user answers "YES" to the question "WOULD YOU LIKE SOMETHING ELSE?" Fig. 8.2 illustrates a possible execution of the program.

8.2.7 Interfaces with Other Systems

dBASE III PLUS can be interfaced with other systems, such as local area networks, spread sheets, and word processors.

The configuration in a computer network, such as the IBM PC network, consists of several computers: one file server and several workstations. The file server must have at least 640K RAM and a hard disk. The file server is multiuser. It can be accessed concurrently by the workstations via the network. The file server implements concurrency control by locking entire relations. Each workstation must have its own copy of the dBASE ACCESS program. A workstation must have at least 384K RAM and does not need a hard disk. Using a computer network allows several cheap workstations (including PC with floppy disks) to share common resources (such as, one PC XT with hard disk, printer, and plotter).

dBASE III PLUS can be interfaced with spread-sheet programs and word processors by copying dBASE files to another software format using the COPY and APPEND commands.

8.3   KNOWLEDGEMAN/2

KNOWLEDGEMAN/2, another popular database system, is marketed by Micro Data Base Systems, which also produces the sophisticated MDBS III.

```
 1: SET CONSOLE ON
 2: SET MARGIN TO 10
 3: CLEAR
 4: ERASE
 5: @ 1,1 SAY "*** HI - WELCOME TO THE BAR DBASE ***"
 6: USE WINE
 7: SET CONSOLE OFF
 8: COUNT ALL TO MAX
 9: STORE "YES" TO ITERATION
10: SET CONSOLE ON
11: DO WHILE "YES" $ ITERATION
12:      @ 3,1 say "**WHICH WINE WOULD YOU LIKE TO TRY
                BETWEEN:"
13:      DISP ALL VINEYARD, VINTAGE
14:      INPUT "** INDICATE YOUR CHOICE BY A WINE NUMBER?"
                TO ANSWER
15:      DO CASE
16:          CASE ANSWER > 0 .AND. ANSWER < = MAX
17:             GO ANSWER
18:             INPUT "** WHAT QUANTITY DO YOU WANT?" TO
                    SERVICE
19:             IF QTY - SERVICE > 0
20:                 @ MAX+8,1 SAY "** ENJOY **"
21:                 SET CONSOLE OFF
22:                 REPLACE QTY WITH QTY - SERVICE
23:                 SET CONSOLE ON
24:             ELSE
25:                 @ MAX+8,1 SAY "**SORRY: I DO NOT HAVE
                        ENOUGH OF"
26:                 @ MAX+8,35 SAY VINEYARD
27:                 @ MAX+8,47 SAY VINTAGE
28:             ENDIF
29:          CASE ANSWER < = 0 .OR. ANSWER > MAX
30:             @ MAX+7,1 SAY "** SORRY! I DON'T HAVE THIS
                    WINE **"
31:          ENDCASE
32:      ACCEPT "WOULD YOU LIKE SOMETHING ELSE?" TO ITERATION
33:      ERASE
34: ENDDO
35: RETURN
```

FIGURE 8.1 Example of dBASE program.

```
*** HI - WELCOME TO THE BAR DBASE ***
** WHICH WINE WOULD YOU LIKE TO TRY BETWEEN: :
00001          VOLNAY              1978
00002          MACON               1980
00003          POUILLY             1978
00004          CHANTURGUES         1979
** INDICATE YOUR CHOICE BY A WINE NUMBER? : 2
    2
** WHAT QUANTITY DO YOU WANT? :   15
    15
** SORRY:   I DO NOT HAVE ENOUGH OF MACON      1980
WOULD YOU LIKE SOMETHING ELSE? :   YES

** WHICH WINE WOULD YOU LIKE TO TRY BETWEEN:
00001          VOLNAY              1978
00002          MACON               1980
00003          POUILLY             1978
00004          CHANTURGUES         1979

** INDICATE YOUR CHOICE BY A WINE NUMBER? : 1
    1
** WHAT QUANTITY DO YOU WANT? :   15
    15
** ENJOY! **
WOULD YOU LIKE SOMETHING ELSE? :   YES

** WHICH WINE WOULD YOU LIKE TO TRY BETWEEN:
00001          VOLNAY              1978
00002          MACON               1980
00003          POUILLY             1978
00004          CHANTURGUES         1979

** INDICATE YOUR CHOICE BY A WINE NUMBER? : 7
    7
** SORRY!   I DON'T HAVE THIS WINE **
WOULD YOU LIKE SOMETHING ELSE?:   NO
```

FIGURE 8.2 Example of dBASE program execution.

KNOWLEDGEMAN/2 is available on PC-DOS and MS-DOS operating systems.

KNOWLEDGEMAN/2 (K-MAN/2 for short) exhibits relational features close to SQL and to those of dBASE III PLUS. It offers a nonprocedural interactive language close to SQL and its own programming language. K-MAN/2 is particularly suited for handling large relations; the limits are 255 attributes per tuple, 65,535 bytes per attribute, and the maximum size of a file limited by the disk size. When some number is constrained only by the hardware capacity, we will qualify it as *unlimited* for short. A relation is stored in a file on which an unlimited number of indexes may be defined. K-MAN/2 supports a multiuser version and access to remote computers. Furthermore it includes many tools for helping application development: screen manager, spread-sheet program, statistical and graphical capabilities, and application generator. Thus K-MAN/2 can be viewed as a large set of integrated programs.

Several relational features are missing. As with dBASE systems, the keys of relations cannot be specified by the user but are assigned by the system. Views and integrity constraints other than domain constraints are not supported.

Detailed information about K-MAN/2 can be found in [Roeder 84, Roeder 86, MDBS 86].

8.3.1 Main Features

K-MAN/2 manages a database composed of relations called tables. The domains are fixed-length character strings, integers, reals, Booleans, and variable-length character strings (of up to 64K bytes). An unlimited number of relations can be simultaneously open and queried (for example, joined). A relation is stored in a unique file and can be indexed. A relation can be accessed by sequential scan or by an index. All indexes are automatically updated when the relation is modified.

K-MAN/2 offers two types of interface: (1) an interactive language for data entry, editing, and retrieval and (2) a portable programming language. The interactive language can be used in three modes: with a natural language interface, using the menu-based system, or directly by typing commands at the dot prompt. With the first mode, the user can query the system with simple English requests. The requests are translated into the interactive language. A built-in vocabulary of 500 words is provided and can be extended by the user. With the menu-based system, the user selects the commands by moving the cursor through the menu options using control function keys. A command area at the bottom of the screen shows the commands generated by choosing menu options. With the last mode, the use enters the commands directly at the dot prompt.

The general format of interative commands is close to that of SQL: <Verb> <Result> [IN/FROM <Object>] . . . [WHERE/FOR <Condition>] [<Option>]. *Verb* indicates the action to do on the relation(s) specified as object. *Result* tells the attributes to display or to modify. *Condition* permits the selection of some tuples. The manipulation of several relations through joins requires several nested FROM statements. Furthermore a scope (which is not part of SQL) can be specified. Some other commands have a format similar to those of dBASE. The interaction with K-MAN/2 is done through a session. The status (context) of a session can be saved on hard disk before exiting the system and restored later.

The programming language is a structured language with data access primitives, constructs such as WHILE DO, TEST . . . CASE, IF . . . THEN . . . ELSE . . . , dialogue and editing capabilities, and many built-in functions.

In addition, K-MAN/2 includes several integrated components that use relations: spread-sheet program, screen manager, report generator, graph generator, text processor, and statistical analysis commands.

K-MAN/2 supports a multiuser version for use in a local area network environment where several PCs are interconnected. K-MAN/2 has also a GATEWAY facility for establishing communication links with remote computers.

8.3.2 Data Description

The definition of a relation schema is done with the command DEFINE <relation>, where *relation* is the name of the created relation. Then the name of the file in which the relation is to be stored must be specified. Thus K-MAN/2 does not confuse the notions of relation and file. For each attribute, the user must specify its domain (STR = character string, NUM = numerical) with the length and the format. The system automatically adds to a relation a Boolean attribute MARK, initialized to false, which is useful for marking deleted tuples. The schema of a relation can be updated with the command REDEFINE <Relation>, which asks the user the new description of the relation.

The internal schema of a K-MAN/2 database includes sequential files and index files. Indexes can be dynamically created on an existing relation with the command INDEX <File> FOR <Relation> BY AZ/ZA <Attribute>. The option AZ/ZA indicates ascending (AZ) or descending (ZA) sort order.

The deletion of a relation is possible with the command DESTROY <Relation>.

8.3.3 Data Manipulation

Each application has a working context defined by a set of variables that maintains the working options chosen. The main options are as follows (the default value is indicated in parentheses):

- E.DECI = number of decimal places (5).
- E.LSTR = length of character strings (15).
- E.OCON = output displayed on screen (TRUE).
- E.ODSK = output written to disk (FALSE).
- E.PAUS = stop display when screen is full (FALSE).

The environment variables may be changed by simple assignment. For instance, writing output to disk is specified by E.ODSK = TRUE.

The working context also includes entry forms, report definitions, and the macrocommands associated with the application. In order to avoid reconstruction for each session, the working context can be saved in a file and loaded at the subsequent session.

Similarly to dBASE, the use of a relation and its index is specified by the command:

    USE <Relation> [WITH <Index-name>]

The addition of tuples at the end of a relation is done using the command CREATE FOR <Relation>. This command opens the EDIT mode to insert subsequent tuples. The EDIT mode can also be invoked with the command BROWSE <Relation> for modifying existing tuples.

The EDIT mode displays vertically on the screen the relation schema and the value of the current tuple if there is one. Control keys permit moving the cursor within attributes of the current tuple or between different tuples. The type of attribute values entered is checked. A sequential record number is automatically assigned to each new tuple.

The retrieval of data can be done with two different modes: one tuple at a time (procedural) and a set at a time (nonprocedural). The tuple-at-a-time mode is invoked with the following statement:

    OBTAIN [FIRST/LAST/PRIOR [n] /NEXT [n] / n]
       [FROM <Relation>] [FOR/WHERE <Condition>]

A current pointer indicates the last tuple accessed in the relation. Moving between records is similar to CODASYL navigation. n is a record number that can be absolute or relative if used with PRIOR or NEXT. The condition is a Boolean expression of single-attribute predicates. Character string comparisons are supported. For example, the first wine of a vineyard starting with V is expressed as:

    OBTAIN FIRST WINES FOR VINEYARD IN ["V"]

The next three wines can then be obtained as follows:

    OBTAIN NEXT 3 WINES

The results are displayed vertically as in the EDIT mode.

The set-at-a-time mode is used with an SQL-like language. The general structure of the retrieval statement is:

    SELECT [UNIQUE] [<Attribute expression>]
          [FROM <Relation>]
          [WHERE/FOR <Condition>][<Scope>]

[GROUP BY <Attribute> ...]
[ORDER BY [AZ/ZA] <Attribute> ...]

Most of the clauses are similar to those of SQL. The Scope (not in SQL) specifies a subset of the relation: ALL, CURRENT, NEXT [n], PRIOR [n], or RANGE [n1, n2].

The following simple examples illustrate the use of the SELECT statement for retrieving information from the WINE relation:

1. Display all wines:
   SELECT W#, VINEYARD, VINTAGE, PERCENT FROM WINE
2. Give the vineyard and vintage of the wines with a percentage greater than 12.
   SELECT VINEYARD, VINTAGE FROM WINE FOR PERCENT > 12
3. Give the vineyard, the vintage, and the logarithm of percentage for the wines with a percentage between 11 and 12 and between the numbers 1 through 10:
   SELECT VINEYARD, VINTAGE, LOG (PERCENT)
   FROM WINE
   FOR PERCENT > 11 AND PERCENT < 12
   RANGE 1, 10

Retrieving data from several relations requires several FROM clauses and join predicates. Relation names may prefix attribute names to distinguish the names that are identical in different relations. For example, the following command, expressed on relations DRINKER and DRINK from the WINES database defined in Chapter 2, retrieves the drinkers having drunk at least one wine in quantity greater than 10:

SELECT NAME
   FROM DRINKER FROM DRINK
   FOR D# = DRINK.D# AND DRINK.QTY > 10

The set-oriented updating of a relation can be done with the CHANGE command, which also uses qualifications of the form [<Condition>] and [<Scope>]. For example, increasing the percentage of wines "Volnay" by 1 percent can be expressed as:

CHANGE PERCENT IN WINE TO PERCENT * 1.01
   FOR VINEYARD = "Volnay"

The deletion of tuples matching a given qualification is done with the statement MARK, which marks true all the tuples to delete. The actual deletion of the marked tuples requires the use of the command COMPRESS < Relation >. Thus tuples to be deleted can be displayed before deletion.

K-MAN/2 includes two other routines, CONVERT and SORT, for generating a file from existing relations. The CONVERT routine permits selecting data from several relations like a SELECT command and writing the result into a file for which a format (called image) is specified or into a spread sheet for which cells are specified or into an array for which dimensions are specified. The SORT routine permits writing a relation sorted on several attributes into a file.

8.3.4 Data Control

K-MAN/2 provides extensive data security features to protect data from multiple users. It also supports type checking when data are entered.

Data protection is of major importance when the system can be accessed by more than one user. Three security levels are supported. First, the access to K-MAN/2 itself is protected by the log-in capability that requires users to enter name and password. Second, relations, attributes, and work-sheet cells may be protected through read and write access codes. Protected data can be accessed by a user only if his or her access codes match those of the data. Third, all tuples are automatically encrypted and therefore unintelligible to unauthorized users. In addition, procedures can be stored in encrypted format.

Semantic integrity control is limited to checking that the types of inserted attributes match those specified at relation definition time.

8.3.5 Report Generation

Many kinds of reports and documents can be quickly generated with the following optional capabilities integrated with K-MAN/2: report writer, text processor, form generator, and graphics.

Custom reports can be prepared with K-REPORT. Designing a report is specified by the command DESIGN < report _ name >, which initiates a question-answering mode in which the structure of the report is specified. The following information characterizes the structure of a report: report header, page headers, group and subgroup headings, selected information, group and subgroup totals, page footers and totals, grand totals, and report footer. Up to twenty-six group levels are available. The report format is saved in a file. A report can be printed with the command REPORT < report _ name > with the specification of the selection and of the grouping and sorting attributes. Thus efficient reports of any format may be generated. Report formats can also be edited. In addition, K-MAN/2 has a predefined report type for mailing labels, similar to that of dBASE.

Letters and documents may be generated using K-TEXT, with which text information can be merged with information in the K-MAN/2 database. Information can be retrieved from the database with all the capabilities of the interactive data language.

K-MAN/2 provides a facility, K-PAINT, for composing forms to be used for data entry or report generation. The definition of a form requires the use of the following commands:

```
FORM  <form_name>
          AT m,n PUT  <Parameters>
          AT m,n GET  <Parameters>
          .
          .
          .
END FORM
```

The form with slots for attribute values can be displayed with the command PUTFORM. Data can then be printed according to the form using the command PRINT <form_name>.

K-MAN/2 also includes a statistical analysis capability that returns to the user various statistics (sum, average, and variance, for example) for each attribute in the result of a SELECT query. The statistical abstract is automatically given if the option E.STAT is set to true. Furthermore the command STAT can be used like SELECT to produce only the statistical results of the query.

Finally the results of retrieval queries can be displayed as graphical forms using a specific capability called K-GRAPH. K-GRAPH permits the drawing of histograms, diagrams, curves, and charts with eight different colors.

8.3.6 Application Development

For developing applications, K-MAN/2 offers a screen manager, an application generator, and its own application programming language.

The screen manager permits the definition of custom screens for editing data. Screens can be defined by composing the forms for editing data with a capability called K-PAINT. K-PAINT can be used with the menu-based system. It accepts color form definitions and form superposition. Form definitions may be saved.

The application generator helps the user in defining simple applications rapidly through the menu-based system. When the application is defined, the application generator produces an application program in the K-MAN/2 programming language.

The K-MAN/2 programming language is a structured language. An application can be programmed using command files of the form <file_name> . IPF, which can be executed with the command PERFORM "<file_name> . IPF". A command file may itself contain PERFORMs for executing subprograms. Returning to the calling command file is done by specifying RETURN. A command file also includes four types of commands:

1. Data management commands as defined in Section 8.3.3.
2. Variable assignments.
3. Program control instructions.
4. Facilities for managing inputs/outputs.

K-MAN/2 variables have a name chosen by the programmer and typed when they are first assigned a value. K-MAN/2 supports numerical, character string, and Boolean typed variables. Assigning a variable may be done with the traditional = sign or by prefixing the assignment with LET. After it is assigned, a variable can be used in any instruction similar to the attribute values of a current tuple.

The structure of a program can be controlled with the standard commands WHILE DO, TEST . . . CASE, and IF . . . THEN . . . ELSE.

K-MAN/2 also includes a number of commands for handling dialogues and data outputs. Environment parameters and options can be set with assignment commands. Possible parameters are the standard length for character strings, the use of the printer, and margins for reports. The output command, [AT m,n] OUTPUT < Parameter >, displays the parameter at the cursor position specified by row m and column n (m and n can be computed by expressions). The input command, [AT m,n] INPUT < Variable > [USING < Image >] [WITH < Message >], prints the message and assigns the entered data to the variable. Furthermore forms can be used in a program for entering or displaying data.

Finally, K-MAN/2 includes a number of built-in functions for standard calculations, string manipulation, conversion, and so on.

To illustrate application programming with K-MAN/2, we have given in Fig. 8.3 the program equivalent to the dBASE program of Fig. 8.1. This program simulates a bar offering the wines available in relation WINES. The main difference with the dBASE program is that the choice of a wine must be indicated by the attribute NW since the system-defined record number cannot be manipulated by program. Fig. 8.4 presents an execution of that program.

8.3.7 Interface with Other Systems

K-MAN/2 is integrated in the C programming language. In addition, it can interface to programs such as spread sheet, word processor, and local area network.

K-MAN/2 is the first microcomputer DBMS to integrate the DBMS functions into a general-purpose programming language. Many K-MAN/2 functions can be called from C programs using K-C. K-C supports most data manipulation commands for creating, modifying, and deleting tuples. K-C is accessible from a variety of C compilers.

```
E.LSTR = 45
E.OCON = TRUE
E.OPRN = FALSE
CLEAR
AT 1,15 OUTPUT "= = = = = EXECUTION EXAMPLE = = = = ="
E.PMAR = 10
AT 2,15 OUTPUT "*** HI - WELCOME TO THE BAR KMAN/2 ***"
USE WINE
E.OPRN = FALSE
ITERATION = "YES"
WHILE "YES" = ITERATION DO
     AT 3,1 OUTPUT "WHICH WINE WOULD YOU LIKE TO TEST
          BETWEEN :"
     E.STAT = FALSE
     SELECT W#, VINEYARD, VINTAGE FROM WINE
     ANSWER = 0
     INPUT ANSWER USING "dd" WITH "** PRECISE THE NUMBER?"
     E.STAT = TRUE
     E.OCON = FALSE
     STAT W# FROM WINE FOR W# = ANSWER
     TEST (£CNT = 1
       CASE TRUE :
          OBTAIN FROM WINE FOR W# = ANSWER
          SERVICE = 0
          E.OCON = TRUE
          INPUT SERVICE USING "dd" WITH "WHAT QUANTITY DO
               YOU WANT?"
          IF QTY - SERVICE > 0 THEN
             OUTPUT "** ENJOY **"
             CHANGE QTY IN WINE TO QTY - SERVICE CURRENT
          ELSE
             OUTPUT "** SORRY: I HAVE NOT ENOUGH OF ",
                     VINEYARD, VINTAGE
          ENDIF
          BREAK
        CASE FALSE :
          E.OCON = TRUE
          OUTPUT "** SORRY: I DON'T HAVE THIS WINE **"
     ENDTEST
     INPUT ITERATION USING "aaa" WITH "WOULD YOU LIKE SOME-
          THING ELSE?"
CLEAR
ENDWHILE
RETURN
```

FIGURE 8.3 Example of K-MAN/2 program.

= = = = EXECUTION EXAMPLE = = = =
*** HI - WELCOME TO THE BAR K-MAN/2 ***
WHICH WINE WOULD YOU LIKE TO TEST BETWEEN:

W#	VINEYARD	VINTAGE
1	VOLNAY	1978
2	CHABLIS	1980
4	TOKAY	1981

** PRECISE THE NUMBER? : 02

** WHAT QUANTITY DO YOU WANT?   : 30

** ENJOY **
WOULD YOU LIKE SOMETHING ELSE?   YES

WHICH WINE WOULD YOU LIKE TO TEST BETWEEN:

W#	VINEYARD	VINTAGE
1	VOLNAY	1978
2	CHABLIS	1980
4	TOKAY	1981

** PRECISE THE NUMBER? : 03

** SORRY: I DON'T HAVE THIS WINE **

WOULD YOU LIKE SOMETHING ELSE?   YES

WHICH WINE WOULD YOU LIKE TO TEST BETWEEN:

W#	VINEYARD	VINTAGE
1	VOLNAY	1978
2	CHABLIS	1980
4	TOKAY	1981

** PRECISE THE NUMBER? : 02

** WHAT QUANTITY DO YOU WANT?   90

** SORRY: I HAVE NOT ENOUGH OF CHABLIS 1980

WOULD YOU LIKE SOMETHING ELSE?   NO

FIGURE 8.4 Example of K-MAN/2 program execution.

K-MAN/2 offers its own spread-sheet program fully integrated with its relational database capability. The spread sheet is a two-dimensional array with rows numbered 1 to nn and columns numbered A, B, C . . . XX. The screen acts as window on the spread sheet. Each cell of the spread sheet is designated by its coordinates. A cell can contain data directly entered at the keyboard or resulting by applying a complex expression or even a program to other cells. The consistency of the spread sheet is automatically maintained so that value modification is propagated to dependent cells. The integration of relations with spread sheet is possible with the command CONVERT (defined in Section 8.3.3) for transferring data from a relation to a spread sheet and with the command ATTACH to copy certain cells into a relation.

K-MAN/2 provides a multiuser version for use in a local area network environment. The configuration in a computer network consists of multiple workstations (up to thirty-two) accessing concurrently a database server. The database server must have at least 640K byte RAM and a hard disk, and run the K-MAN/2 multiuser version. Concurrent accesses are controlled with a locking mechanism that applies locks to relations (if prescribed by the user) or tuples (the default mode). Network interfaces are available for Novell, 3Com, and the IBM PC networks.

Finally, data may be exchanged between K-MAN/2 and computers at remote locations using K-COM. K-COM uses a GATEWAY facility to establish communication links with remote computers.

8.4 R:BASE 5000

R:BASE 5000 is the powerful successor of R:BASE 4000, marketed by Microrim Inc. R:BASE systems are RDBMSs that run on the PC-DOS environment. Unlike dBASE and K-MAN/2, R:BASE systems derive from a mainframe DBMS: the Relational Information Management (RIM) System. R:BASE 5000 is fully relational according to the definition given in Chapter 1. An R:BASE database is a set of relations satisfying user-defined rules including unique key, domain, and referential integrity constraints. R:BASE is one of the rare DBMSs (including systems for mainframes) to support semantic integrity control completely. A relational database can be manipulated through relational algebra operations. R:BASE 5000 includes many tools. It offers an interactive relational algebra language usable in both menu-driven and command-driven mode and a procedural programming language. Excellent integrity control and limited security control facilities are provided. The development of applications is significantly facilitated by an outstanding report generator and a powerful application generator EXPRESS for rapidly creating a database, customized data entry screens, and reports. Performance of the applications may be increased by using indexes and also by compiling application files. Compilation is rarely supported by most other microcomputer database systems. A File Gateway utility is also provided for converting files of different formats into R:BASE format. Finally a multiuser version of R:BASE 5000 is available and enables several R:BASE workstations to access concurrently an R:BASE file server via a local area network. In the rest of this section, we briefly describe the most salient features of R:BASE. More complete information on R:BASE 5000 is available in [Taylor 86].

Interaction with R:BASE 5000 may be guided with the PROMPT mode, which provides on-line help for entering commands with parameters. PROMPT mode may be used in the menu-driven and command-driven interfaces. It explains the correct syntax of the commands and asks the user for each parameter of the command.

The definition of a relational database must be initiated with the DEFINE (< Database _ name >) command, where Database _ name refers to a new or existing database. Then the following actions may be undertaken for specifying attributes, relations, data security, and semantic integrity constraints.

1. The definition of an attribute requires the association of an attribute name with a type and a length. The type must be one of INTEGER, REAL, TEXT, DATE, DOLLAR, or TIME. Attributes can have fixed or variable length (the maximum is 1500 characters). Furthermore an attribute may be specified as a key of a relation, in which case the system will enforce its uniqueness. Several key attributes may be defined on the same relation. An index is automatically built for each key attribute.

2. A relation is defined by associating the relation name with a set of attributes.

3. Limited data security is provided by a capability that enables the database creator to associate passwords with data objects. Two types of passwords are supported: *owner password* and *relation passwords*. The owner password is associated with a database and protects the database schema (but not the database data). Database data are protected by associating two passwords with each relation: a read password (RPW) and a modify password (MPW).

4. A relation's key definitions may be added any time during the relation's lifetime with the command BUILD KEY. This command also implies the construction of an index on the key attribute.

5. Domain integrity constraints may be associated with an attribute of a relation. The constraint is expressed as an assertion applied to the attribute. A message must also be given; it is printed when the constraint is violated.

6. Referential integrity constraints may be specified between two attributes of two different relations. Functional dependencies may be specified in the same way.

When the database structure is complete, data can be entered in the relation either directly in PROMPT mode or in a mode guided by predefined forms (customized screens). Data can also be loaded from a file.

R:BASE 5000 provides an interactive language that implements a superset of relational algebra. The interactive language may be used in two types of interfaces: menu driven or command driven. The menu-driven interface combined with the PROMPT mode is suitable for nonprogrammer users. This interface, however, consumes a large part of the computer resources (in particular, main memory). Therefore the command-driven interface is also available for users concerned with performance. Up to forty relations may be simultaneously opened and used.

R:BASE relational language supports six relational operations (select, project, join, union, intersection, and difference) compared to only three with dBASE III PLUS (select, project, and join). This language is a superset of relational algebra since it includes a sort routine and a command for computing simple functions (COUNT, MIN, MAX, AVE, SUM) on a single attribute in a relation subset.

A relation may also be updated using various commands. The EDIT mode applied to a relation allows the user to browse a relation and to modify its content. The EDIT mode may be used with the default screen format or with predefined custom screens. Furthermore set-oriented commands allow updating of relations. For example, a subset of a relation defined by a qualification can be updated (CHANGE) or deleted (DELETE).

R:BASE 5000 includes a powerful report-writing capability, the Extended Report Writer (ERW). ERW allows the user to define headers and footers and to lay out data in any order. Reports may be defined from several relations with up to forty report variables and ten levels of subtotals.

For developing applications, R:BASE 5000 offers an application generator, a programming language, and a compiler. The application generator APPLICATION EXPRESS lets the user create an application quickly in a menu-driven and question-answering mode. It eases and guides the task of defining the application components such as the database, customized entry screens, reports, and menus. After it has been defined, the object code of the application is automatically generated.

The R:BASE programming language is a structured language (similar to these of dBASE or K-MAN/2) that includes data management commands, variables, program control structures, and input/output facilities.

R:BASE 5000 also has a compiler, RCOMPILE, which can convert all application files (command file, screen file, report file, menu file) into binary code. The main value of compiling applications is that the object code is smaller and more efficient, which makes the application run faster.

R:BASE 5000 can be interfaced with other systems using the File Gateway, a copy program that converts a file from a popular format such as Lotus 1-2-3 into an R:BASE relation. Therefore interfacing with programs such as spread sheets or word processors can be done simply but indirectly.

An R:BASE 5000 Multiuser version is available for use in the IBM Personal Computer Network environment. In such a context, several R:BASE workstations are allowed to access concurrently an R:BASE file server that manages the databases. The file server must have at least 640K of RAM and a hard disk. A workstation must have at least 512K of RAM, 320K of which must be user addressable. The file server supports concurrency control by automatically locking entire relations. Deadlocks are avoided; users willing to access a locked relation must wait until it is unlocked. An entire database may be locked by a user.

8.5 EXCEL

Unlike dBASE, K-MAN/2, and R:BASE systems, EXCEL, marketed by Microsoft Corp., is not a complete relational DBMS. Rather it is a system that integrates spread-sheet, database, and graphics capabilities. We include it here for four reasons. First, it is representative of many other integrated spread-sheet programs such as VISICALC (the first one, released in 1978), LOTUS 1-2-3, MULTIPLAN (also from Microsoft Corp.), and SYMPHONY, which are available on microcomputers. Second, it provides an interesting relational functionality that interfaces nicely with the spread-sheet capability. Third, it is available only on the Apple Macintosh, the main competitor of IBM PCs and compatibles, and fully exploits Macintosh features such as menus and icons. Fourth, it is important to see how the database capabilities of an integrated system differ from those of a complete RDBMS. EXCEL is an example of contextually integrated system since it integrates three capabilities (spread sheet, database, and graphics) used in the same context. EXCEL is designed for numerical data processing applications that require extensive data analyses. Examples of applications are investment analysis, tax planning, marketing analyses, and inventory management. Worksheets are particularly suited for creating complex models and perform what-if analyses. The EXCEL database capability permits selection and sorting of data from a single relation to produce cell values in a work sheet. The main constraint is that a relation must fit in main memory. In summary, EXCEL provides capabilities for work-sheet management, database management, graph and chart generation, and advanced features for what-if analysis, linking several work sheets, and customized macros. Finally, EXCEL can be interfaced with other systems using the Switcher. A more complete presentation is given in [Townsend 85].

A work sheet is a two-dimensional table with up to 16,384 rows and 256 columns in each row. The columns are designated by letters A, B, . . . , Z, AA, . . . , IV, and the rows are numbered 1 to n. The intersection of a column and a row is a *cell,* which may be referred to by its coordinates — for example, B3. A work sheet is created by selecting the EXCEL icon from the main menu. By browsing through the spread sheet and highlighting a cell, using the mouse to select the submenus, the user may enter data in the current cell. The user can also define the value of a cell by a formula such as = B2 + B4 or by a function applied to different cells. EXCEL provides eight types of functions, such as mathematical, statistical, trigonometric, and financial, totaling eighty-six functions. For each cell, the user must specify a value and the format for displaying that value. A comment may be attached to a cell and made visible only in entry mode (and not display mode). Names may be assigned to cells or cell ranges. Names are useful for making formulas explicit — for example, = DEBIT − CREDIT. After creation, a work sheet may be saved on disk and given a name. An existing work sheet can then be loaded from disk and modified in EDIT mode by browsing through the work sheet. The EDIT operations include: deleting a cell or a set of cells, editing the content of one cell for further modification, inserting and deleting rows and columns, and adding comments to cells. After editing, the updated work sheet can be saved on disk.

The EXCEL on-screen database management capability is different from specialized DBMSs such as dBASE or K-MAN/2. dBASE, K-MAN/2, and R:BASE systems can handle databases whose size is limited only by the size of the hard disk. With EXCEL, the size of a relation is limited by the amount of available main memory. A relation is stored in a file on disk and is loaded entirely in main memory for use. One advantage is that database operations are very efficient because they do not incur any I/O. The main drawback is that large relations cannot be supported by EXCEL and should be managed by another DBMS such as dBASE using the EXCEL Switcher. The primary use of the EXCEL database capability is to retrieve data associatively and to sort data. A relation is similar to a spread sheet where rows represent tuples. Thus the maximum number of tuples in a relation is the maximum number of columns in a spread sheet (16,383). A relation (called database in EXCEL terminology) must be defined as part of a work sheet. Thus the same features and commands available for work sheets may be used for database data.

The definition of a new relation requires the opening of a new work sheet and the specification of an area of this sheet that will contain the relation. Then attribute names and data can be entered in the relation in the same way as cell values in a work sheet. Type checking is not automatic, however. Saving the created data on disk is done by saving the work sheet that contains the relation.

Data from an opened relation can be retrieved by specifying query qualifications as spread-sheet formulas. Thus all the power of the spread-sheet program can be used to retrieve data based on complex conditions (for example, with mathematical functions), which would be difficult or impossible to express with other RDBMSs. The first selected tuple is displayed in the upper part of the spread sheet. Subsequent selected tuples may be displayed by using the scroll arrows. Complex conditions can also be employed to designate tuples to be deleted. The updating of a relation must be done in the spread-sheet EDIT mode, which requires the user to scroll through the relation for modifying some attribute values. There is no way to perform modifications associatively (with a condition). EXCEL also provides a limited sort capability that can sort a relation based on up to three attributes in ascending or descending order.

Two or more work sheets can be linked based on some defined cells. An update of one common cell is automatically propagated to the corresponding cells in linked work sheets. This capability may be used for linking different relations on common (join) attributes, where referential integrity is automatically enforced. The modification of a common attribute in one relation automatically generates the update of the corresponding foreign attribute in other relations. Data in one opened work sheet or relation may be selected based on complex formulas that involve data stored in other linked work sheets or relations. This type of operation is similar to a semijoin. Data in the linked work sheet or database that may not be in main memory are designated by external references that EXCEL resolves.

Work sheets (and relations) are always displayed as windows. The manipulation of several relations is possible through EXCEL's multiple window management. Several relations can thus be displayed simultaneously, facilitating the expression of queries with multiple relations.

EXCEL provides an impressive set of built-in functions for manipulating work sheet and database data. It also includes a function macrolanguage that allows the user to define his or her own functions with its arguments and result. Macros are particularly useful for saving complex functions or database functions that are executed repetitively.

Because relation data are part of the work sheet, reports can be generated using EXCEL capabilities that control work-sheet reports. The associated formatting information is useful for generating presentation-quality documents. We should emphasize that these capabilities are particularly well suited for work sheets and also usable for database; however, they cannot be compared with sophisticated report generators such as those of R:BASE 5000.

Results of work-sheet analyses or database queries may be presented using graphics. EXCEL's graphics capability enables the user to create graph and chart representations of the data. A graph or a chart definition is associated with the data. EXCEL permits the creation of many kinds of graphs (column graphs, bar graphs, pie graphics, and so on) and charts (histograms) well adapted to data analysis. The graphics capability of EXCEL is far superior to those of more traditional database systems.

Like most other systems for microcomputers, EXCEL provides a copy routine for transferring data between EXCEL and other software programs, such as word processors, database systems, and other spread-sheet programs. Another capability, the Switcher, allows the user to use another program, such as MacWord, and EXCEL simultaneously. With the Switcher, data can be copied and pasted between the two programs.

8.6 Conclusion

In this chapter, we have presented four DBMSs, with some relational capabilities, available on microcomputers. Three of them — dBASE III PLUS, KNOWLEGE-MAN/2, and R:BASE 5000 — offer rather complete relational features. They represent the most successful relational systems for microcomputers. We have also looked at EXCEL, which provides more limited database capabilities but is representative of many powerful integrated software packages that are available on microcomputers. Tables 8.1 and 8.2 summarize the main features of these four systems.

Database management systems for microcomputers are increasing in number. They range from simple file systems to relational database systems. The best of them, including those discussed in this chapter, exhibit powerful relational features such as a set-oriented data language. They often contain some advanced features suitable for a wide range of business applications: spread sheet, graphics, statistics, and so on. The strongest advantage of microcomputer DBMSs is user-friendly interfaces. This reflects the fact that a large number of microcomputer users are nonprogrammers. Therefore microcomputer DBMSs typically include a menu-driven interface, sometimes a limited natural language interface (K-MAN/2), customized screens for easing data entry, an EDIT mode for browsing and updating a relation, and an application generator. In addition, they offer more efficient facilities, such as a command-driven interface, and their own programming language for more skilled users.

With the advent of local area networks for microcomputers, such as the IBM Personal Computer Network, DBMSs can now provide multiuser support. In such a context, several workstations are allowed to access concurrently, via a network, a multiuser database server that manages the shared database. Workstations run the single-user version of the DBMS, while the database server runs the multiuser version. The database server can be a microcomputer with a hard disk (dBASE, K-MAN/2, R:BASE) or even a mainframe computer (INGRES, ORACLE, FOCUS). The integration with a mainframe DBMS provides many opportunities to tailor the configuration to user needs.

Many integrated software programs for microcomputers often include a database capability. As we saw with EXCEL, this capability is not as complete as those of dBASE, K-MAN/2, or R:BASE; however, they illustrate the trend of contextually integrated systems that provide a few capabilities such as spread sheet, database, and graphics, which are useful in the same application context.

Performance of microcomputer DBMSs is quite acceptable for simple queries (with not many joins) when indexes are available. Some interesting performance measurements have been obtained in [Zeller 86] for dBASE III, R:BASE 5000, and the microcomputer versions of INGRES and ORACLE. Measurements are done on PC-XT – compatible computers (with 512K RAM and a hard disk) by applying the Wisconsin Benchmark [Bitton 83]. Performance results for select and join are given in Tables 8.3 and 8.4, respectively.

TABLE 8.1 List of basic features.

	dBASE	K-MAN	R:BASE	EXCEL
Data description				
Max. attribute size	5K	64K	1500	255
Max. attributes per tuple	255	255	400	256
Max. tuples per relation	Disk	Disk	Disk	16K
Attribute types[a]	B,C,D,N,S,	B,C,N,S	B,C,D,N,S,T,$	B,C,D,N,S,T,$
Max. indexes per relation	7	Unlimited	Max. primary keys	No
Max. relations per database	1	Unlimited	40	1
Data manipulation				
Interactive language	Relational alg.	SQL like	Relational alg.	Worksheet
Menu driven	Yes	Yes	Yes	Yes
Command driven	Yes	Yes	Yes	No
Max. open relations	10	Unlimited	40	Main memory
Max. joined relations	10	Unlimited	40	Main entry
Max. sort fields	7	Unlimited	10	3
Functions[b]	A,D,L,M,T	A,D,L,M,S,T	A,L,M,S,T	A,D,F,L,M,R,S,T
Data control				
Type checking	Yes	Yes	Yes	Yes
Protection	Yes	Yes	Passwords	Passwords
Views	For retrieval	No	No	Hiding attributes
Semantic integrity[c]	No	No	D,F,K,R	No

[a] B:Boolean, C:character, D:date, N:number, S:variable size text, T:time, S:dollar.
[b] A:aggregate, D:date, F:financial, L:logical, M:mathematical, R:trigonometric, S:statistical, T:text.
[c] D:domain, F:functional dependency, K:primary key, R:referential.

TABLE 8.2 List of advanced features.

	dBASE	K-MAN	R:BASE	EXCEL
Report and form management				
Headers	Yes	Yes	Yes	Yes
Footers	Yes	Yes	Yes	Yes
Max. subtotals	7	26	10	Unlimited
Report summaries	Yes	Yes	Yes	No
Custom screens	Yes	Yes	Yes	No
Statistical analysis	No	Yes	No	Yes
Graphics	No	Yes	No	Yes
Color	Yes	Yes	No	No
Application development				
Application generator	Yes	Yes	Yes	No
Programming language	Yes	Yes	Yes	No
Compiler	No	No	Yes	No
Multiuser version	Yes	Yes	Yes	No
Protection	Encryption	Encryption and passwords	Passwords	
Concurrency control	Relation locks	Relation and tuple locks	Relation and database locks	
Interfaces with other systems	COPY APPEND	CONVERT Integrated spread sheet	File Gateway	COPY, Switcher
Other features	No	Integrated in C Natural language interface	Compatible with RIM	What-if analysis
Environment	PC-DOS MS-DOS	PC-DOS MS-DOS CP-M	PC-DOS	Macintosh

TABLE 8.3 Performance of select for four microcomputer DBMSs.

Index	Result size	dBASE III	INGRES	ORACLE	R:BASE 5000
No	50	65	84	75	40
No	500	88	76	198	72
Clustered	50	5	4	15	41
Clustered	500	39	28	141	70
Secondary	50	8	8	18	42
Secondary	500	70	72	163	72

Source: [Zeller 86].
Notes: Selection in 5000 tuple relation; time in seconds; result written in a relation.

Although microcomputer DBMSs are constantly evolving, they nevertheless have limitations (which will be probably overcome in the near future). Menu-driven interfaces are useful for guiding the user in expressing language syntax; however, complex queries with several relations remain difficult to express because many relation schemas must be manipulated. We believe a QBE-like interface [Zloof 77], where relation structures are graphically displayed, would overcome this difficulty.

With the ability of multiuser access, data protection is becoming crucial.

TABLE 8.4 Performance of join for four microcomputer DBMSs.

# select	Clustered index	dBASE III	INGRES	ORACLE	R:BASE 5000
No	No	—	905	45000	—
No	JAs	325	424	946	1179
1	No	—	389	49918	—
1	SA, JAs	432	257	239	186
2	No	—	330	—	—
2	SAs, JAs	553	320	271	303

Source: [Zeller 86].
Notes: Time in seconds; result written in a relation; SA: select attribute, JA: join attribute; join of two 5000 tuple relations; — means undoable.

Current microcomputer DBMSs provide little support for data protection. Only dBASE systems have a simple view mechanism limited to retrieval queries. Data security consists of only password protection and data encryption. Semantic integrity control is limited to type checking when data are entered. R:BASE 5000 is a notable exception since it provides impressive semantic integrity control, including referential integrity.

Although multiuser systems support the notion of transaction and concurrency control, there is no provision for recovery management, which remains the responsibility of the user through the operating system; however, support of recovery management such as logging will affect system performance.

Since their release, microcomputer DBMSs have shown constant performance improvements, but much more progress is needed. File access methods are quite simple and limited to a small number of secondary indexes per file. Most systems interpret their commands. Compilation, provided only by R:BASE 5000, can improve performance dramatically.

The interface of the DBMS with other systems or subsystems of the DBMS is generally achieved with a COPY routine. There is no integration with other programming languages such as C, Pascal, or COBOL. K-MAN/2 is a notable exception, since its database functions may be called from C. Even the interface between different modules of the same system (for example, spread sheet and relation in K-MAN/2) must be done by copying data from one format to another. We believe that a unified integration of various subsystems like OBE [Zloof 81, Zloof 82] would make these systems extremely powerful. The trend has already started with contextually integrated systems for spread-sheet applications.

References

[Bitton 83] D. Bitton, D. J. DeWitt, C. Turbyfill, "Benchmarking Database Systems: A Systematic Approach," Int. Conf. on VLDB, Florence, Italy, 1983.

[Kruglinski 83] D. Kruglinski, *Data Base Management Systems: A Guide to Microcomputer Software,* Osborne-McGraw-Hill, Berkeley, 1983.

[McCharen 84] J. D. McCharen, *Using dBASE II: Programming dBASE II,* Hayden Book Company, N.J., Fast Reference Guide, 1984.

[MDBS 86] MDBS, "KM/2: The Universal Knowledge Management System," in *User's Guide,* Micro Data Base Systems, Lafayette, Ind., 1986.

[Roeder 84] G. M. Roeder, *The Book of KnowledgeMan,* Vol. 1, All-Hands-On Press Chelmsford, Mass., 1984.

[Roeder 86] G. M. Roeder, *The Book of KnowledgeMan,* Vol. 2, All-Hands-On Press Ed., Chelmsford, Mass., 1986.

[Simpson 86] A. Simpson, *Understanding dBASE III PLUS,* SYBEX, Berkeley, Cal., 1986.

[Taylor 86] A. G. Taylor, *R:base 5000 User's Guide,* Que Corporation, Indianapolis, 1986.

[Townsend 85] C. Townsend, *Mastering EXCEL,* SYBEX, Berkeley, Cal., 1986.

[Zeller 86] H. Zeller, "Performance Measurements of PC Database Systems," Technical Report, University of Stuttgart, West Germany, April 1986.

[Zloof 77] M. M. Zloof, "Query by Example: A Data Base Language," IBM Systems Journal, Vol. 16, No. 4, pp. 324 – 343.

[Zloof 81] M. M. Zloof, "QBE/OBE: A Language for Office and Business Automation," IEEE Computers, Vol. 14, No. 5, May 1981.

[Zloof 82] M. M. Zloof, "Office-by-Example: A Business Language That Unifies Data and Word Processing and Electronic Mail," IBM Systems Journal, Fall 1982.

9
DATABASE MACHINES

9.1 Introduction: The Database Machine Approach

Usually a DBMS is a set of system and application programs executed by a single computer. This approach has several shortcomings. Because of recent advances in database theory and technology, the size of the databases and the variety of applications have significantly increased. Now some databases have several giga-bytes. Their management by a classical DBMS results in poor utilization of computer resources, which are shared between applications and other complex software programs. The DBMS can easily congest the main memory with useless data and saturate the central processor when selecting the relevant data. This situation stems from the excessive centralization of data and application management functions.

A solution to that problem appeared in early 1970 [Canaday 74]. The idea is to offload the central processor by isolating the database management functions from the main computer, or host computer, and group them in a specialized computer, called a *database machine* (DBM) or sometimes *database computer* or *back-end,* dedicated to their execution. The objectives of the database machine approach are multiple. Better utilization of computer resources, better functionality (such as increased reliability), and higher performance due to specialized technology (such as parallel architectures) are expected. Furthermore the recent advances in hardware (microprocessors, interconnection networks, and others) and distributed systems allow the use of a DBM as a server of various hosts such as workstations and classical computers linked via a local network (such as Ethernet) or general network (such as Arpanet). A DBM can thus be used in a distributed context where a modular expansion of computer resources is possible. The development of DBMs in the 1980s is similar to the development of front-ends in the 1970s to manage communications as shown in Fig. 9.1.

The advantages of this approach must be balanced against the overhead introduced by the communication host-DBM. Navigating through the database one record at a time incurs a prohibitive communication cost. The communication cost can be amortized only if the DBM interface is of sufficiently high level to allow the expression of complex queries involving intensive data processing. The relational model, which favors set-oriented manipulation of data, has therefore been largely assumed by DBM designers.

Hardware progress has greatly influenced the history of database machines. The classical Von Neumann architecture was designed primarily for the efficient execution of numerical operations. The prohibitive cost of primary memories of these computers made a single processor sufficient. But this type of architecture is not suited to the requirements of database functions. The first DBM architects adopted an extreme solution: the implementation of most database functions in hardware. The best example is the realization of the selection operation by filter processors associated with disks. Most of the first DBM projects were unsuccess-

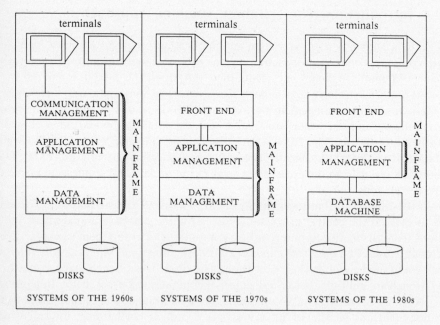

FIGURE 9.1 Evolution of system architectures.

ful for two reasons: the difficulty and the high cost of building prototypes and the poor price-performance ratio compared to the classical solutions (seen in the previous chapters). The first DBMs [Lin 76, Su 75] optimized only a few primitive database functions (such as selection) at the expenses of others (such as join) that must be executed in cooperation with the host computer. As a result, the first successful DBM products [Epstein 80] were more software oriented than hardware oriented. Nonetheless the recent advances in semiconductor technologies have decreased significantly the development cost of all components used with DBMs (processors, main memory, interconnect, disks, and so on). Furthermore research on DBMs has become more mature, and algorithms for exploiting parallelism are now better understood. DBMs based on multiprocessor and large main memory (RAM) architectures are now viable with a better price-performance compared to the classical solution. The recent DBC/1012 Database Computer is a good example of a highly parallel and fully relational database machine that promises great success.

In Section 9.2, we introduce a generic architecture for database machines by isolating the components. Then we present four commercial DBMs representative of different design approaches: CAFS-ISP by Int. Computers Limited (England) in Section 9.3, DBC/1012 by Teradata (United States) in Section 9.4, DORSAL 32 by Copernique (France) in Section 9.5, and IDM 500 by Britton Lee (United States) in Section 9.6. For each of these machines, we specify components of the generic architecture. In Section 9.7, we present the various research projects from many countries (United States, Japan, Canada, France, Italy, West Germany) and their novel features.

9.2 Database Machine Architecture

9.2.1 Variety of Approaches

Among the database machines marketed are CAFS/ISP by ICL [Babb 79], DBC/1012 by Teradata [Teradata 84], DORSAL 32 by Copernique [Armisen 81], and IDM 500 by Britton Lee [Epstein 80]. All over the world, research projects have attempted or are attempting to develop relational database machines [Hsiao 83], in particular SABRE [Gardarin 83a] and VERSO [Bancilhon 83] in France, RDBM [Leilich 78] in West Germany, DBMAC [Missikoff 82] in Italy, RAP [Ozkarahan 77] in Canada, DELTA [Murakami 83] and GRACE [Fushimi 86] in Japan, and CASSM [Su 75], DIRECT [DeWitt 79], DBC [Banerjee 78] and Gamma [DeWitt 86] in the United States.

A wide variety of DBM architectures and designs has been proposed; none of the architectures can be considered generic. Thus we have attempted to abstract from these early proposals a generic architecture for a DBM; we can then compare the proposals in terms of the generic architecture.

9.2.2 Generic Architecture

All database machines are generally computers with a variable number of processors and a variable degree of specialized hardware, interfaced to one or several host computers. A DBM receives commands in encoded messages from a host computer and returns answers (data and state), also in encoded format. The set of message types that permits the dialogue between host and DBM is called a *data manipulation protocol*. This protocol is an essential feature of a DBM.

Starting from the user and application program interface (in a top-down description), most systems with a DBM offer four functions (see Fig. 9.2) provided in four layers:

1. The management, analysis, and encoding of user queries in internal format are performed by an external software layer, the *database interface manager*. This layer is located in the host computer and usually provided by the DBM designer as host resident software.

2. The messages between the host and the DBM are generally managed by a *communication controller* distributed between the host and the DBM. The data manipulation protocol that defines the dialogues host-DBM is used at this level. This layer calls the communication subsystem specific to the connection type: network or channel.

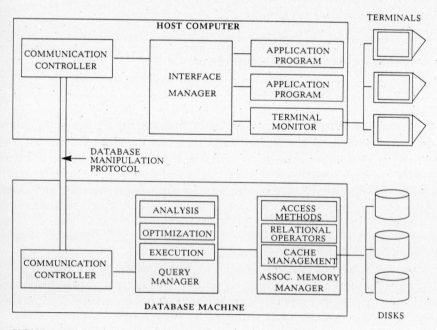

FIGURE 9.2 Generic architecture with database machine.

3. The third layer performs the decomposition of external data manipulation commands (search, update) into internal and simpler operations (generally select, sort, join, aggregate, and others), their optimization and their execution. This layer also manages the database schemas. And it is in charge of selecting the best access paths to the data in order to reduce data access time. We call this layer *query manager.*

4. Data management and associative access constitute the primary functions of the last layer, *associative memory manager.* In a relational DBM, the emphasis is on the efficient execution of relational operators using parallel algorithms and/or special-purpose processors. The most famous special-purpose processor is the filter, designed primarily for select operations. A filter can be associated with a group of disks, one disk, or a disk channel. There could be other specialized processors, such as joiner, sorter, hasher, merger, or index processor. Generally these processors access data in a large cache memory. This layer also manages the disk space and can support basic access methods.

In addition, a DBM provides a number of important functions:

- Control of access rights during data retrieval and update.
- Semantic integrity control of data during updates. The system must ensure that the updates do not violate the database consistency, as defined by the integrity assertions.
- Concurrency control among multiple users. Each individual user must be unaware of concurrent accesses to data, which must be synchronized by the system.
- Transaction management. The updates are generally grouped in functional units, called *transactions,* which must be entirely executed (committed) or not executed at all. This control is particularly difficult because of data distribution and the probability of soft and hard failures. Recovery routines must exist.

The generic architecture of a system with a DBM is represented in Fig. 9.2. It is difficult to place the four main functions in specific layers because of the variety of DBM approaches; the functions may not always appear in the same layer or layers.

9.2.3 Study of DBM Products and Projects

In the following, we will study four database machines. To facilitate their comparison, we describe them using the following standard outline: architecture; external interfaces offered to the users; features of the data manipulation protocol; query management and optimization; associative memory management; and control mechanisms. We will also examine research projects. In general, many elements are not well documented in research projects since they are more incomplete than products, but they often present novel features. Therefore for each project, we look at its architecture and the components that we consider original.

9.3 CAFS-ISP by Int. Computers Limited

9.3.1 Architecture

CAFS-ISP (Content Addressable File Store-Information Search Processor) is described in [Babb 79, ICL 82]. CAFS-ISP is not a complete database machine; rather it is an efficient filter component that can be added to an ICL disk controller. A host CPU can be interfaced with up to six CAFS components. The CAFS components are used as associative search processors by the VME operating system. The VME system includes the IDMS (CODASYL database system) routines to access records directly and the CAFS routines to access data associatively.

The hardware architecture of a CAFS component is illustrated in Fig. 9.3. A CAFS component is divided into four modules: logical format unit, key channel, search evaluation unit, and data selection unit.

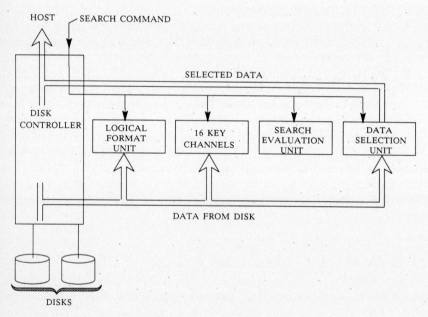

FIGURE 9.3 Architecture of a CAFS component.

The *logical format unit* receives and identifies the data coming out from disk. This module also detects the critical points, such as beginning of record and beginning of field. It signals these critical points to the other modules.

The *key channel* evaluates a simple search criterion of the form <attribute> <operator> <value>, where the operator is in $\{=, \leq, <, >, \geq, \neq\}$. A key channel can also test for the presence or absence of an attribute and uses masks for hiding characters or character strings. A CAFS component has sixteen key channels, which allow it to evaluate complex predicates composed of up to sixteen simple predicates in parallel.

The *search evaluation unit* receives the Boolean results of the sixteen key channels and decides whether the tuple satisfies the complex predicate. This module is composed of sixteen simple processing components, each associated with a different key channel; together they evaluate the logical expression corresponding to the selection criterion of the search command. Also a counting function records the total number of selected tuples.

The *data selection unit* includes two modules: the *retrieval unit*, which selects the tuples satisfying the criterion, and the *retrieval processor*, which projects the tuples on some specified attributes. The retrieval processor also manages a buffer for the selected tuples.

In addition, *bit arrays* may be managed by the search evaluation unit. These are used to improve the processing of semijoin operations [Babb 79].

9.3.2 Data Manipulation Protocol

Because CAFS is a filter processor interfaced with ICL disk controllers, the data manipulation protocol is composed of internal commands not visible to the users.

9.3.3 External Interface

CAFS-ISP is an optional component of the ICL database system. This DBMS offers a procedural interface (based on the network model) and a nonprocedural interface (based on the relational model). The network model is the basic model of IDMS, which implements a rather complete CODASYL system. IDMS can be accessed from COBOL and FORTRAN. Relational views may be derived from data described in an IDMS subschema. A relational view can be seen as a file of virtual records. Rules for deriving virtual records include selection and join operations. Relational views may be queried but not updated by (1) a nonprocedural query language, QUERYMASTER, which permits all types of selections on a given view, including complex textual search expressions, and (2) a specialized relational interface to COBOL, providing capabilities similar to those of QUERYMASTER.

9.3.4 Query Management and Optimization

Without CAFS, the queries are managed by the IDMS database system. The value of CAFS is the optimization of query execution. Therefore when the CAFS component is present, this optimization is exploited by both IDMS and QUERY-MASTER for performing selections that do not include indexed attributes, selections on text attributes, and semijoin operations, which are not implemented by CODASYL sets.

Furthermore IDMS uses CAFS only for the files that have been declared searchable by CAFS in the SEARCHABLE AREA of the schema. An empirical rule provided to the DBA to decide when to declare a file searchable by CAFS is:

$$T > 4*V$$

where T designates the period in seconds between two file scans and V is the volume of the file in M-bytes. For example, a 5 M-byte file may be declared searchable if it is accessed less than once every 20 seconds. The reasoning behind this is that frequently accessed files should not be scanned (as with CAFS) but cached in main memory.

9.3.5 Associative Memory Management

This is the only layer that CAFS implements. The CAFS filter processor can evaluate any complex Boolean expression with up to sixteen simple predicates. The simple predicates are evaluated in parallel in each component. The filtering operation can be done in parallel over multiple disks when several disk controllers are used, each having its own CAFS component. In addition, CAFS realizes the semijoin operation, which has been proved to be useful for processing join operations. The semijoin algorithm is original: the first relation is hashed on the join attribute to produce a bit array that summarizes the join attribute values, and then the second relation is filtered using this bit array, thereby producing the semijoined tuples. Because bit arrays are much smaller than the list of join attribute values, the operation is efficient.

The CAFS file formats are specialized and not compatible with the IDMS file formats. This implies that all CAFS files must be converted to "searchable."

9.3.6 Control Mechanisms

CAFS does not support any control mechanism. All the control operations are under the responsibility of IDMS and VME.

9.3.7 Summary

CAFS-ISP is an intelligent filter component able to perform selection, semijoin, and textual search operations. Thus it is not a full-function DBM. This component can be interfaced to all ICL disk controllers. ICL has been successful in integrating this component in its main database systems. However, there are some limits in the level of integration: the DBA must decide to use CAFS or not (it is not a "system" decision). The direct access provided by IDMS and the associative access provided by CAFS are not compatible. Some performance measurements have been made for QUERYMASTER statements with and without CAFS. CAFS has been shown to improve performance by a factor of approximately 5 for associative queries.

9.4 DBC/1012 by Teradata

9.4.1 Hardware Architecture

The DBC/1012 Database Computer [Neches 85, Teradata 84], recently marketed by Teradata, has a highly parallel architecture. The modular design allows the integration of 6 to 1024 processors. DBC/1012 is an example of Multiple Instruction stream Multiple Data stream (MIMD) architecture (see Section 9.7 for a description of MIMD design). The implementation consists of two types of processors built with off-the-shelf components, called interface processors (IFPs) and access module processors (AMPs), communicating via a proprietary interconnection network, Ynet. Each component processor (IFP or AMP) runs a copy of the Teradata Operating System (TOS). An overview of the architecture of DBC/1012 is given in Fig. 9.4.

Interface Processors (IFPs)
IFPs manage the communication with the host computer and perform the functions of query manager-optimizer. They control query execution by communicating with AMPs over the Ynet.

An IFP contains four hardware components: channel interface, CPU, memory, and Ynet interface. The channel interface manages the communication with the host via a block multiplexer channel. Currently the CPU uses the Intel 80286 microprocessor and 80287 arithmetic coprocessor. It includes a 32K byte two-way set-associative cache with either 2M byte or 4M byte of error-corrected main memory. The future system will be based on the Intel 80386, which is expected to provide a two and a half times improvement as compared with the 80286. The Ynet interface manages transmissions on the Ynet. More precisely, since the Ynet is composed of two networks, Ynet-A and Ynet-B, the Ynet interface has two components.

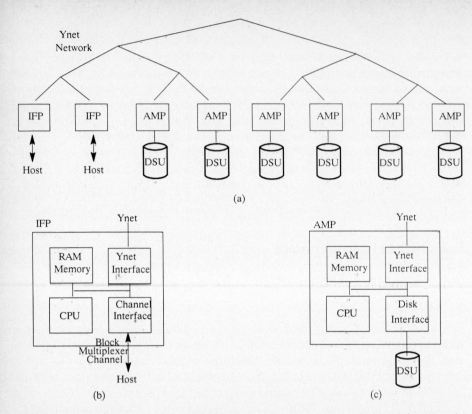

FIGURE 9.4 Architecture of the DBC/1012. (a) Interconnection of IFPs and AMPs, (b) Interface Processor (IFP), and (c) Access Module Processor (AMP).

Furthermore the system console of the DBC/1012 is connected to one of the IFPs.

Ynet

The Ynet is a network connecting IFPs and AMPs. To increase reliability and performance, the DBC/1012 employs two independent Ynet networks, Ynet-A and Ynet-B. Both Ynets interconnect all processors and operate concurrently. If one fails, the other continues to operate as a backup.

The Ynet is not a classic bus. It has a binary tree topology, where each node of the tree contains active logic to perform sort-merge functions. The leaves of the tree are IFPs and AMPs, as shown in Fig. 9.4(a). Messages are merged in the Ynet so that one message at a time travels from its origin to the root of the tree and then is broadcast to all processors. The merge capability of the Ynet is also useful to sort data as they travel from AMPs to IFPs.

Access Module Processors (AMPs)

AMPs primarily perform the associative memory management functions. They also support important database functions such as logging and data reorganization.

The hardware configuration of an AMP is similar to that of an IFP except that the channel interface of IFP is replaced by a disk interface. The disk interface controls the communication with the disk storage units (DSUs). An AMP can be connected to two DSUs, each a 500M byte Winchester disk.

9.4.2 External Interface

The DBC/1012 supports a pure relational model. Users access data managed by the DBC/1012 through host resident software supplied by Teradata. The interface language of the DBC is DBC/SQL, an implementation of SQL. DBC/SQL is a unified language for data definition, data manipulation, and control. DBC/SQL is close to IBM's SQL language (introduced in Chapter 3). DBC/SQL includes high-level statements for:

- The creation of databases in which relations, views, and macros can be defined.
- The retrieval of data from views and relations, as well as the formatting of the output (report generation).
- The updating of relations.
- Data control (definition of authorizations and integrity constraints).
- Transaction management (Begin, End, and Abort Transaction).

In addition, DBC/SQL offers general-purpose services that enhance usability and performance. The most important facilities are:

- The creation or deletion of secondary indexes on one or more attributes.
- The definition of parametric macros composed of several DBC/SQL statements.
- The archiving and restoring of a database.
- The copying of bulk data from or to a host.
- The reconfiguration of data placement over multiple AMPs for increasing reliability and/or performance.

DBC/SQL is the only entry point to the DBC/1012. The host resident software permits the use of DBC/SQL in various modes with the following components:

1. The interactive DBC/SQL enables an end user to interact with the DBC/1012 from a terminal attached to the host CPU.
2. The Batch DBC/SQL facility is useful for executing in batch a set of DBC/SQL statements.
3. The COBOL and PL/1 preprocessors permit the integration of DBC/SQL statements in COBOL or PL/1 programs. The preprocessors convert the DBC/SQL commands into calls to service routines that interface with the DBC/1012. The mapping from the nonprocedural mode of DBC/SQL to the procedural mode of COBOL or PL/1 is done by using explicit cursors with FETCH statements, similar to DB2.
4. The Call-Level Interface (CLI) may be invoked by high-level programs using a CALL statement. CLI interfaces these programs with the DBC/1012.

In addition, a variety of third-party interfaces has been added to the DBC/1012. These include interfaces with the NOMAD2 and FOCUS systems (presented in Chapter 7) and the INTELLECT natural language system. An interface with ADR's IDEAL and DATACOM/DB systems (presented in Chapter 7) is forecast.

9.4.3 Data Manipulation Protocol

The data manipulation protocol of the DBC/1012 is an encoded form of DBC/SQL. One or several DBC/SQL statements can be sent to the DBC/1012 in a request message. A message is composed of a message header, a request number, and message data. These messages are created by the Teradata Director Program (TDP), which runs on the host computer. The TDP manages communication between the host resident applications and the DBC/1012 via the multiplexer channel. The TDP also receives the result messages from the database computer.

9.4.4 Query Management and Optimization

This layer is implemented on IFPs by two modules: the DBC/SQL parser and the scheduler. The parser analyzes a DBC/SQL request and interprets it into an optimized sequence of lower-level operations corresponding to the request execution plan. The target language generated by the parser is probably close to relational algebra with synchronization commands. The DBC/SQL parser has access to the data dictionary to get information on relations, views, users, access rights, and so on. Unlike DB2, the DBC/1012 does not save the execution plans for repetitive use. Therefore interpretation has to take place for each execution of the request; however, execution plans may be cached in memory in case they are used again soon.

The scheduler controls and synchronizes the execution of the operations in the execution plan. Operations are sent over the Ynet to be executed by the appropriate AMPs. The control of execution of one request is thus centralized in one IFP. However, the data of each relation are horizontally partitioned (spread) over many AMPs by hashing on an attribute. Therefore the execution of a single operation, like selection in one relation, can be done in parallel by many AMPs, each performing a subset of the operation.

9.4.5 Associative Memory Management

This layer is implemented by the AMPs. In addition, all the data controls are done partially by the AMPs. Because of horizontally partitioned placement of data, a centralized controller (the IFP's scheduler) is necessary. Each AMP runs a copy of a low-level database system on the Teradata Operating System (TOS). TOS provides services suitable for database management (such as buffer management). The high performance of the associative memory manager is due to its implementation on many AMPs together with the horizontally partitioned data placement. Furthermore a merge operation used frequently for producing sorted results is done by the Ynet when the data are transferred to the IFP. (The initial sorts are done locally on each AMP; then the final merge is done.) A hash-based join algorithm is supported. For increasing reliability, data duplication is supported; the same tuples can be redundantly stored on two AMPs.

9.4.6 Control Mechanisms

The control mechanisms of the DBC/1012 are as follows:

1. Control of access rights. The management of privileges on database objects is powerful and similar to that of System R.
2. Semantic integrity control. Only unique key constraints are supported using the definition of primary and secondary keys.
3. Concurrency control. Concurrency control uses the two-phase locking algorithm. The locks can be acquired on variable-size granules: database, relation, or tuple. Locks can be implicitly or explicitly acquired. Deadlocks are detected using a distributed graph checking algorithm because data are distributed. In case of deadlock situation, a victim transaction is chosen to be restarted.
4. Transaction atomicity control. This control is done using a transient journal that contains the data images before modification and the transaction actions (begin, end, and so on). Undoing a transaction is accomplished by reconstituting the before-images of the transaction. Committing a transaction requires a two-step commit protocol synchronized by the scheduler of that transaction.

5. Restoration. The RESTORE command enables the restoration from archives of a database image after a disk crash. Furthermore there is a log of after-images that permits reconstituting the updates done by committed transactions between the last savepoint and the crash. If the lost data were duplicated on other AMPs, an accurate copy of the crashed disk can be rebuilt more efficiently without using archives.

9.4.7 Summary

The DBC/1012 is a powerful relational database machine. It employs intensive parallelism for increasing performance and reliability. Except for semantic integrity control, the relational capabilities are rather complete. The hardware architecture is modular and can accommodate up to 1024 processors. The largest configuration currently installed is 168 processors. Performance measurements [Decker 86] have shown its price and performance superior to that of a conventional DBMS. The DBC/1012 achieves the same performance as a mainframe for approximately a fourth of the cost. It shows linear capacity growth; the addition of components results in proportionally increasing performance. The DBC/1012 has been primarily designed for the IBM processing environment but is being interfaced with others. The DBC/1012 can be connected to IBM 370, 43xx, or 30xx mainframes, plug-compatible machines (such as Amdahl and Fujitsu), or any machine that supports an IBM block multiplexor channel (such as CDC and Honeywell).

The host operating systems supported are MVS, VM/CMS, TPF, and several non-IBM host OSs. With the addition of a third processor type, the Communications Processor (COP) supporting Ethernet physical protocols and either TCP/IP or ISO/OSI logical protocols, host support will be available for UNIX and PC/DOS.

9.5 DORSAL 32 by Copernique

9.5.1 Architecture

DORSAL 32 [Copernique 82] is both a network and a relational database machine. It is composed of two main machines, each with a multiprocessor architecture: the *logical management machine* (LMM), in charge of query management and optimization functions, and the *physical management machine* (PMM), which performs the associative memory management functions. The DORSAL 32 architecture is portrayed in Fig. 9.5. The logical machine LMM has a multiprocessor architecture composed of a principal processor (PP); from one to seven coprocessors (CP) based on the 68000 microprocessor; a control unit for interact-

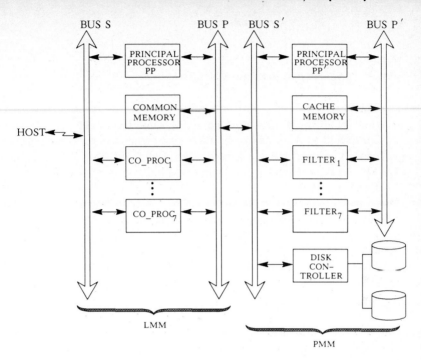

FIGURE 9.5 Architecture of DORSAL 32.

ing with an operator; and MOS memories, common memory (CM), and local memory (LM), from 1 to 256 megabytes.

Each processor can access the entire common memory through a common bus (P). It can also access a local memory via a private path. A second bus (S) interconnects various communication units to the principal processor, in particular communication units for the hosts.

The physical machine (PMM) manages the disks and the cache memory and performs filtering operations. PMM has a multiprocessor organization similar to the LMM, which acts as a host for PMM. Thus a specific interface processor interconnects bus P of LMM to bus S' or PMM; this unit manages a FIFO queue containing the requests from LMM to PMM. Also, bus S' of PMM is linked to the principal processor PP' of PMM. Besides this principal processor, PMM has a disk formatting unit, which can manage up to sixteen disks; a cache memory (CM') of 1 to 16 megabytes for caching the most frequently accessed data; and from zero to seven filtering processors (FPs), each having a private memory of 256K bytes and a 68000 processor.

PMM is marketed separately by Copernique as an intelligent cache memory, called DIRAM 32. DIRAM 32 can manage up to sixteen disks, each having a storage capacity up to 600 megabytes.

9.5.2 External Interface

Data Models
DORSAL 32 supports two data models:

1. The *network model,* with the limitation that the records must be flat; that is, all the atoms must be at the same level. The records may be connected by 1-*n* links going from one owner record to *n* member records. The records have a maximum predefined size.
2. The *relational model* permitting manipulation of relational tables of fixed-size tuples.

The same database may be manipulated with the functions of both models. A record type is assumed to be a relation scheme. Users can manipulate base data directly or data derived from base data by the use of subschemas (with the network model) or relational views. A subschema is simply a subset of a base relation with the possibility of data restructuring within a record. A view is the result of an arbitrary relational query.

Data Manipulation Languages
DORSAL 32 offers three data manipulation languages:

1. A *navigational language* close to the CODASYL DML, accessible from COBOL, allows the manipulation (retrieval and update) of network databases. The data manipulation commands are translated into calls to the DORSAL 32 library. This language permits access to the DBM one record at a time. Transaction management commands are also supported (Begin Transaction, RollBack, Abort, Commit).
2. A *network manipulation language,* CNQL (Copernique Network Query Language), allows the composition of complex network manipulation requests using the operator For-Each. With For-Each, a set of occurrences can be defined for processing using either a known access path (such as record, key, or link) or a selection on record type. Furthermore CNQL allows the manipulation of variables, the transfer of records or subrecords between DORSAL 32 and the host, and the conditional processing of records. In general, CNQL is a macroprogramming language for network database. Complex programs can thus be processed by the DBM, thereby avoiding the record-at-a-time communication overhead of DML. It is possible to mix DML and CNQL commands in the same transaction.
3. A *nonprocedural SQL-like language,* CSQL (Copernique Structured Query Language), exists for manipulating relational databases. The language is similar to SQL (see Chapter 3). CSQL can also be embedded into programming languages such as COBOL. The conversion

from the nonprocedural mode of CSQL to a procedural mode is accomplished through cursors associated with results of CSQL queries.

9.5.3 Data Manipulation Protocol

The data manipulation protocol is based on procedure calls with parameter passing. The existing protocol allows either step-by-step navigation or the execution of complex queries. With complex queries, navigation is automatic, and only relevant tuples are transferred to the host. The latter type of execution is also used for the relational interface.

9.5.4 Query Management and Optimization

This layer is designed for navigation in network databases. The problems of query decomposition and join ordering specific to the relational model have not yet been described in the technical reports. This layer is called the *kernel* of the DBMS. It is handled by the logical machine LMM. The kernel is structured in five modules:

1. An internal module, STAR, is responsible for tuple or record placement in files. A file is a set of pages that can dynamically evolve according to need. It can contain several record types. Records are arranged by hashing or by placing them close to the owner of a link occurrence.

2. The second module manages the secondary indexes, which associate with each data value (atom or attribute) the list of record logical addresses in the file. Secondary indexes are implemented as specific record types called management records.

3. The third module manages keys and links. A *key* associates a group of attributes with a record occurrence. A *link* associates an owner record with a group of member records. Keys and links are organized as inverted lists.

4. The fourth module manages the user record types, that is, the relations users see when using the relational interface. This module realizes the ordering of attributes within tuples, as well as the ordering (sorting) of tuples according to a sort key. This module also manages the automatic links. An automatic link associates owner and member records based on the equality of a common attribute value. When a member record is inserted into the database, it is also automatically linked to the owner record with some common attribute value.

5. The last module manages the navigation. Scans are dynamically created for that purpose. A scan is a set of ordered record occurrences having a common property, such as belonging to the same record type or hav-

ing the same secondary key value. A scan can be used sequentially forward and backward.

A separate module does the schema compilation of schema source code submitted
by the host or the LMM console. The compiled schema is stored in a metabase,
which is loaded in main memory when opening a database. The schema can be
dynamically modified.

9.5.5 Associative Memory Management

This layer is located on the PMM. It performs three main functions:

1. *Caching.* A MOS memory from 1 to 16 megabytes is used to store the
    most frequently accessed disk sectors so as to provide access times of 1
    millisecond per sector. The cache memory is divided into two parts: a
    static part for loading sectors whose addresses are prespecified (in a
    file) and a dynamic part for keeping the most frequently accessed sec-
    tors. Writes can be done either immediately after updates or deferred
    and done periodically (for example, when the disk is idle).
2. *Associative search.* This function is performed by the filter processors,
    which use a finite state automaton. They are capable of exploring a
    disk area (set of sectors) sequentially to select the records satisfying
    a search qualification (encoded in the automaton). Up to seven filter
    processors can work in parallel.
3. *Logging.* Two types of logging are possible: a static logging where an
    entire disk is copied to another one (upon user's decision) and a dy-
    namic logging where two disk units are mirrored so that each write is
    done simultaneously on both disks. Logging is used for media recovery.

9.5.6 Control Mechanisms

DORSAL 32 supports the following control mechanisms:

1. Control of access rights. Rights can only be assigned to users for a
    database or a subschema.
2. Semantic integrity control. Only key constraints and some basic do-
    main integrity constraints are supported.
3. Concurrency control. Concurrency control is based on two-phase lock-
    ing. The records are locked incrementally according to the accesses by
    the transaction. As in System R, three consistency degrees are provided,
    where degree 3 ensures complete consistency (equivalent to a mono-user
    system). Deadlocks between transactions are detected using a graph-

checking algorithm. Two options are possible: the list of transactions involved in the deadlock is sent to the host or the transaction that created the deadlock is aborted (and then restarted automatically).

4. Transaction atomicity control. This control is done using two logs: the transaction log, which records the history of actions on the database (such as begin and end transaction), and the page log, which records the page images before modification. A transaction can be undone by applying the before-images for that transaction. Atomic commitment is done by writing a COMMIT record in the transaction log. In addition, DORSAL 32 generates periodical warm checkpoints to support warm restart (after soft failures). A transaction may contain several atomic units and thus can be partially undone.

5. Cold restarts must be done in case of data loss on disk (for example, after a disk crash). A cold restart uses an after-image log, which records the page images after modification, and the transaction log. Operator commands can define cold checkpoints when no other transaction is running. A cold restart requires loading the last image of the database and applying the after-images until the last cold checkpoint.

9.5.7 Summary

DORSAL 32 is a network and relational DBM. The machine has a multiprocessor architecture, which can accommodate up to sixteen microprocessors. Network interface and transaction management are well supported. Relational capabilities remain restricted. DORSAL 32 can be connected to the following computers: MITRA (BULL SEMS) and MINI 6 (BULL).

9.6 IDM 500 by Britton Lee

9.6.1 Architecture

The Britton Lee's IDM500 database machine [Ubell 85] is a full-function relational database machine built around a high-speed bus. This bus can interconnect up to sixteen modules, each of which accomplishes a specific function. The classical configuration has five types of boards, one of them optional:

1. A *host interface channel* manages the communication with various host CPUs in four different modes: serial (up to 1920 bytes per second), byte wide (up to 170K bytes per second), Ethernet, and IBM block multiplexor. The byte-wide channel can handle eight connections with different hosts.

2. The *database processor* is a standard 16-bit microprocessor (Zilog

Z8000) that can execute all the functions of a database system similar
to INGRES. This database system runs on a specific operating system
tailored for database support. The database processor supports the
main part of the IDM software. It has all the advantages of specialized
software. It exploits the use of the database accelerator when present.
All database code (55,000 lines) is shared among the tasks and kept
resident in memory.

3. The *database accelerator* is a special-purpose processor of 8.5 (8.5
   MIPS). It is built with standard ECL medium-scaled integration (MSI).
   The database accelerator provides an instruction set for relational database primitives that are most often used. This instruction set is micro-
   coded. This processor performs mainly multiattribute selections and
   therefore acts as a filter. The database accelerator is optional. The addition of the accelerator in the IDM improves performance by a factor
   up to 10 depending on the application. A factor of 4 is typical.

4. The *memory modules* are accessible from any module via the bus and
   can be as large as 6M bytes each.

5. The *disk controllers* manage up to four 600M byte disks each. Up to
   four controllers may be supported.

The overall architecture of the IDM machine is depicted in Fig. 9.6. In addition,
a magnetic tape controller, an administration console, and a maintenance console
can be connected to the IDM.

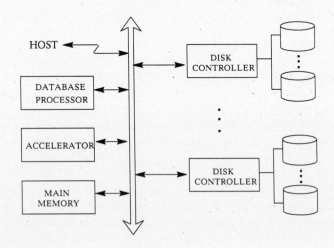

FIGURE 9.6 Architecture of IDM 500.

9.6.2 External Interface

The IDM fully supports the relational model. High-level nonprocedural languages enable the user to define, manipulate, and control relational databases. The supported high-level languages are SQL and IDL (Intelligent Database Language). The latter is similar to INGRES's QUEry Language (QUEL). IDL provides:

- Relational data management statements: Creation/deletion and opening of databases, data control, nonprocedural querying and updating, index creation/deletion, and transaction management.
- Additional service facilities: Many service routines are provided to facilitate the IDM utilization. For instance, stored commands can be defined as sets of IDL statements with parameters. A stored command is executed by the command EXECUTE <macro name> with parameter values. Also bulk copy routines are provided to load or unload relations and to dump a database.

In summary, IDL is a complete relational language that offers many additional services. Furthermore IDL statements or IDL macros can be embedded in general-purpose programming languages (COBOL, Pascal, and others). A specific preprocessor per host language is necessary to recognize the IDL statements.

In addition to the language processors, a variety of user-interface and host-IDM communication functions is provided as host resident software. Host IDM communication is supported by software device drivers (serial, parallel, Ethernet, and IBM block multiplexor) and a run-time library of communication routines that interface the IDM users and administrators with the IDM from the host. An end user on a terminal can also interact with the IDM through the interactive session monitor and run ad hoc queries written in IDL. Finally IDL can be interfaced with fourth-generation languages, which provide powerful application generators and report writers.

9.6.3 Data Manipulation Protocol

The IDM data manipulation protocol is based on an internal format of the IDL language. Each command is encoded by the host resident software, which manages the communication with the database machine according to the following format:

1. Command code.
2. Definition of the variables used in the command (if any).
3. Search tree composed of a left part representing the list of target attri-

butes in internal form, a root node describing the different parameters, and a right part representing the qualification in internal form.
4. End command code.

The command is then sent by the host to the IDM, which, after having accepted and processed the encoded query, returns the result data in the following format:

1. Attribute format with length or variable-length mark.
2. Sequence of tuples, each tuple being preceded by a "tuple" code and each variable-length attribute being preceded by its length.
3. A code indicating either error code or OK, followed by the number of transmitted tuples.

At the communication level, for the serial and byte-wide channels, a packet may be refused if there is not enough room in the channel. Each command sent to the IDM machine may be executed immediately or wait for resources. A command will wait when the database machine is overloaded. This simple solution, which lowers the multiprogramming level, avoids thrashing of the database machine. The result of a query must be explicitly requested by the host. Also in case of data input from the host (for example, to insert new tuples), the communication is controlled by the host, which makes the host resident software simpler.

9.6.4 Query Management and Optimization

The query management and optimization layer is implemented in the database processor. Each IDL request is analyzed, validated, decomposed, optimized, and then executed. Defining stored commands bypasses most parsing and validation activities at execution time and results in better performance of frequent queries. Primary and secondary indexes are exploited to perform selections and joins. For each relation in the query, the optimizer chooses an index if there is one. If there is none, an index can be dynamically constructed on the useful subset of the relation.

The database processor manages a relational metabase that can be accessed by DBAs. This metabase contains the following relations:

- DATABASE, describing the current state of the databases.
- RELATION, defining the relations of each base.
- ATTRIBUTE, describing the attributes of each relation.
- INDEXES, defining the primary and secondary indexes.
- PROTECT, prescribing the user access privileges.
- QUERY, containing the stored commands and the views.

- DESCRIPTION, containing the description in readable text provided by the DBAs of certain objects of the databases.
- USER, defining the database users.

9.6.5 Associative Memory Management

The associative memory management layer is implemented in the database processor and (in a different way) in the database accelerator. If the accelerator is not present, the database processor behaves exactly like a conventional DBMS except that it does not share the processor with other complex software systems of applications, and it runs on a dedicated operating system that makes database functions more efficient. In the IDM, the database system code, and the operating system kernel are highly integrated, resulting in effective database management support [Nyberg 86].

The database accelerator can filter, sort, and move data in memory via the bus. The database accelerator executes the most useful low-level routines, which are mainly involved in inner loops. It also contains arithmetic logic unit chips to perform computations. The database accelerator performs one operation at a time. The multitasking is therefore under the responsibility of the database processor. This allows the database accelerator to avoid context switching.

9.6.6 Control Mechanisms

The control mechanisms offered by the IDM are:

1. Control of access rights. All privileges are granted by the DBA with the primitives PERMIT and DENY. The read-write operations can be authorized on an entire relation or on specific attributes of a relation. The execution of predefined requests can also be authorized. The operation rights on the database objects can be given to users and groups of users. The group notion facilitates flexible data administration.
2. Semantic integrity control. The IDM supports domain and unique key constraints. In addition, the IDL language enables the validation of parameterized data used in updates. When defining a parametric macro, it is possible to add predicates to verify its parameters.
3. Concurrency control. A two-phase locking protocol with intention modes is done first to the relations and then to the data pages. A relation can be locked in the following modes: global read, global write, read with intention of page write, intention of page read, and intention of page write. A page can be locked because of a write or read operation. The intention locking is applied during the search for a page or

several pages to be read or written. This technique attempts to avoid the incompatibilities (read/write, write/write) for the modes global read or write with the intention modes. The locks are automatically handled by the system (as opposed to the user transaction). They are managed in a special lock relation. IDM supports three degrees of increasing consistency and increasing cost. The user may specify the degree of consistency. Degree 3 (the highest) is default.

4. Transaction atomicity control. Atomicity control is classical, using the notion of commitment and a log containing the updates. The log contains both the old and new values of modified objects. The commitment itself is achieved by writing a record "committed transaction." A transaction is either a sequence of IDL statements between BEGIN and END TRANSACTION or an individual IDL statement. When a transaction is aborted, all its modifications are undone by using the log to replace the new object values by the old ones.

5. Restoration. The IDM system performs periodic checkpoints that are recorded in the log. At a checkpoint, the database on disk is made consistent by flushing to disk the after-images of committed transactions still in buffer. In case of a failure of the host program, computer, or the network, the affected transactions are aborted. When the IDM machine suffers a soft failure (for example, power failure where data in main memory are lost), the database integrity is recovered through a warm restart procedure, accomplished by using the log as follows: all transaction updates that occurred after the last checkpoint are undone, and the updates of the committed transactions are redone.

The database is regularly saved on magnetic tape on the host or in an IDM file. Furthermore the log is periodically copied on tape or on disk (the disk having the copy should be different than the one having the current log). In case of hard failure (such as a disk crash) where data on disk are lost, a cold restart procedure must be performed. A consistent version of the database is reconstituted from the last archive and the after-images of the committed transactions (found in all copies of the log since the database dump). It is important to perform the log dump frequently in order to avoid the loss of transactions updates.

Another important standard feature of the IDM is mirrored disks, which permit the user to duplicate the critical part of the database (such as logs) on a redundant set of disk drives. Mirrored disks provide faster recovery after media failure or disk crashes.

9.6.7 Summary

The IDM is a complete and powerful relational database machine. The machine is more software than hardware oriented. The only special-purpose component is the database accelerator, which can increase performance by a factor of up to 10. The IDM machine can be connected to the following host computers: DEC VAX under UNIX, VMS and ULTRIX, microVAX under VMS, IBM PC under PC/DOS, IBM 43xx under VM/CMS, ATT under UNIX and PYRAMID under UNIX, Univac 100, Alpha Micro, and Apollo. One main application of the IDM is as a database server connected via a local area network to personal workstations.

IDM provides excellent price-performance ratio. A comparison with commercial INGRES, considered one of the most popular relational DBMSs, in a multiuser environment [Boral 84] showed that the IDM is three times faster for single user queries, and it improves as the multiuser load increases. The IDM can achieve six to thirty-five debit-credit transactions or single-retrieve transactions per second [Britton Lee 86]. The future Britton Lee OMEGA database machine based on a parallel and RISC architecture should support forty to four hundred such transactions per second.

9.7 Research on Database Machines

This section is devoted to the presentation of DBM research projects. We will limit ourselves to describing their architecture and their original features. Because there are so many projects, we propose a taxonomy of database machines, which will simplify the subsequent presentations, and then look at only the best known. Additional information on DBM research can be found in [Boral 85, DeWitt 81, Hsiao 83].

9.7.1 Database Machine Taxonomy

Generally database machines are based on multiprocessor architectures in order to avoid the so-called uniprocessor bottleneck. Thus they can be classified according to Flynn's approach [Flynn 66]. Conventional database systems perform database requests sequentially on a single CPU; however, pseudo-parallelism can be achieved by multitasking. The idea behind most database machine designs is to achieve absolute parallelism in two ways: by executing several requests in parallel and by processing several data flows in parallel.

Machine architectures can be divided into four classes [Flynn 66]: SISD, MISD, SIMD, and MIMD. An SISD (single instruction stream single data stream) machine is a classical Von Neumann (sequential) machine. An MISD (multiple instruction stream single data stream) machine can execute simultaneously several instructions on a unique data stream. An SIMD (single instruction stream multiple data stream) machine can perform the same instruction on several parallel data flows. An MIMD (multiple instruction stream multiple data stream) machine can execute several different instructions on several parallel data flows. MIMD machines are the most powerful but the most complex to realize.

Fig. 9.7 presents a taxonomy of the main DBMs according to the number of parallel data flows and the number of database instructions (for example, selections) executed simultaneously. CAFS-ISP is a limited MISD machine since it uses sixteen key channels acting in parallel on the same data flow. CAFS also may be used in an MIMD mode if several filter components are used in parallel. Although its architecture allows an MIMD mode, DORSAL 32 processes one request at a time and thus remains SISD. DBC/1012 is highly MIMD. We will detail some machines specific to each class except for the SISD class, exemplified by DORSAL and IDM, which we have already discussed above.

9.7.2 Hardware Architecture Classification

Each database machine has a hardware architecture with specific features that make it unique. In order to simplify our presentation, we will abstract and classify these architectures. This classification is also useful to evaluate alternative designs quickly. As we will see, this classification is not orthogonal to the DBM taxonomy. DBM architectures may be characterized based on the most important hardware components: secondary storage media, main memory, cache memory, interconnect, and processors. We have isolated five generic hardware architec-

	Parallel Instructions	
Parallel Data Flows	*SI (one)*	*MI (several)*
SD (one)	DORSAL	CAFS-ISP
	IDM	VERSO
MD (several)	CASSM	DBC
	DIRECT	DBC/1012
	RAP	DBMAC
	RARES	DELTA
		GAMMA
		GRACE
		MBDS
		RDBM
		SABRE

FIGURE 9.7 Database machine taxonomy.

tures that we present in chronological order of appearance in the literature. The classification also gives a short history of DBMs. These architectures are: (1) multifilter, (2) multiprocessor multifilter, (3) multiprocessor cache memory, (4) multiprocessor cache filter, and (5) shared nothing multiprocessor. To describe these architectures uniformly, we will assume that secondary storage media are always disks. The interconnects will be represented as buses. In addition, we will distinguish between two types of processors: general- or special-purpose processor (PROC) and filter processor (FILTER). A processor or a filter is assumed to have a local memory.

Multifilter Architecture (MF)

MF architecture is illustrated in Fig. 9.8. A filter is attached to each disk or disk subset (for example, cylinder, track). Filters perform all unary operations such as selection with complex predicates. Selected data are transferred via an interconnect (generally a high-speed bus) to a general processor's local memory. This general processor is responsible for other database functions and can run a complete DBMS.

Depending on the number of filters per disk, MF captures the processor per track, processor per cylinder, and processor per disk approaches characterized in [DeWitt 81]. The MF architecture can be used in SIMD or MISD mode. The following DBMs use the MF architecture: CAFS-ISP (presented in Section 9.3), CASSM [Su 75], RAP [Ozkarahan 77], RARES [Lin 76], and VERSO [Bancilhon 83].

The MF approach is efficient for all unary operations that have high selectivity. However, the database processor or the interconnect rapidly can become a bottleneck because operations have low selectivity. The high probability of interconnect bottleneck precludes a large number of filters (for example, as in the processor per track approach). The main drawback of this architecture is that operations of nonlinear complexity (for example, join) on large relations are poorly supported.

Multiprocessor Multifilter Architecture (MPMF)

MPMF architecture, illustrated in Fig. 9.9, is similar to the MF architecture and differs from it only in the number of processors in charge of nonfiltering func-

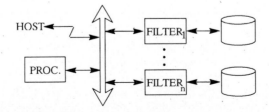

FIGURE 9.8 Multifilter architecture (MF).

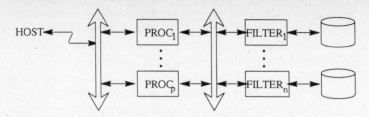

FIGURE 9.9 Multiprocessor multifilter architecture (MPMF).

tions. These processors are generally interconnected with a specific device. The MPMF architecture can be used in SIMD or MIMD mode. Examples of MPMF designs are DBC [Banerjee 78] and DBMAC [Missikoff 83].

Like the MF architecture, MPMF is efficient for unary operations performed by filters. In addition, it enables the parallel execution of more complex operations, which is efficient if the operand relations can be entirely contained in the processor's local memories. Large temporaries must be written back to disk, thereby making the system I/O bound (the processors may remain idle). Similar to the MF approach, this architecture is limited by the filter-processor interconnect bottleneck for queries with low selectivity.

Multiprocessor Cache Memory Architecture (MPCM)

MPCM architecture does not employ filter processors. As portrayed in Fig. 9.10, it is based on a three-level memory hierarchy composed of the disk units, a large cache memory, and processors' local memories. The processors always access the data in cache memory. Thus frequently accessed data or temporaries will remain in cache. The MPCM architecture may be used in SIMD or MIMD mode. DIRECT [DeWitt 79], DELTA [Murakami 83], and GRACE [Kitsuregawa 83] are representative of MPCM designs.

This approach more efficiently supports complex operations such as join or sorting than the preceding architectures; however, since any processor must be able to access any cache cell, the shared cache memory is likely to be a highly contended resource even for doing a simple select. This limits the number of processors and cache cells that can be interconnected.

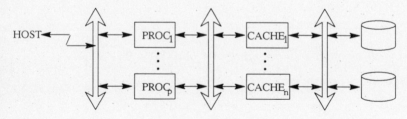

FIGURE 9.10 Multiprocessor cache memory architecture (MPCM).

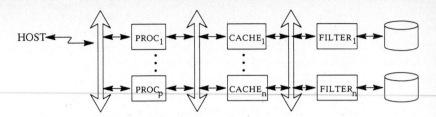

FIGURE 9.11 Multiprocessor cache filter architecture (MPCF).

Multiprocessor Cache Filter Architecture (MPCF)
This architecture is a combination of the MPCM and MPMF approaches. With MPCF, the most frequently accessed data can be maintained in cache. As shown in Fig. 9.11, a filter is able to process data either on disk or in cache. This recent capability of filters broadens their application domain and increases their value [Faudemay 85]. The MPCF architecture can be used in SIMD or MIMD mode. It has been experimented with in RDBM [Schweppe 83] and SABRE [Gardarin 83b]. The advantages of this architecture are those of the MPCM and MPCF approaches: efficient processing of unary and complex operations. However, like the MPCM, the shared cache memory is a potential bottleneck.

Share Nothing Multiprocessor Architecture (SNMP)
Surprisingly the SNMP is the most recent and simplest architecture. It stems from a critique of the previous DBM designs, which suffer from various bottlenecks, in particular, the I/O bottleneck [Boral 83] and the cache memory bottlenecks. Fig. 9.12 illustrates the SNMP approach. The architecture consists of disk-processor pairs and, usually, a set of diskless processors interconnected via a common high-speed network.

Except for the interconnect, these processors share nothing; there is no

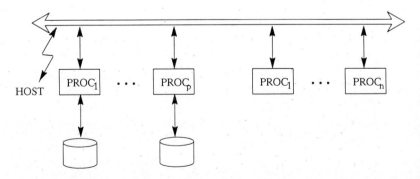

FIGURE 9.12 Share nothing multiprocessor architecture (SNMP).

common memory. As a result, this architecture is modular and extensible. Although current technology allows the development of high-speed interconnects, it is critical for the DBM software to avoid interconnect network contention. It is intended for MIMD operational mode. Examples of SNMP approaches are the DBC/1012 introduced in Section 9.4, GAMMA [DeWitt 86], and MBDS [Demurjian 86].

This approach can lead to high performance if many processors and small-capacity disks are used. The key problem is to achieve load balancing so that all processors remain equally busy. The horizontally partitioned data placement strategy [Livny 87] and parallel execution strategies [Khoshafian 88] are the main solutions toward this goal.

9.7.3 SIMD Machines

SIMD machines perform the same database instruction (for example, selection) on several parallel data flows coming directly from disks or a multiport cache memory.

CASSM (University of Florida)

CASSM [Su 75] is the oldest example of MF design where the same instruction is executed on several parallel data flows. This machine is based on magnetic disks having parallel outputs, one per read-write head. The basic assumption was a disk technology with one read-write head per track. Therefore there is one filter per track. A prototype has been built using fixed-head disks. All filters receive the same search command from a controller (located in the front end). Thus each filter executes this instruction on a different track. Each filter returns its result in turn.

CASSM supports a hierarchical storage model. CASSM's interface includes the selection and semijoin operations (called "match"), which are directly supported in hardware. Semijoin is implemented as a selection on the target relation where the selection predicate is $A = V1$ or $V2$ or . . . $Vn,$ where A is the semijoin attribute and $V1, . . . , Vn$ the list of join values of another relation. If this list is too long, several passes are necessary.

The advantage of the processor-per-track approach is that the entire database can be filtered in a single disk revolution. The drawbacks of this approach are multiple. First, it requires a special and expensive disk technology that is not cost-effective to build. Second, if the selection has low selectivity (many tuples are selected), the bus becomes a serious bottleneck. Third, this design, like all the other first DBM designs, supports only the selection and semijoin operations and poorly supports the more complex and time-consuming operations (such as join).

DIRECT (University of Wisconsin, Madison)

DIRECT [DeWitt 79] introduced the MPCM design. A DBM prototype has been built around the INGRES DBMS. The processors, implemented with LSI.11s, do not work directly on the disk data flows but on a cache memory realized with charge coupled device (CCD) memory modules. The CCD modules hold data pages coming from disk. In theory, all CCD modules can be accessed in parallel by all processors via a cross-bar-type interconnection matrix. Actually the cross-bar has not been built because of its high cost and has been replaced by a multi-port memory. (Note that cross-bar switches are now easily feasible.) The interconnection matrix enables the transfer of data pages from the CCD modules (used as a cache memory) to any number of processors. Each processor has a private memory to perform its task locally. Each processor executes code generated by the INGRES system residing on the host CPU (VAX) and distributed by a central "controller." The processors perform relational algebra operations and updates on data read from the CCD modules. The parallel algorithms for performing relational algebra operations are described and analyzed in [Bitton 83a]. The prototype has been demonstrated with four processors.

DIRECT has two serious performance problems. The first is the I/O bottleneck. DIRECT docs not support indexes but instead employs parallelism and sequential scans for performing all relational operations. The presence of indexes would have avoided many I/O operations. The second problem with DIRECT is the high communication overhead for controlling the execution of parallel algorithms. DIRECT adopted page-level granularity. To start an I/O operation on a page, a processor must first obtain the page address from the controller and then read or write the page. Therefore the number of messages to perform a join operation is proportional to the product of the operand relation cardinalities. It was shown in [Bitton 83b] that the time incurred in managing messages largely dominated the I/O and CPU time for join-type operations.

The lessons learned from DIRECT led to the design of a new high-performance DBM, GAMMA.

RAP (University of Toronto)

RAP [Ozkarahan 77] is similar to CASSM in design and purpose but with more generality. RAP has an MF (processor-per-track) architecture. It is composed of a controller, a set function unit, and an array of parallel memory components, each attached to a filter processor. Memory components and processors are, respectively, similar to disk tracks and filters in CASSM. The memory components used in the prototype were CCD modules but could have been disk tracks. A processor is a special-purpose microprocessor that performs specific functions on its memory component. The set function unit is connected to all processor-memory couples and performs aggregate functions on sets of values obtained from them. The controller interfaces with the host CPU, performs some RAP routines, directs the coordination of the processors, controls the set function unit, and integrates the results to be communicated to the host.

RAP implements low-level primitives for relational database support. Functions like selection, semijoin, and aggregates (COUNT, SUM, and so on) are directly supported in hardware. Furthermore RAP supports two important features: multiprogramming and virtual memory management. Multiprogramming permits the pseudo-simultaneous processing of simple (fast) and complex (slow) queries. Virtual memory management is an extension useful to manage databases that are too large to fit in the array of memory modules.

The same observations made for CASSM hold for RAP.

9.7.4 MISD Machines

A few machines perform the execution of multiple instructions on a single data flow coming from disk or memory. CAFS-ISP, with its use of parallel key channels, is based on this principle. This principle, together with the advances of VLSI technology, are explained in [Faudemay 85] where the design of an MISD filter processor based on parallel comparators is proposed.

VERSO (INRIA, France)

Although not really an MISD machine, the VERSO machine, of which a prototype has been built at INRIA, can be viewed as such. The reason is that the physical data model used in VERSO, called V-relations [Bancilhon 83], enables the processing of several relations at the same time. A V-relation is a hierarchical and compacted representation of several relations where repetitive attribute groups are supported. For example, the relational database describing courses taught by professors, where each course is associated with a set of results (student, grade) and a set of locations (time, room), would be classically represented by the three relations: COURSE (Course, Professor), RESULT (Course, Student, Grade), and LOCATION (Course, Time, Room). The corresponding V-relation is R ((Course, (Student, Grade)*, (Time, Room)*, Professor)*), where $(A)^*$ denotes that the attribute group A can be repeated from 0 to n times.

The value of V-relations is that some frequent join operations are avoided. The VERSO machine has an MF design based on a hardware filter capable of executing all relational algebra operations (selection and merge type operations) and updates at the speed of the disk bandwidth. The condition for handling binary operations (such as join) is that the operand relations are already assorted (for example, on join attribute). The DBMS kernel, which offers a relational interface, resides on a separate microprocessor.

The filter is based on a finite state automaton [Bancilhon 80]. It returns the results in its memory, which constitutes a disk extension. This filter has been integrated as a disk controller in a multiprocessor machine, the SM90 [Finger 80]. In addition, a "software" version of the filter (implemented on a standard microprocessor) has been compared with the hardware one [Gammerman 85]. The comparison results for select operations show that hardware filtering is IO bound, while software filtering is CPU bound. The hardware filter spends half the time waiting for data from disk. Although slower than hardware filtering, software filtering provides acceptable performance. Furthermore it is simpler and easy to port to a new and faster microprocessor.

9.7.5 MIMD Machines

Compared to the machines seen above, MIMD designs are more recent and thus have benefited from the experience gained in working on the previous designs. MIMD machines can process several parallel data flows simultaneously for different database instructions. These machines are the most general; they offer both horizontal storage modularity and vertical processing modularity [Missikoff 83].

DBC (Ohio State University).
The database computer DBC [Banerjee 78] was the first design of an MIMD machine. The DBC has an MPMF design that can be seen as two loops, one corresponding to a set of processors and one composed of filters, each attached to a disk track. A control processor is responsible for host interface and control of the two loops. The first loop manages the schema and indexes and maps a query into a list of disk page addresses that contain data satisfying the query. The second loop manages the access to data and selects the tuples on disk satisfying the query. The commands corresponding to queries are pipelined in the loops so that interoperation parallelism is achieved. This machine has not been built because of the high cost of developing specialized hardware, in particular, a special disk technology.

Another MIMD machine, MBDS [Demurjian 86], has been developed at the Naval Post Graduate School in Monterey, California, by the DBC designers. MBDS is a software-oriented DBM that uses a highly parallel architecture, similar to those of Gamma and GRACE. The MBDS design is simple and general so as to provide easy growth and high performance. The architecture is a set of minicomputers interconnected via a high-speed bus and managed by a central controller that interfaces MBDS to the host computer. Each minicomputer runs the same centralized DBMS. Data of the same relation are spread (horizontally partitioned) over many minicomputers in a round-robin fashion. A prototype has been built on VAX 11/750s connected via Ethernet.

DBMAC (CNR, Italy)
DBMAC [Missikoff 83] is an MIMD relational database machine and also implements the MPMF approach. DBMAC's unique contribution is the storage model: tuples are stored by domain. Each tuple is split into binary tuples of the form < attribute value, tuple identifier > and stored in files corresponding to the same domain. These files are managed by a filter per disk called *intelligent memory interface*. The parallel processors are in charge of logical functions, such as query decomposition and optimization, and of some physical functions, depending on the configuration. The value of the domain-based model is that join queries with a few projected attributes are very efficient. The worst type of query is the retrieval of a single entire tuple; this operation will involve many join operations over the different files storing the domains of the relevant tuple.

DELTA (ICOT, Japan)

DELTA [Murakami 83] is an important component of the Japanese Fifth-Generation Computer Project, which began in 1981. This new generation of computers is aimed at supporting a large number of inferences on large knowledge bases. A knowledge base is composed of facts and rules about these facts. In its simplest form, inference enables the generation of new facts by applying rules to existing facts. The fact base can be a relational database on which complex queries (with possibly many joins) are given.

This architecture is composed of a sequential inference machine (SIM) connected with a relational DBM (DELTA) through a local area network or a common memory. SIM is responsible for mapping knowledge base queries onto relational queries. In the future, SIM will be replaced or helped by a parallel inference machine.

The DBM offers a relational algebra interface and is understood as a highly parallel MIMD machine based on the MPCM design. The DELTA interface includes operations of extended relational algebra and transaction management commands. Several commands can be formed simultaneously on several parallel data flows.

DELTA is functionally distributed into three subsystems: the control processor, the relational database engine, and the hierarchical memory manager. The control processor and relational database engine are processors in Fig. 9.10, and the hierarchical memory manager is made of caches and disks. Other subsystems are responsible for the interface with the local area network or the cache memory. The role of the *control processor* is the scheduling of relational operation execution on other processors and the multiuser control. Each *relational database engine* (there may be several) performs mainly the select, join, and sort operations. This processor is based on a sort-merge cell [Shibayama 84]. This cell can merge two sorted strings incoming from FIFO buffers or perform a complex selection by using one FIFO buffer for the selection predicate and controlling the output. The sort-merge operation on large relations can be accomplished using a large tree of cells communicating in pipelined mode. The *hierarchical memory manager* manages two high-capacity memories: a silicon disk of 128M byte of RAM and four 1 Gbyte magnetic disks. It accomplishes secondary memory management, data placement, transaction restart, and data transfer from and to the relational database engines.

Like DBMAC, DELTA stores data in binary relations, associating each attribute value with its tuple identifier. A higher degree of parallelism can be obtained for relational queries. Compared to the classical approach, which stores all the tuple's attributes together, this method requires more operations but on smaller data sets. A prototype of DELTA has been developed and demonstrated. The coupling with the inference engines remains to be shown.

Gamma (University of Wisconsin – Madison)

Gamma [DeWitt 86] is a recent relationally complete DBM whose design stems from the lessons learned with the DIRECT prototype. DIRECT had two major performance problems: I/O bottleneck and high communication control overhead. Gamma solves these problems by exploiting distributed data placement, indexes, and data-flow query processing techniques. The architecture of Gamma, based on the SNMP paradigm, is quite simple and is similar to many recent DBM designs such as DBC/1012 and MBDS.

Gamma is composed of a set of disk drives, each attached to a processor, interconnected via a high-speed ring network. Some diskless processors are used to interface with the host CPU or to help in processing complex CPU-intensive operations. The main idea of this design is to use a large number of small disk drives instead of a small number of large disk drives in order to maximize the parallel I/O bandwidth. Each processor can run the same DBMS code, which simplifies the addition of new components.

The critical issue with this type of design is data placement on multiple disk drives. Data placement must be such that all disk drives are used in parallel with about the same load. Otherwise one node can be overloaded and become a bottleneck while the others are idle. This is, in fact, the key problem of parallel processing. In Gamma, all relations are horizontally partitioned over all the disk drives. Several methods are used to define the relation partitionings. One efficient method is to hash all the relation tuples on a specified attribute. Therefore when a query involves one relation (such as selection), all the disk drives and their processors presumably will participate in parallel to the execution of the query. Data placement is also used to limit the amount of work to be done; an exact match or range queries will be sent only to the disk drive that contains the matching tuples.

Each processor runs a copy of a relational DBMS supporting an extension of the QUEL language. The DBMS is implemented on top of an ad hoc operating system that provides specific features for database functions (such as hints to the buffer manager). Clustered and secondary indexes are employed to minimize the number of local I/Os.

The communication control overhead is minimized in two ways. First, efficient hash-based algorithms are used for complex operations (like join) [DeWitt 85] so as to maximize local processing. Second, Gamma exploits data flow query processing techniques to minimize the control of synchronization of different operations of the same query (interoperation parallelism). This control is decentralized and predefined by the optimizer. As soon as a data packet is produced by a processor, it is sent directly to the next (predetermined) processor for further processing. Under the classical approach, the processors must wait until all the results of the previous operation are available.

Gamma has been implemented on twenty VAX 11/750 processors, eight attached to 160 M byte Fujitsu disk drives. The processors are interconnected via an 80 Mbit per second token ring network. The preliminary performance measurements of Gamma [DeWitt 86] encourage this type of DBM design.

GRACE (University of Tokyo)
GRACE [Kitsuregawa 83, Fushimi 86] is a parallel relational DBM under development at the University of Tokyo. GRACE employs innovative solutions for mini-

mizing the number of I/Os and the overhead in controlling the execution of parallel operations.

The basic GRACE architecture follows the MPCM approach. Processors, cache memory modules, and disks are interconnected via two high-speed ring buses: the processing ring between processors and memory modules and the staging ring between memory modules and disks. Control processors are associated with each ring to manage the interface with the host CPU and control the various modules in the DBM. They also perform transaction management and query decomposition, optimization, and scheduling. Several processors perform the execution of relational algebra operations. They operate on the memory modules that are used for temporary storage, called staging storage. The GRACE machine may be extended with special-purpose hardware modules (filter, hasher, sorter).

As in Gamma, data placement on multiple disks is critical for minimizing the number of I/Os. In GRACE, tuples of the same relation are horizontally partitioned over all disks using the adaptive multidimensional clustering algorithm [Fushimi 85]. This algorithm stores on the same disk all tuples that satisfy a multiattribute predicate. The algorithm adapts itself to variations in the content of relations. A query involving clustered attributes will access a single disk, while queries on nonclustered attributes will be executed in parallel on all disks. Joins on clustered attributes can be performed efficiently with this multidimensional clustering.

Another major performance issue with this type of architecture is the overhead incurred in controlling the execution and synchronization of relational operations. In order to reduce control overhead, GRACE employs a query data flow processing technique. With this technique, the unit of execution and control is a whole set of tuples involved in the operation. A processor can start an operation as soon as an operand tuple (or some operand tuples) is (are) present in its associated memory module. The algorithms for complex relational operations (such as join) are therefore based on pipelined execution. These algorithms use a combination of hashing and sorting. Hashing is employed first to partition two operand relations into buckets. Sorting is then used to complete the operation between buckets having same number. The GRACE pipelined sort merger performs sorting in linear time, provided that enough memory is available. The most important problem of a pipelined execution strategy is the overflow of the memory space. The GRACE solution is the virtual memory management of the memory modules, which are associated with working disks for that purpose.

The GRACE software has been implemented on a simulator. The GRACE DBM is being implemented with SMD disk drives and 68000 microprocessors.

RDBM (University of Braunschweig, West Germany)

RDBM [Schweppe 83] is a DBM that extensively uses special-purpose hardware. Its architecture is based on the MPCF approach. RDBM is composed of a multiprocessor filter processor derived from SURE [Leilich 78] and a set of four processors in charge of sorting, interrecord operations, conversion, and query management and control. The processors are interconnected through a high-speed bus.

The RDBM filter processor is composed of a page buffer and a set of retrieval and update processors. These processors perform selections and updates on the page buffer, which is used as a disk cache memory. Results are transferred to a common cache memory.

The rest of the RDBM processors work on the cache memory, as well as on their private memory. For example, the sort processor maintains pointers in private memory to tuples stored in main memory. The interrecord processor is responsible for all operations with more than one tuple, such as the join of two tuples or an aggregate function on two tuples. RDBM implements the sort-merge join algorithm, whose efficiency strongly depends on the hardware sort processor. Finally one processor acts as the query manager and the controller of the machine. Since special-purpose hardware is used for almost all database functions, the price-performance advantage of this architecture is difficult to evaluate.

SABRE (INRIA, France)

In Chapter 5, we describe the system SABRINA as a relational DBMS. A DBM version of the system, SABRE [Gardarin 83], has also been developed at INRIA. SABRE is an MIMD database machine based on MPCF architecture. One version of the SABRE DBM has been emulated on a French multiprocessor machine, the SM90 [Finger 81]. The hardware architecture of the SM90 is composed of up to eight MC 68000 microprocessors, each having a local memory, interconnected through a 10M byte bus and sharing a common memory. To achieve system portability, SABRE has two architectures: a functional architecture, composed of functional processors and interfaces between them, and an operational architecture, which maps the functional architecture on a real machine with the addition of a low-level operating system kernel.

The functional processors are the host resident processor managing the interaction with users, the view and integrity processor, the query processor, the join and sort processor (also in charge of other complex operations), the cache manager, the transaction manager, and the filter processor (in charge of updates and select operations). Depending on the hardware configuration, each of the functional processors can be replicated on several real processors (for example, the filter, join, and sort processor). Conversely, several functional processors that do not require high processing power (for example, the query processor) can be grouped on the same physical processor.

The SABRE DBM attempts to achieve the following performance objectives: (1) decrease the number of I/Os, (2) increase the parallel IO bandwidth and hence the system throughput, (3) increase the degree of parallel execution and minimize CPU time, and (4) increase the system reliability.

Objective 1 is attained with the access method based on predicate trees [Valduriez 84a], which enables the user to cluster a relation according to multiple attributes. A predicate tree (PT) specifies a hash function that encodes a multikey into a bit string, called a *signature*. Tuples are clustered on disk by digital hashing on the signature. Tuples with the same signature prefix (having the same partial hash value) and possibly satisfying a multiattribute predicate are stored together in the same disk page. The association signature prefix-page address is maintained efficiently in a directory itself hashed on signature prefix [Gardarin 84]. Queries referring to clustering attributes of the PT incur a minimum number of I/Os, however, queries on nonclustering attributes must scan the entire relation. To decrease the number of I/Os for accesses based on nonclustered attributes, secondary indexes may be implemented as secondary predicate trees [Chesney 86a] associating secondary signatures (made up of several secondary attributes) with primary signatures. Secondary PTs make the secondary indexes much smaller and thus more cost-effective than in the traditional approach.

Objective 2 is also achieved through predicate trees. PTs are useful for clustering data according to some predicates. In a parallel environment, PTs can also be used to partition each relation horizontally over multiple disks. Thus the access to tuples of a relation (such as select) may be done in parallel, thereby increasing the parallel I/O bandwidth. The distribution of a relation among many disks is done according to the first PT level describing a hash function applied to one attribute chosen as the partitioning attribute. Therefore this first level serves as a global index to the disks. The subsequent levels of the PT are used to cluster data locally on the relation partitions.

Objective 3 has been initially tackled in [Valduriez 84b] where parallel algorithms for performing join, semijoin, and sort operations in the SABRE DBM are described and analyzed. A multiprocessor hash-based join algorithm was shown generally to outperform the parallel versions of the nested-loop and sort-merge join algorithms. In [Chesney 86b], the hash-based join algorithm is extended to exploit the case where the join attribute is the partitioning attribute. If the operand relations are partitioned according to the join attribute, then a simple access to the digital directory is required to reject the pages that have no matching tuples. The algorithm is also adapted to the case in which one or both relations are not partitioned according to the join attribute by adding a partitioning phase. This algorithm provides an improvement factor of 3 to 5 compared to the ones in [De-Witt 85].

Since most queries are select-join-project queries, a new primitive operator, select-prejoin, is introduced in [Chesney 86b]. Select-prejoin is a pipelined operation that preprocesses the subsequent join (partitioning phase) as the selected data are produced. Select-prejoin increases the degree of parallel execution.

To decrease the CPU time, which becomes significant for evaluating complex predicates, a hardware filter based on VLSI technology has been proposed in [Faudemay 85]. The filter is composed of a large number of similar basic comparators that perform important database operations. The functionality of this processor is quite general; selection, text search, join, and sort operations are supported. The processor is being built in CMOS technology.

The parallel architecture of SABRE and the data placement strategy offer opportunities for increased reliability [Viemont 84]. Data are replicated (mirrored) over separate disks. In case of disk failure, a degraded working mode is achieved by correcting the partitioning function in order to avoid accessing the failed disk. Whereas most other systems would be down because of disk failure, the SABRE DBM is virtually nonstop.

The experience with the SABRE relational DBM has guided the design of a new knowledge base machine at INRIA [Gardarin 86] that provides higher usability while maintaining high performance. This machine makes extensive use of the data structures, large main memory, and parallelism.

9.8 Conclusion

Although the idea of database machine (DBM) appeared in the early 1970s, it took about ten years to develop the first DBM products. Current DBM designs have evolved significantly from earlier ones. The first DBM designs suffered from three main problems. First, it is difficult to develop special-purpose hardware for supporting database functions in an academic environment. The time required to develop a filter prototype (three to four years) is about the same required to produce a new generation of microprocessors. Second, they did not provide a significant price-performance ratio compared to the conventional DBMS approach. Third, early DBM proposals provided incomplete functionality, including low reliability. Thus integration in real environments was difficult.

Only recently have database machines looked promising. The DBM products are now relationally complete (because relational technology is better understood) and provide many additional features, which increase their usability. Because of their specialization, they can provide high-performance benefits compared to the conventional approach, as shown in first measurements [ICL 82, Bitton 83b].

The classic argument against the DBM approach is that a good DBMS (like those described in this book) running on a powerful mainframe (for example, with a few high-speed processors accessing a large main memory connected to multiple disk drives) may be as efficient. This argument is valid but ignores the higher cost (for same performance) of the classic approach. The main difference between the conventional and DBM approaches is that the latter closely integrates the database system code and the operating system kernel tailored to database system needs. The conventional approach suffers from a serious mismatch between the database software and the overly general (and complex) operating system [Stonebraker 81]. In other words, performance of the database system is traded off against the generality of the operating system. For example, the DB2 system (see Chapter 3) in the MVS environment has to traverse many software layers to operate on the data. This overhead has a dramatic effect on performance. The advantage of the DBM approach is exemplified by the IDM 500, which employs a rather traditional hardware architecture but a tight integration between database software and operating system kernel. The specialized approach can be a big winner.

The advent of standard multiprocessor architectures enables the development of highly parallel DBMs without the need for special-purpose hardware. The most recent DBM designs, such as DBC/1012, Gamma, and SABRE, are based on the parallel architecture paradigm, whose main value is to increase significantly the disk I/O bandwidth (and thus performance) and to provide higher reliability. For example, the DBC/1012 provides a price-performance improvement factor of approximately 4 over the conventional approach. Also a DBM fits naturally in a distributed environment, for example, by acting as disk server connected to personal workstations. The new applications of databases (AI, CAD/CAM, and others) require both functionality and performance that the conventional approach cannot easily provide.

References

[Armisen 81] Armisen J. P., Caleca J. Y., "A Commercial Back-end System," Int. Conf. on VLDB, Cannes, France, 1981.

[Babb 79] Babb E., "Implementing a Relational Database by Means of Specialized Hardware," ACM TODS, Vol. 1, No. 2, June 1976.

[Bancilhon 80] Bancilhon F., Scholl M., "Design of a Back End Processor for a Data Base Machine," ACM SIGMOD Int. Conf., Los Angeles, 1980.

[Bancilhon 83] Bancilhon F. et al., "VERSO: A Relational Backend Database Machine," in [Hsiao 83].

[Banerjee 78] Banerjee J., Hsiao D. K., Baum R. I., "Concepts and Capabilities of a Database Computer," ACM TODS, Vol. 3, No. 4, 1978.

[Bitton 83a] Bitton D., Boral H., DeWitt D. J., Wilkinson W. K., "Parallel Algorithms for the Execution of Relational Database Operations," ACM TODS, Vol. 8, No. 3, September 1983.

[Bitton 83b] Bitton D., DeWitt D. J., Turbyfil C., "Benchmarking Database Systems: A Systematic Approach," Int. Conf. on VLDB, Florence, November 1983.

[Boral 83] Boral H., DeWitt D. J., "Database Machines: An Idea Whose Time Has Passed? A Critique of the Future of Database Machines," Int. Workshop on DBM, Munich, September 1983.

[Boral 84] Boral H., DeWitt D. J., "A Methodology for Database System Performance Evaluation," ACM-SIGMOD Int. Conf., Boston, June 1984.

[Boral 85] Boral H., Redfield S., "Database Machine Morphology," Int. Conf. on VLDB, Stockholm, September 1985.

[Britton Lee 82] Britton Lee Inc., "IDM 500 Reference Manual," Britton Lee, Inc., Los Gatos, Ca., 1982.

[Britton Lee 86] Britton Lee Inc., Vol. 3, No. 1, Los Gatos, California, Summer 1986.

[Canaday 74] Canaday R. H., Harrisson R. D., Ivie E. L., Ryder J. L., Wehr L. A., "A Backend Computer for Data Base Management," Comm. of the ACM, Vol. 17, No. 10, 1974.

[Chesney 86a] Chesney J. P., Faudemay P., Michel R., "An Extension of Access Paths to

Improve Joins and Selections," Int. Conf. on Data Engineering, Los Angeles, February 1986.

[Chesney 86b] Chesney J. P., Faudemay P., Michel R., Thevenin J. M., "A Reliable Parallel Backend Using Multi-Attribute Clustering and Select-Join Operator," Int. Conf. on VLDB, Kyoto, August 1986.

[Copernique 82] Copernique Company, "DORSAL 32: Technical Documentation," Paris, 1982.

[Decker 86] Decker J., "C31 Teradata Study," RADC-TR-85-273, Rome Air Development Center, New York, March 1986.

[Demurjian 86] Demurjian S., Hsiao D., Menon J., "A Multi-Backend Database System for Performance Gains, Capacity Growth and Hardware Upgrade," Int. Conf. on Data Engineering, Los Angeles, February 1986.

[DeWitt 79] DeWitt D. J., "DIRECT—A Multiprocessor Organization for Supporting a Relational Database Management System," IEEE TC, Vol. C28, No. 6, June 1979.

[DeWitt 81] DeWitt D. J., Hawthorn P. B., "A Performance Evaluation of Database Machine Architectures," Int. Conf. on VLDB, Cannes, France, September 1981.

[DeWitt 85] DeWitt D. J., Gerber B., "Multiprocessor Hash-Based Join Algorithms," Int. Conf. on VLDB, Stockholm, September 1985.

[DeWitt 86] DeWitt D. J. et al., "GAMMA — a High Performance Dataflow Database Machine," Int. Conf. on VLDB, Kyoto, August 1986.

[Epstein 80] Epstein R., Hawthorn P., "Design Decisions for the Intelligent Database Machine," NCC 1980, AFIPS Press, Montvale, N.J. 1980.

[Faudemay 85] Faudemay P., Valduriez P., "Design and Analysis of a Direct Filter Using Parallel Comparators," Int. Workshop on DBM, Grand Bahama Island, 1985.

[Finger 81] Finger U., Medigue G., "Multiprocessor Architecture and Availability: The SM 90" (in French), CNET, L'Echo des Recherches, No. 105, July 1981.

[Flynn 66] Flynn M. J., "Very High Speed Computing Systems," Proc. IEEE, Vol. 54, No. 12, December 1966.

[Fushimi 85] Fushimi S. et al., "Algorithm and Performance Evaluation of Adaptive Multidimensional Clustering Technique," ACM-SIGMOD Int. Conf., Austin, Texas, May 1985.

[Fushimi 86] Fushimi S., Kitsuregawa M., Tanaka H., "An Overview of the System Software of a Parallel Relational Database Machine GRACE," Int. Conf. on VLDB, Kyoto, August 1986.

[Gammerman 85] Gammerman S., Scholl M., "Hardware versus Software Data Filtering; The VERSO Experience," Int. Workshop on DBM, Grand Bahama Island, March 1985.

[Gardarin 83a] Gardarin G., Bernadat P., Temmerman N., Valduriez P., Viemont Y., "Design of a Multiprocessor Relational Database System," IFIP 83 World Computer Congress, Paris, September 1983.

[Gardarin 83b] Gardarin G., Bernadat P., Temmerman N., Valduriez P., Viemont Y., "SABRE, a Relational Database System for a Multiprocessor Machine," in [Hsiao 83].

[Gardarin 84] Gardarin G., Valduriez P., Viemont Y., "Predicate Trees: A Way for Optimizing Relational Queries," Int. Conf. on Data Engineering, Los Angeles, April 1984.

[Gardarin 86] Gardarin G., Abiteboul S., Scholl M., Simon E., "Towards DBMS's for Supporting New Applications," Int. Conf. on VLDB, Kyoto, August 1986.

[Hsiao 83] Hsiao D. K., *Advanced Database Machine Architecture,* Prentice-Hall, 1983. 394 pages.

[ICL 82] International Computers Limited, "ICL CAFS-ISP," Commercial Documentation, 1982, London.

[Kitsuregawa 83] Kitsuregawa M., Tanaka H., Moto-oka T., "Application of Hash to Database Machine and Its Architecture," New Generation Computing, Vol. 1, No. 1, 1983.

[Khoshafian 88] Khoshafian S., Valduriez P., "Parallel Execution Strategies for Declustered Databases," in *Database Machines and Knowledge Base Machines,* edited by N. Kitsuregawa and H. Tanaka, Kluwer Academic Publishers, 1988.

[Leilich 78] Leilich H. O., Stiege G., Zeidler H. C., "A Search Processor for Database Management Systems," Int. Conf. on VLDB, Berlin, 1978.

[Lin 76] Lin S. C., Smith D. C. P., Smith J. M., "The Design of a Rotating Associative Memory for Relational Database Applications," ACM TODS, Vol. 1, No. 1, 1976.

[Livny 87] Livny M., Khoshafian S., Boral H., "Multi-Disk Management," ACM-SIGMETRICS Int. Conf., 1987.

[Missikoff 82] Missikoff M., "A Domain-Based Internal Schema for Relational Database Machines," ACM SIGMOD Int. Conf., Orlando, Fla., June 1982.

[Missikoff 83] Missikoff M., Terranova M., "The Architecture of a Relational Database Computer Known as DBMAC," in [Hsiao 83].

[Murakami 83] Murakami K., Kakuta T., Miyazaki N., Shibayama S., Yokota H., "A Relational Database Machine: First Step to Knowledge Base Machine," ICOT Technical Report TR-012, Japan, May 1983.

[Neches 85] Neches, P. M., "The Anatomy of a Data Base Computer System," COMPCON Int. Conf., San Francisco, February 1985.

[Nyberg 86] Nyberg G., "An Operating System for a Database Machine," IEEE Bulletin on Database Engineering, Vol. 9, No. 3, September 1986.

[Ozkarahan 77] Ozkarahan E. A., Schuster S. A., Sevcik K. C., "Performance Evaluation of a Relational Associative Processor," ACM TODS, Vol. 2, No. 2, June 1977.

[Schweppe 83] Schweppe H. et al., "RDBM — A Dedicated Multiprocessor System for Database Management," in [Hsiao 83].

[Shibayama 84] Shibayama S., Kakuta T., Miyazaki N., Yokota H., Murakami K., "The Delta Data Base Machine," ICOT Technical Report TR-064, Japan, April 1984.

[Stonebraker 81] Stonebraker M., "Operating System Support for Database Management," Comm. ACM, Vol. 24, No. 7, July 1981.

[Su 75] Su S., Lipowski G. J., "CASSM: A Cellular System for Very Large Data Bases," Int. Conf. on VLDB, Boston, 1975.

[Teradata 84] Teradata Corporation, "Database Computer System Concepts and Facilities," Document No. C02-0001-01, Teradata Corporation, Los Angeles, October 1984.

[Ubell 85] Ubell M., "The Intelligent Database Machine," in *Query Processing in DBMS,* edited by W. Kim, D. S. Reiner, and D. S. Batory, Springer-Verlag, 1985.

[Valduriez 84a] Valduriez P., Viemont Y., "A Multikey Hashing Scheme Using Predicate Trees," ACM-SIGMOD Int. Conf., Boston, June 1984.

[Valduriez 84b] Valduriez P., Gardarin G., "Join and Semi-Join Algorithms for a Multiprocessor Database Machine," ACM TODS, Vol. 9, No. 1, March 1984.

[Viemont 84] Viemont Y., Michel R., "An Update Algorithm Integrating Concurrency and Reliability," (in French), AFCET Workshop on Security and Intelligence, Paris, October 1984.

APPENDIX: SYSTEM DESIGNERS

CAFS-ISP
International Computers Limited, World Headquarters, ICL House, Putney, London, SW15 1SW, England
(01) 788-7272

DATACOM/DB
Applied Data Research, Inc., Route 206 and Orchard Road, CN-8, Princeton, New Jersey 08543
(201) 874-9000

DBASE
Ashton-Tate, 10150 West Jefferson Boulevard, Culver City, California 90230
(213) 204-5570

DBC/1012
Teradata Corporation, 12945 Jefferson Boulevard, Los Angeles, California 90066
(213) 827-8777

DB2 and **SQL/DS**
IBM Corporation, Programming Publishing, P.O. Box 50020, San Jose, California 95150

DORSAL 32
COPERNIQUE, 10-12 rue Yvan-Tourguenieff, 78380 Bougival, France
(1) 39-18-04-32

EXCEL
Microsoft Corporation, 16011 Northeast Thirty-sixth Way, P.O. Box 9097017, Redmond, Washington 98073
(206) 882-8080

FOCUS
Information Builders, Inc., 1250 Broadway, New York, New York 10001
(212) 736-4433

IDM
Britton Lee, Inc., 1919 Addison Street, Suite 105, Berkeley, California 94704
(415) 548-3211

INGRES
Relational Technology, Inc., 1080 Marina Village Parkway, P.O. Box 4006, Alameda, California 94501
(415) 769-1400

KNOWLEDGEMAN
Micro Data Base Systems, Inc., P.O. Box 248, Lafayette, Indiana 47902
(800) 344-5832

NOMAD
MUST Software International, 187 Danbury Road, Wilton, Conneticut 06897
(212) 754-1700

ORACLE
Oracle Corporation, 20 Davis Drive, Belmont, California 94002
(415) 598-8000

R-BASE
MICRORIM Inc., 3925 159th Avenue, Redmond, Washington 98052
(206) 885-2000

SABRINA
INFOSYS, 15 rue Anatole France, 92800 Puteaux, France
(1) 47-78-85-35

SUPRA
CINCOM Systems, Inc., 2300 Montana Avenue, Cincinnati, Ohio 45211
(800) 543-3010

SYBASE
Sybase, 2910 Seventh Street, Berkeley, California 94710
(415) 548-4500.

UNIFY
UNIFY Corporation, 3870 Rosin Court, Sacramento, California 95834
(916) 920-9092

INDEX